Fair Exotics

Fair Exotics

Xenophobic Subjects in
English Literature, 1720–1850

RAJANI SUDAN

PENN

UNIVERSITY OF PENNSYLVANIA PRESS

Philadelphia

Copyright © 2002 University of Pennsylvania Press
All rights reserved
Printed in the United States of America on acid-free paper

10 9 8 7 6 5 4 3 2 1

Published by
University of Pennsylvania Press
Philadelphia, Pennsylvania 19104-4011

Library of Congress Cataloging-in-Publication Data

Sudan, Rajani.
  Fair exotics : xenophobic subjects in English literature, 1720-1850 / Rajani Sudan.
     p.cm
  Includes bibliographical references and index.
  ISBN 0-8122-3656-4 (acid-free paper)
  1. English literature—18th century—History and criticism. 2. Exoticism in literature. 3. English literature—19th century—History and criticism. 4. Xenophobia—Great Britain—History—18th century. 5. Xenophobia—Great Britain—History—19th century. 6. Foreign countries in literature. 7. Aliens in literature. I. Title.

PR448.E85 S83 2002
820.9'1—dc21   2002018723

For my parents,
Ravindra Nath and Dipali Sudan,
and to the memory of
Michael David Bunsey, 1964–1998

Contents

Introduction 1

1. Institutionalizing Xenophobia: Johnson's Project 24

2. De Quincey and the Topography of Romantic Desire 65

3. Mothered Identities: Facing the Nation in the Works of Mary Wollstonecraft 96

4. Fair Exotics: Two Case Histories in *Frankenstein* and *Villette* 117

Afterword 148

Notes 153

Works Cited 181

Index 189

Acknowledgments 199

Introduction

> For what the unconscious does is to show us the gap through which neurosis recreates a harmony with the real—a real that may well not be determined. . . . It is not without effect that, even in a public speech, one directs one's attention at subjects, touching them at what Freud calls the navel—the navel of the dreams, he writes, to designate their ultimately unknown centre—which is simply, like the anatomical navel that represents it, that gap of which I have already spoken.
> —Jacques Lacan, *The Four Fundamental Concepts of Psycho-Analysis*

Shortly after Robinson Crusoe makes his providential landing on the island, he takes stock of his situation and makes a list of the "good" and "evil" aspects of his circumstances. Most of his laments have to do with his complete isolation (or at least his isolation from anything recognizably British); but he also notes that he has no clothes. He reasons, however, that even were he to have them he could hardly wear them for the heat.[1]

Of course this sort of reasoning doesn't go very far with either Crusoe or the reader because the weather isn't the point: clothes, quite obviously, mark the difference between Crusoe's sense of himself as British and the great mass of naked savages he encounters in his many travels. What is curious, however, is to see how the issue of clothing collapses into his fetishization of skin: Crusoe's need to make difference visible, if only to himself, primarily because of the increasingly attractive possibilities of not establishing visible difference.

Defoe's champion of moral progress represents arresting problems of identity that post-colonial studies might usefully consider. Critiques of colonialism, despite their various disclaimers, tend to iterate imperialist models and attribute a monolithic agency to Eurocentric "legacies."[2] What is often missing from these critical inquiries is an account of the profound insecurities upon which those legacies rest. These largely unnamed fears take shape in Defoe's novel as strange episodic eruptions in the relatively contiguous narrative of literary realism. Crusoe's general uneasiness with being a stranger in a strange land explodes into a series of arbitrary, incapacitating worries: his trouble with cats, his apprehensions about cannibals, or his anxieties about clothing.

Eventually Crusoe's clothes rot off his body and he is forced to fashion others from the outlandish materials he has on hand. Indeed, he claims, "had anyone in England been to meet such a man as I was, it must either have frighted them or raised a good deal of laughter; and as I frequently stood still to look at myself, I could not but smile at the notion of my traveling through Yorkshire with such an equipage and in such a dress" (134). With his clothes and skin here signifying his non-Englishness, Crusoe jokingly entertains the idea of positioning himself as the foreign body, thus implying a certain attraction to the idea.[3] However laughable a figure he might cut for himself (as the only appreciative member of his audience), he insists on wearing this "equipage" even "though it is true that the weather was so violent hot that there was no need of clothes" (120). To explain this apparent perversity, Crusoe falls back on a naturalized physical inability to withstand the intensity of the sun, which we can read as a fairly clear ideological inability of an Englishman to be a "savage": the "very heat," he writes, "blistered my skin" (120). He goes on to describe "a great clumsy ugly goatskin umbrella," which "after all, was the most necessary thing I had about me, next to my gun." As for his face, he writes, "the color of it was really not so Mulatto like as one might expect from a man not at all careful of it and living within nineteen degrees of the equinox" (135). These various incidental details concerning Crusoe's outfit do far more than describe his physical person: they inscribe an ideological position that makes such a description possible. In some ways, however, these details return our focus to the presence of the physical body.

What concerns Crusoe the most is the problem of skin—or skins. He must protect a skin that doesn't have the capacity to withstand extreme heat, and yet the very geographical location and meteorological conditions of this island may, if care is not taken, transform British fairness to an island "Mulatto." Crusoe is quite meticulous on this detail: his skin is, in fact, not as Mulatto as the British reader would expect, even given the fact that he hasn't been "at all careful of it." There is, then, something "natural" about his skin's inclination towards fairness. Given this, it seems odd that Crusoe has to police this fairness continually, always carrying his umbrella, which is "the most necessary thing I had about me, next to my gun." The gun has already established Crusoe's physical dominance on the island (and in earlier travels as well). His umbrella, manufactured from the skins of native goats, performs an equally crucial function as a visible sign of ideological dominance based on the color of his skin. Even if the "large pair of Mahometan whiskers" he sports are "monstrous" by English standards, and, perhaps, signify a potential fall into otherness, his clothing and general mien will now protect his dominant position.

Crusoe describes the clothing he makes for himself:

I had a short jacket of goatskin, the skirts coming down to about the middle of my thighs; and a pair of open-kneed breeches of the same; the breeches were made of the skin of an old he-goat, whose hair hung down such a length on either side that, like pantaloons, it reached to the middle of my legs. (134)

As with the umbrella, Crusoe uses materials furnished by the island's animal population in order both to protect the fragility of his own skin—and, therefore, the fragility of his identity as an Englishman—and to insure by the most discernible display the limitlessness of his own power; he has been able to tame and husband a flock of goats for his consumption. These goats both nourish him and provide him with a protective skin, so to speak, against other hostile elements.[4] The goats are figures of self-consolidating otherness—their skins establish Crusoe's difference because as animals, quite naturally, they are available for exploitation and sustenance. It is also crucial to Crusoe's narrative that they are goats and not sheep; breaking away from an English economy that is dependent on the consumption of sheep, Crusoe manages both to replicate a British cultural consumerism and yet to differentiate his own place within such an order as perfectly discrete. Crusoe makes a point of specifying the gender of the old he-goat that becomes his breeches; Crusoe, that sly old goat, can brandish the phallus even under cover of another, more "barbarous" skin. It is no accident as well that this item of clothing has "skirts"; skirting issues of the problematics of race and gender, Crusoe supplements British or European economies producing "legitimate" clothing with his own island fashions.

Skin operates as a place where identities are negotiated: Crusoe's representation of a self directly depends on what he perceives to be visibly other. Crusoe, however, does more with the goats than use their skins: he also eats them, as well as turtles and birds. The difference between skin and flesh is strikingly marked in this novel in terms of consumption. While Crusoe is able to use the skins of the animals he eats—even the turtle's shells come in handy—the reverse is not always true. One of his first encounters with wild beasts on this island presents interesting possibilities of reading the ways in which the natural and the feminine resist incorporation and ingestion.

Crusoe writes in his journal: "This day went abroad with my gun and my dog, and killed a wild cat; her skin pretty soft, but her flesh good for nothing" (63). Goats (and turtles, and dogs, and birds) are one thing, cats are quite another. While her skin is attractive, the feminine flesh of this cat is "good for nothing": her meat is inedible, her loyalty suspect; even as a procreative member of his household the cat is resistant, forming, rather, a family of its own. As members of Crusoe's privileged household, cats (always female) are equally inconsistent and thoroughly unreliable. Crusoe proudly likens his table to that of "a king . . . attended by my servants," who consist of his parrot Poll (the only one able to "speak" to Crusoe) and his dog, as well as his two cats. These cats, however,

> were not the two cats which I brought on shore at first, for they were both of them dead . . . but one of them having multiplied by I know not what creature, these were two which I had preserved tame, whereas the rest run wild in the woods and became indeed troublesome to me at last; for they would often come into my house and plunder me too, till at last I was obliged to shoot them, and did kill a great many. (133–34)

Poll the parrot ventriloquizes his master's language, the dog provides for his master's sustenance, the goats are husbanded for their flesh, but the cats are wild cards. Even Friday, whose skin and cannibalistic habits at first situate him as absolutely othered in relation to Crusoe, later (primarily because he gives up those habits) functions as the figure who most confirms Crusoe's ideological superiority.[5]

While Crusoe can consolidate these various other members of his household into predictable and fairly reliable reflections of his own position of power, the cats pose a continual challenge and threat to the integrity of this image. They function as border cases: tamed, and yet indistinguishable from their "native" counterparts. They don't need to depend on Crusoe's household skills; they are, in fact, more than able to proliferate successfully (with unidentifiable creatures, moreover) in this "native" environment. Even their skins—the mark of their domestication and difference—are useless to Crusoe. At the end of the novel, Crusoe recovers his ability to monitor and regulate reproduction, previously threatened, perhaps, by those unruly cats, by bringing to the island women appropriate to its inhabitants:

> I touched at the Brazils, from whence I sent a bark, which I brought there . . . and in it, besides other supplies, I sent seven women, being such as I found proper for service, or for wives to such as would take them. As to the Englishmen, I promised them to send some women from England, with a good cargo of necessaries. (275)

Crusoe repopulates the island with especial attention to likeness of skins. The Spaniards receive their due measure from the Brazils, while the Englishmen, who quite naturally could not expect to be serviced by seven Brazilian women, can anticipate their proper allotment from the next cargo Crusoe deploys.

Skin is cosmetic: it is superficial, it covers things up. Skin's opacity functions to separate outside from in, and yet, curiously, it is this very opacity that enables skin also to negotiate between internal and external borders. Skin makes ideological differences perceivable ostensibly by making interiorities externally obvious. Jame Gumb from the film *The Silence of the Lambs* (and also from the Thomas Harris novel of the same name) constructs a suit of women's skins in order to make clearly visible an interior identity—his sense that he "really" is a woman—despite his outward appearance. Robinson Crusoe assembles a suit of goat skins in order to cover and protect an identity based on external attributes that nonetheless supposedly embody an internal condition of being.

The solid ground of British national identity from which Crusoe claims his subjectivity becomes acutely contested territory particularly when it comes to the issue of colonizing property. The random problems of clothes, cats, and cannibals—three especially cogent forms of property for Crusoe—contribute both to assure and to destabilize Crusoe's footing as the principal authoritative figure, prompting him to represent his island life rather xenophobically. His journal allows him to resituate himself on more familiar ground as colonist and patriarch rather than as shipwrecked isolate. More interestingly, his journal is also the place where he turns the material problems he encounters on the island—the impediments to his material authority—into the narrative that demonstrates his discursive authority. But, not surprisingly, this sublimation often depends upon a strategically employed xenophobia. Crusoe, faced with multiple material threats to his very survival, manages his own anxiety by defining these threats as the mere challenge of the foreign to his British ingenuity. Crusoe's xenophobia, however, may also stave off his more compelling—and romantic—desire, his desire to give himself over to the other.[6] Crusoe's xenophobia may be a sign of his xenodochial desire: his desire to invite and entertain the foreign. His compulsion to establish visible difference vis-à-vis skin color, therefore, marks the territory of identity in clear, constative terms.

Thus Defoe's great novel of moral psychological development replicates the emergence of identity—social, national, cultural, personal—as a process that sublimates external material problems into an internalized coherence. Quite a wrench from our conventional understanding of eighteenth-century literature as devoted to rational order, regularity, and the prevailing public arena, Robinson Crusoe in fact articulates romantic issues, if we are to understand romantic affect as traditionally invoking the internal workings of subjectivity. In fact, even if we consider the more specific definitions of romantic authorship, Robinson Crusoe fits the bill. Crusoe's journal functions in its capacity as an inventory of his daily life, an empirical catalogue of "new" knowledge (even if this knowledge turns out suspiciously to replicate what Crusoe has always known). It is, however, also the place for introspection, a place made "safe" for convoluted expressions of xenodochial desire because of the emergence of a disembodied writing self. Such an example of rendering resistant desire "safe" by authorial reason occurs when Crusoe discovers an alien footprint that he at first reads as the sign of the devil, then of "some more dangerous creature, viz . . . the savages," and finally, with (short-lived) relief, "a mere chimera of my own" (139–40).

There seems to be a moment in literary representation when ideas about the externality of difference shift toward the introjection of that difference as a strategy of national self-identification. Defoe's novel is not only a tour-de-force celebration of eighteenth-century commercialism; it stands more insistently as just such a transitional text. Crusoe figures his island as a supplement to British economic structures, but part of its appeal (especially for Crusoe himself, the archetypal merchant adventurer) is that it both replicates and resists Britain's imperial model and demonstrates the ways in which commercial traffic becomes a barometer of moral traffic.[7]

These moments from *Robinson Crusoe* serve to illustrate early imperial constructions and contestations of "race," the "natural," and the "feminine," especially as they are manifested in Crusoe's consumerism and husbandry. But especially at issue in this novel are two crucial features that mark it as a transitional text. First, is the relationship between xenophobia and xenodochy. The initial attraction of the foreign becomes frightening to the British subject, thus giving rise to the repudiation of the thing that provoked illicit or dangerous desire by xenophobia. The second feature is the striking similarity (and difference) this relationship has with the tenets of romanticism. Harbored within British cultural consciousness is the mutual dependence of self and other. In the first two definitions of "xenodochy" supplied by the *Oxford English Dictionary*, the "entertainment of the foreign" may take shape either as an expression of a mutual intertwining or as a form of maintenance. In either expression, foreign entertainment implies that the apparently radical differences between familiar and foreign are in fact contingent on each other and can therefore be the source of an equally radical anxiety on both parts.[8] Xenophobia and xenodochy work as an economy because they are mutually constitutive, and it is through this economy that national and cultural identity is manifested. Particularly resonant with romantic discourse is the desire and loathing for the foreign thing that establishes a distinct place for the self.

Xenophobia is firmly fixed within the symbolic register of representation and its referents are produced through the paranoic construction of the "other." Like the ways in which we erase the historical aspect of paradigms of race, however, the condition of xenophobia seems to exist similarly a priori as a psychic impulse or drive without the historicizing accorded most cultural events. Long perceived and accepted as a "phobia," the fear of the foreign may, in fact, signify something quite different. This phobia may work as a fetish, as something in which we invest and cathect a great deal of cultural meaning in order to organize our own national identities. The fear of something foreign presupposes that "we" can understand what counts as foreign, but how are we to come to an understanding of the foreign without recognizing it within some signifying system that makes sense to us? Xenophobia is the process by which the "other" is constructed, but its definition is contingent on previous interest or attraction to the foreign (xenodochy). Freud's understanding of the fetish help explicate the xenophobic drive. Freud writes:

One would expect that the organs or objects selected as substitutes for the penis whose presence is missed in the woman would be such as act as symbols for the penis in other respects. This may happen occasionally but it is certainly not the determining factor. It seems rather that when the fetish comes to life, so to speak, some process has been suddenly interrupted—it reminds one of the abrupt halt made by memory in traumatic amnesias. In the case of the fetish, too, interest is held up to a certain point—what is possibly the last impression received before the uncanny traumatic one is preserved as a fetish.[9]

The fetish first emerges as a "cover" for the missing penis; accidentally and arbitrarily a part of the scene in which the castrated woman is first observed, an object is literally dis-placed from its proper location and "stands in" for what is really absent. As such a disavowal of that absence, however, the fetish clearly also testifies to the knowledge of castration that it negates. The care and attention that Freud argues we give to fetish objects because they both signify and nullify castration—because they mark a troubling and disturbing eruption while simultaneously dismissing it—is evocative of the ways in which xenophobia constructs cultural identities through a grid of abjection: the fearful foreign body signifies our difference and negates the possibility of our own castration by negating the castration itself. In the case of eighteenth-century Britain, cultural difference was fetishized as color difference, and hierarchical codes were erected that could only benefit the British and abject the foreign. The complications of foreign identity and agency were thus reduced to the material body. Early modern infatuation with commercial traffic increased the physical boundaries of "home," but it also supplied multiple opportunities for contaminating domestic identity with xenodochial desire. Nineteenth-century industrialism may have been, therefore, compelled to divorce the sordid details of exploitation and dominance from commercial enterprise and fetishize its moralizing aspects. Such a focus would then have provided a way of situating English cultural identity as the body of an idealized imperial authority.

It should not be possible to think about romanticism without invoking xenophobia. Perhaps philosophical models of the production of knowledge, especially a model that is an acknowledged "bridge" between Enlightenment and post-Enlightenment thought in the philosophical tradition, may help us understand how such a claim is possible. Kant is one of the clearest systematizers of the Enlightenment, and yet the dualism between the noumenal and the phenomenal that, according to his logic, makes room for God, also happens to accommodate an early model for the split subject: the unconscious. It is this split that profoundly influenced romantic formulations of subjectivity. This model may also help locate the histories of the internalization of psychic space. For example, in the *Critique of Pure Reason*, at the beginning of the "Transcendental Aesthetic," Kant describes the intuitive mediation of phenomenological knowledge: "In whatsoever mode, or by whatsoever means, our knowledge may relate to objects, it is at least quite clear, that the only manner in which it immediately relates to them, is by means of an intuition."[10]

It seems that Kant, spending his entire life in Königsberg, never venturing forth from this tiny East Prussian town, would have been hard put not to have developed an entire critique of reason that turned the internal processes of the mind into a transcendental object, a representation of the sublime.[11] His sequestered material life demonstrates the dramatic turn self-definition took toward the end of the eighteenth century both across Europe and in Britain—a turn that privileged a radical implosion of the external world into the consciousness of the individual. In early eighteenth-century Britain, a primary strategy of national self-definition was the xenophobic differentiation of self from nonwhite colonial others; the strategy was naturalized. By the end of the eighteenth century, as we see with Johnson and his strong influence, self-definition, nationalist or otherwise, involved a conviction of the existence of an essential inner self—and of existence as an essential inner self, ostensibly independent of any external context or dependence on an "other." These beliefs were wholeheartedly espoused by British and European intellectuals. Kant's notions of the sublime, of pure reason, and the domain of the transcendental aesthetic, produced in this milieu, reflect these changing accounts of subjectivity. Such an aesthetic shift promised an existential or subjective freedom to the individual imagination and suggested, in part (though class difference in literary production was always an issue), a liberating departure from the rigid standards of poetic practice established by eighteenth-century men of letters. In short, this aesthetic shift reflected other forms of revolution that championed the emancipation of the individual; for example, Thomas Paine's The Rights of Man and the French Revolution itself.

Kant continues his explication of the intuitive. On the transcendental exposition of the conception of time, he writes:

I shall add that the conception of change, and with it the conception of motion, as change of place, is possible only through and in the representation of time; that if this representation were not an intuition (internal) *a priori*, no conception, of whatever kind, could render comprehensible the possibility of change. . . . Time is nothing else than the form of the internal sense, that is, the intuitions of self and of our internal state.[12]

Embedded in the understanding of an a priori category is a curious trust in the stability and universality of the mind. In fact, the notions of both "intuition" and "a priori" rest in unknowing, on the opposite side of eighteenth-century reasoning that purports to use external cultural properties to shape individual or private sentiment. "Intuition" suggests by definition an immediacy of reaction or the lack of a conscious process of reasoning: an unconscious response. "A priori" (especially as Kant popularized the term) also defines the categories as innate to the mind, not based on visible experiential evidence.

These terms upon which he sustains his critique of "pure" reason are conditioned by Enlightenment thinkers (such as Kant himself) who understood difference as only an external phenomenon and therefore inconsequential and ephemeral, while the internal structure of the mind and reason were universal, eternal, and essential. The faith in this belief justifies imperialism, material and imaginative, as the overcoming of "mere" material differences (of the natives) by means of education: as "we" educate the other to use his divinely sanctioned reason, he will become more like us because while we are the embodiment of realized reason, "natives" are only reason in potentia. But the fact that such reasoning depends on the representation of difference embodied by the "native" suggests that there is something suspect about disembodied reason. We may have to account for the success of Enlightenment reasoning because of the threat that difference posed to Western beliefs in the infallibility of their system. In other words, the idea that difference existed, even if it was cast as cultural inferiority, raised the specter of an always differential identity in the seamless integrity of European (and, in the context of this argument, specifically British) mastery. If something could be visibly different and if that difference were crucial in producing the notion of an internalized, transhistorical identity, it spelled an inability of the all-knowing capacities of Western discursive practices to account for phenomenology.

The Kantian model of mind, certain of its own universality and trusting the legitimacy of its constitution of the outside world, nevertheless acknowledges the existence of its own internal "other": what will come a hundred years later to be called "the unconscious," Kant called "the thing" itself. Although Kant claimed the noumenal to be outside the scope of human knowledge, many of the romantic philosophers and artists who followed him could not resist the appeal of the unknown self. Little wonder that almost a century later Freud began using these aesthetically produced ideas in order to define the psyche in a scientific discourse. It seems then that Kant's understanding of the outside world—of a world outside Königsberg or Eastern Prussia or Europe—could only exist, a priori, as an internal projection. In this way, his *Critique of Pure Reason* can so glibly and successfully exclude history. This exclusion, of course, is nothing new; the cultural privilege Western nations place on historiography may well portend other forms of the successful exclusion of history. Latent anxieties that the impingement of an other, unknown world poses to the integrity and coherence of the "known" world are mitigated by historiographical discourse: our understanding of "universal" events is defined by what we know about ourselves and project onto others. Such a discourse consequently produces Western fantasies of its own political and cultural control. In the case of Kant and the romantic writers who deployed his understanding of the transcendental sublime through poetics, however, the putative incorporation of exotic otherness effectively masked an intense xenophobia that structures the internal life of the mind and the unconscious.[13]

The belief in an essential internal life of the mind that is able effectively to transcend the material circumstances of its own production has served the academy well, both in Kant's time and ours. Cultural studies, however, identify the ways aesthetics are politically motivated and manifested as products of power. But while the field of romanticism acknowledges the crucial need for such politicizing, it also holds some particular "truths" to be self-evident. Prominent among these professed truths is the successful foreclosure of xenophobia as a constitutive factor in the production of romantic ideas about subjectivity, inwardness, and authorship. It strikes me, however, that articulations of such "truths" may also usefully uncover the complexities of xenophobia as a cultural phenomenon. Following Freud's accounts of the processes of incorporation and introjection in which the first notion provides the bodily model for the second psychological operation, xenophobia dictates how (foreign) objects are situated and resituated within domestic discourse. Thus the bodily incorporation of difference that is identified as a "thing" is itself later transposed to its sublime form, the introjection of an idea. Our language embodies the cultural unconscious that rests both within and without the privileged internal space of individual agency.[14] In other words, as part of the symbolic, language acts as both basilisk and signpost to conscious ideas and unconscious impulses that make up what we define as "personal" subjectivity, one that may turn out to be more public than private.

A perfectly disembodied and idyllic "life of the mind" will always crucially depend on the dirty work performed by the "life of the body" for its articulation, resting precisely on material hierarchies of gender, race, class, and sexuality that it purports to transcend. Romantic writing—especially its preoccupation with subjectivity, the sublime, or other forms of transcendental philosophy—also rests on the messy material hierarchies that are both invoked and eradicated by xenophobia. Despite the radical changes cultural studies have wrought in the academy, it may nonetheless unconsciously retain older formulations of subjectivity that both depend on and reinforce notions of the internal and the external for their articulation. Romantic writing in particular struggles with its attachment to the imagination: a privileged internal space of unproblematized knowledge (as in Kant's exposition of the transcendental aesthetic), uncomplicated by the problems that race and gender pose to the production of epistemology. The meaning of race in early eighteenth-century Britain takes shape only as a projected materiality, an external reality far removed from ideas of Cartesian subjectivity. Color that is mapped out on an external skin functions exclusively in relation to the "uncolored" or white body privileged with the capacities of an internal life and a clearly defined "self."

But exactly how do these internal and external spaces get codified as hierarchies in cultural discourse? One way of addressing this problem is to look at Lacan's formulations of the unconscious. One of the most difficult—and most transparent—claims Lacan makes about the unconscious is its externality: the fact that the "unconscious is outside." Like the anatomical navel whose material presence marks a prior connection with someone other and therefore visibly contests the notion of an autonomous body, the ultimately unknown center of a psychic truth is equally visible: only available as a representation, it is out there, waiting to be uncovered, recovered, and situated within some ideological matrix. Ideological assumptions about the difference between external and internal sites of identity have privileged the internal: the enduring Enlightenment belief that the internal carries more meaning than the external turns out, according to Lacan, to be exactly the opposite.

Governed by epistemological interests in order and knowledge produced through a largely taxonomic discourse, Enlightenment thinking focuses on the empirical study, the Cartesian paradigm. Romanticism has been commonly understood as a reaction against Enlightenment reasoning, focusing on the erratic and the uneven rather than the regular, harkening back to older models of romance (medieval) for its paradigmatic shift. M. H. Abrams writes, for example:

in the several decades beginning with the 1780s, however, a number of the keenest and most sensitive minds found radically inadequate, both to the immediate human experience and to basic human needs, the intellectual ambiance of the Enlightenment, with (as they saw it) its mechanistic world-view, its analytic divisiveness (which undertook to explain all physical and mental phenomena by breaking them down into irreducible parts, and regarded all wholes as a collocation of such elementary parts), and its conception of the human mind as totally diverse and alien from its nonmental environment.[15]

While I believe that the "minds" that produced these objections certainly perceived themselves as making radical moves away from Enlightenment ideology, perhaps those moves were not quite as radical as they might appear. Or, conversely, perhaps the very radicalness of their representation is a sign of disturbing contiguities. Embedded within romantic discourse is a commitment to the idea of the author produced through inward contemplation, celebrating the imagination as the primary space for a revolt against a secured public arena of thought. It is against the popular eighteenth-century understanding of the author as voicing the collective thinking of a reasoning public that romanticism has come to be conceptualized.

Interestingly, however, as *Robinson Crusoe* makes abundantly clear, these ostensibly different discourses of Enlightenment and romantic thought share many similar currents, particularly in relation to their definitions of national identity. Appropriating the old meaning of "romance" from "romans/romauns," the vernacular language of France (as opposed to Latin), romantic writers consecrate the colloquial or common tongues, firmly believing these languages to articulate "true" feeling. That is, the historical motives for the "original" turn to the vernacular among medieval and renaissance writers, philosophers, politicians and the like had to do with the rise of nation states. Speaking the vernacular as an expression against Latin, against another authority, also suggests the production of one community in opposition to another one that has since been linked to the emergence of nation.[16] Likewise, Crusoe's taxonomic efforts, recorded in his journal as putatively free from any colonizing desire except "necessity," appropriate island artifacts (with crucial exceptions) and translate them into an eighteenth-century British commercial vernacular.

Wielding the technical facility Crusoe enjoys as a British subject to fashion his circumstances according to models of trade and commercialism, Defoe makes quite visible the ways in which subjectivities are fabricated through the fetish of xenophobia. Conscious of the outlandish figure he cuts with his goatskins, Mahometan mustaches, and not-quite-Mulatto skin, Crusoe is still able both to acknowledge his othered position (as when he becomes enslaved earlier in the novel) and to brandish the kind of authority granted a British subjectivity. We may be able to situate Defoe on the cusp of eighteenth- and early nineteenth-century formulations of the self in relation to others. Eighteenth-century constructions of subjectivity reproduce selves in relation to external reflections of exotic others. Jonathan Swift's *Gulliver's Travels*, for example, depicts the national and what we would now term cultural differences inhabiting the bodies of Lilliputians, Brobdingnagians, or Yahoos as externally manifested in the smallness, largeness, or darkness of their bodies, all of which are so conceptually distinct from Gulliver's own British body as to be incapable of sharing the same epistemological space.[17] Even if romantic conceptions of the self also deploy national identities as ways of insuring the discreteness of the self, the crucial difference is in their capacity to identify with otherness and incorporate it within the boundaries of the self. Thus when Wordsworth expresses his "personal wish / To speak the language more familiarly," it takes shape as his gradual withdrawal into the French revolutionary cause: "I gradually withdrew / Into a noisier world, and thus did soon / Become a patriot—and my heart was all / Given to the people, and my love was theirs."[18] Defoe's *Robinson Crusoe*, on the other hand, performs the important task of negotiating between these positions, which reinforces the argument that the "origins" of romantic identity may be deeply embedded in eighteenth-century epistemology.[19] My particular contribution to the large and longstanding literature on this subject is to argue that the shared inflections between these ostensibly incompatible discourses are primarily xenophobic and get represented in terms of nation.

The phenomenon of xenophobia remains largely untheorized in current postmodern and postcolonial studies; this telling absence may well attest to the ways in which it functions so successfully in social structures. This book will demonstrate the ways our academic belief in romantic principles (inward subjectivity, the solitary voice, the authority of writing) can be understood only through xenophobia and the language it produces.

Recent critics have persuasively claimed the influence of imperialism, orientalism, and colonialism on the production of romantic literature after Jerome J. McGann's important study, *The Romantic Ideology*, "precipitated a return to historical and political readings of the Romantic period."[20] John Barrell, Marilyn Butler, Nigel Leask, Robert Young, Jerome McGann, Saree Makdisi, Charles Rzepka, Alina Clej, Josephine McDonagh and others address the importance of attending to historical materialism in relation to romanticism, thus shifting our understanding of the discipline as a field without history. Collections such as Tim Fulford's and Peter J. Kitson's *Romanticism and Empire*, Sonia Hofkosh's and Alan Richardson's *Romanticism, Race, and Imperial Culture*, or John Beer's *Questioning Romanticism*, among others, conduct very useful cultural inquiry into the concept of romanticism, and problematize the material conditions of romantic discourse. Few arguments, however, have addressed the psychological conditions attendant upon imperialist ideology that make possible the production of romanticism. Little work in romantic studies or in the field of history has addressed the relationship between imperialism and nationalism that together with historical materialism forms the ideological apparatus for cultural representation.[21] Leask and Saree Makdisi make important arguments regarding Britain's sense of national self-enclosure: that imperial cultural incomparability results from internal or domestic anxiety about empire (Leask) or that the move away from trade and commerce and entry into industrialism happened well before the mid-eighteenth and nineteenth centuries (Makdisi). I place my own study in relation to these as an investigation of the psychological structures set up to account for these internal anxieties about national identity—for example, Johnson's trepidations about language or Defoe's uneasiness with trade—and claim that these concerns are historically based on an economy of xenophobia and xenodochy.

I will argue that British romantic writing, produced from imperialist ideology, is also constituted through the psychological hinge between imperialism and nationalism: xenophobia. The aesthetic focus dominating representations of romanticism (both of the literature and the critical discourse but also of more recent cultural and material readings) have emerged as a result of territorial claims. Not unlike the historical ways in which unknown worlds were incorporated—and introjected—within the parameters and perimeters of a "known" culture, academic definitions of historical periods as intellectual (or historiographical) territories repeat the imperial impulse to nationhood. As early eighteenth-century novels like *Robinson Crusoe* demonstrate, however, the connections between discourses long believed to have been antithetical to one another may also demonstrate the ways in which we lock certain paradigms of identity into fixed meanings, whether or not we associate them with a specific literary period. It stands to reason, then, that the romantic period is not simply an isolatable historical phenomenon which we have since "passed."

Saree Makdisi argues that the

> distinction between modernism and romanticism . . . is not so much in their engagement with modernization . . . but rather in that romanticism merges with the beginnings of modernization and persists alongside it to the end; whereas modernism emerges specifically at the climax of that process and helps to constitute that climax in overall cultural terms.[22]

I would add, however, that romanticism does not simply give way or fade out to modernism but is continually renewing itself according to new historical models even in the guise of modernity and postmodernity. For example, Makdisi locates the "much earlier, more deeply and stubbornly held view about overseas European hegemony" near the end of the eighteenth century. Defoe's *Robinson Crusoe*, however, demonstrates a much earlier belief in the epistemological superiority of British national subjectivity (one that develops from trade and commercial activity, but that later evolves into a form of island industrialism—the manufacture of skins into textiles). This belief is contingent upon a romantic understanding of the internalized self as wholly sufficient to articulate British national hegemony. What happens earlier than the end of the eighteenth century is also possible on the other end of the historical spectrum: that romantic celebration of the "archaic" at whatever point of "eradication" (as Makdisi argues) is an ongoing process that makes possible new definitions of (post)modernization (10).

My question addresses why the belief in the romantic understanding of an essential, inward authorial subjectivity and a persistent belief in aesthetic sensibility as a free-standing phenomenon is so enduring, particularly in the face of a postmodern culture with increasingly sophisticated capacities for self-consciously reinventing aesthetics. What epistemological ends does this tenacity serve?

This study addresses these questions by analyzing the ways xenophobia has historically created and sustained the belief in an essential authorial subjectivity. How xenophobia disarticulates and rearticulates this need, I argue, is crucially connected to the strategic and complex understanding and definition of orientalism and imperialism in late eighteenth and early nineteenth-century Britain. I am especially concerned with the ways the idea of containment—most often figured as containment of the literal mass of territories that constitute Britain's ideological imperial identity—is prominently represented in romantic literature. That is, to contain something—to draw boundaries around that "thing"—is to give it definition, whether this definition is produced discursively (lexicography), economically (commerce), or ideologically (nationality).[23]

Definitions, especially as they emerge as representations of containment, are critical to the ways in which colonial relations operate. Britain's relation to India seems to offer a particularly convincing example of how containment works. The relation India has had to Britain has been understood as politically, culturally, and aesthetically subordinate. However, India was crucial to the production of British identity: one has only to remember Gauri Viswanathan's crucial contribution to postcolonial studies when she argued that the solidification of a canon of literature marking English cultural identity was principally invented in India before it was deployed in Great Britain.[24] According to this model, there are no independent freestanding nations of "Britain" and "India" because their political, aesthetic, and cultural identities are mutually constitutive. It is not possible to "have" an India free from the cultural signification with which Britain has endowed it, or the reverse.

The popular dualism between "England" and "India," often postulated as the binary relation between "self" and "other," has conventionally situated these locales as utterly distinct from one another, sharing only a colonialist relation based on dominance and subordination. If we think of these territories, however, not as endpoints or fixed modular units but only as spaces for cultural negotiation—as intermediary planes occupying "in-between" spaces, in which neither place is automatically endowed with a natural(ized) authority over its own meaning—then the ideological structures sustaining beliefs about dominance and subordination become more transparent. The same insecurities defining the subaltern space for the British also delineate their own domestic space. Thus, from a British standpoint, what connects the "home" country, the domestic habitat (in the sense of native) to its fantasy of the East (an India that is continually being reinvented as ever more foreign), also subjects the domestic to a need for continual recontainment.[25] The ideological circuits that attach far-flung colonies to their "mother" country entangle those faraway places with the home base; foreign colonies, therefore, may not always be figured as outlandishly different from the mother country. These circuits also problematize the material things that identify the domestic space (the incorporation of tea, for example, as a signifier of Englishness); in short, they deterritorialize the domestic. While it is true that the national identity displayed by both colonial and postcolonial "India" is constructed within a European discourse, it is also true that British national identity is absolutely dependent on those "Indias" for its articulation. I argue that any British insistence on its own domestic interiority—or at least on the independence of that interiority from the colonial exterior—requires a disavowal or repression of the material practices that define Englishness.

As an academic discipline, romanticism is no longer understood as the self-referential celebration of art and the dehistoricized artist. Rather, romanticism provides us with ways of making things outside the scope of that nucleus, outside our domesticated space, "safe" for our consumption. Xenophobia similarly operates as a crucial ideological force in the task of organizing a space, of making and remaking the territories that, among other things, demarcate what is and what is not "home."

I am arguing, however, that xenophobia is not a free-standing entity, out of which is produced imperialism. As I've suggested earlier, xenophobia also depends on an economy with another less familiar term, xenodochy. Articulations of xenophobia—such as those occurring in imperialism—thus crucially depend on inviting the "foreign" to inhabit domestic grounds. Nigel Leask and John Barrell both argue that the consumption of the other is a form of maintenance; in Leask's terms, sporting "the sign of the Other in order to disengage the signifier from any semantic substance, to parody it, and also to innoculate himself and his culture from the threat which it poses" accounts for the sustained interest in and often excessive consumption of Oriental artifacts in tandem with a continual abjection of Oriental identity.[26] The difference my argument brings to their important formulations is in thinking through and historicizing the psychic impulses that drive such forms of consumption and vilification.

Slavoj Žižek argues that fantasy "constitutes our desire, provides its coordinates . . . teaches us how to desire."[27] What one incorporates or introjects within one's desire is always going to be articulated in the context of phobic markers. Crusoe's desires to resituate himself within a foreign signifying system take shape as the intense phobias that mark his difference. For example, Friday's habits, particularly his predilection for cannibalism—a practice that for his people is a way of negotiating political power—need to be instantly and radically relearned because of the threat they pose to Crusoe. Despite the fact that Friday willingly learns Crusoe's lessons and is an admirable companion to him, Crusoe remains skeptical, fearing the return of other savages even while admitting to the pleasantness of his life.

> But to return to my new companion: I was greatly delighted with him and made it my business to teach him everything that was proper. . . . now my life began to be so easy that I began to say to myself that could I but have been safe from more savages, I cared not if I was never to remove from the place while I lived. (188–89)

Such fears remain as the introjected phobic markers that critically mark the difference between Crusoe and Friday despite Crusoe's desires for assimilation.

The two parts of this book examine the ways xenophobia informs the relations between colony and mother country through the reification of romantic authorship. British romantic ideology, I argue, is first codified in the heart of the Enlightenment.[28] Later, during the period customarily understood as romantic, this ideology may have been more dramatically exemplified by its "outcasts" than by the main characters themselves. In other words, while Wordsworth, Coleridge, and Byron, for example, write about the relation between romanticism and orientalism, more marginal figures like De Quincey, Wollstonecraft, and Mary Shelley demonstrate the incorporation of oriental exoticism within English intellectualism. Foucault's injunction to seek history (genealogy) in "the most unpromising places, in what we tend to feel is without history" suggests that a field's central texts are not the only persuasive representations of literary movements.[29] The authors and texts I choose to examine, therefore, do not belong to a conventional roster of romantic writers; in fact, because I am situating the "origin" of romanticism well within the Enlightenment, I spend a good deal of time discussing the eighteenth century. I am arguing that the initial codification of romantic ideology as an articulation of xenophobic/xenodochial drives occurs within eighteenth-century documents. I am not examining literary texts that self-consciously raise the specter of the Orient (for example, Johnson's *Rasselas* or Byron's *Eastern Tales*), but, rather, am interested in the unselfconscious invocation of Oriental metaphor.

The first chapter situates the beginnings of a romantic ideology in the mid-eighteenth century with attention to Johnson's corpus. Although there have been many compelling arguments about eighteenth-century imperialism in Johnson's work, I argue that his imperialism informs romantic ideology and the shifting strategic deployments of imperial identity. Chapter One uncovers the ways in which his *Preface* to the *Dictionary, London,* and the *Life of Savage* institutionalize Englishness in its most invisibly authoritative form—the reference work—as well as in the more visible (works with identifiable authors) genres of poetry and biography through a self-consciously strategic xenophobic apology. These genres radically depart from earlier eighteenth-century representations that figure otherness and the exotic as external. Johnson clearly demonstrates the romantic move toward incorporating otherness within the self and the importance of exclusionary sensibilities to a "stable" national identity. His fictional and nonfictional works define the necessity for a privatized authorial space, dominated by his own sense of possessing an internal psychic self plagued by the vicissitudes of the unconscious.

This eighteenth-century hypostatization of the unconscious constitutes what we should recognize as the beginning of romantic ideology. The move Johnson makes toward interiorization may have been appropriated ex post facto forty-five years later to formulate the structures of a "new" romantic ideology.[30] Thus while his corpus figures mightily in the established history of eighteenth-century men of letters, it is also clear that it gestures toward a romantic ideology; ironically, he may embody an Oedipal figure against which "canonical" romantics rebel even as they carry on his legacy.

In some ways, De Quincey's relation to romanticism, while more obviously canonical than Johnson's, is less trustworthy because of his infamous addiction to opium. That is, his autobiographical confessions to opium-eating demonstrate a pathological relation to romantic scholarship, as John Barrell and Nigel Leask have so provocatively uncovered. It is this addiction, however, that keenly problematizes his romantic xenophobia. My second chapter demonstrates the internalization of exoticism in De Quincey's works, particularly his *Confessions*. I argue that his obsession with cultural monstrosity—"exotic" creatures like tigers and crocodiles that for him blur the boundaries of animal and human—functions as part of an impulse to derive histories of meaning that serve to situate, contextualize, and eventually mythologize the place of British imperial history. De Quincey's traffic in opium, his problems with addiction, and his struggle to maintain his intellectual status in the circle of Lake District poets all manifest the ways in which the xenophobia is institutionalized through the process of xenodochy. In other words, the fear of the foreign that informs so much of British cultural identity is negotiated in De Quincey and other romantics only by entertaining that which is most feared: the foreign. Thus De Quincey is able to slide between registers of familiarity and difference—between the domesticity of Dove Cottage and the network of oriental fantasies it produces—with ostensibly writerly ease. The Žižekian symptom of phobic markers of desire and loathing for the foreign that Crusoe deploys to his advantage returns in De Quincey's writing to mark off the limits of a "stable" identity.

What difference does gender make to the ways in which xenophobia is produced in romantic culture? Perhaps our attention should turn to the paradigms of xenophobia that depend on notions of reproduction. Maternal bodies represent the national body: more specifically, the mother's body provides colonialism with a material identity and imbues imperial authority with the innocence typically attributed to motherhood. Romantic models of solitary, inward-looking authorship are more vexed in relation to female writing because the material conditions providing such roles for authors were simply not commonly available to women in the late eighteenth or early nineteenth centuries (although both Mary Wollstonecraft and Shelley defy these conventions). Mary Wollstonecraft's relation to romanticism is, therefore, more overtly political. Like Wordsworth's interest in the French Revolution, Wollstonecraft's political, fictional, and personal writings all addressed the interests of common citizenry that the Lake District poets endorsed. Such articulations are, however, particularly vexed by gender. On the one hand, writers like Hannah More, Ann Yearsley, Wollstonecraft, and others demonstrate a keen sense of identification with the social oppressions wrought by imperialist traffic such as the slave trade. On the other, their own authorial positions are contingent upon same the kinds of power structures associated with imperialism.

In these interests, the second half of this study examines the mechanism through which a recently disclosed "female" canon complicates but does not overcome the xenophobic erection of such models of imperialism. Feminist recovery of the writings of Mary Wollstonecraft, while very crucially shifting the parameters of the canon, may have foreclosed our attention to some of the difficulties of her fictional and nonfictional work. For example, even while vociferously speaking for the need for women's political and intellectual agency in *Vindication of the Rights of Woman,* Wollstonecraft's own xenophobia determines the boundaries of which groups of "women" can claim subjectivity. Her fictional work, focusing on problems of mothering and female education, similarly reflects the insidiousness of the ideological structure of imperialism. Wollstonecraft's interest in romantic politics is primarily centered around the overtly political causes Wordsworth and Coleridge ended up discussing in their *Preface to the Lyrical Ballads.* The French Revolution with its concerns of republicanism and enfranchisement dramatized for poets like Wordsworth a material means to engage his revolutionary poetics. For Wollstonecraft, her interest in radical views on education, particularly those of Rousseau, her unorthodox ideas about marriage and domesticity, her attachment to Richard Price, place her within the intellectual parameters that have come to be known as romantic. Her anti-Jacobin *An Historical and Moral View of the Origin and Progress of the French Revolution* seems to align her with De Quincey's similar sentiments, though her opposition to the tyranny of the politically disfavored and the poor alike seems much less encoded by class (and gender) than De Quincey's. However, they share an untroubled sense of British hegemony articulated by xenophobia. Here the paradigm Samuel Johnson uses to formulate conceptions of the definitive other through a self-assimilating francophobia is repeated by both De Quincey and Wollstonecraft (ironically for the latter, given her attachment to Talleyrand and Rousseau).

I begin my argument on female authorship with Wollstonecraft partially because of her stature in a canon of "feminist" writing. Like Johnson, Wollstonecraft carves out a new lexicography but her feminist language is subject to the same ideological conflicts complicating Johnson's project. Specifically, I examine Wollstonecraft's representation of mothering as a phenomenon informed by general maternal images of the body of colonial power. These images are complicated by her equally fervent representations of the Rousseauian model that advocate a specific relationship between mothering, patriotism, and national (imperial) identity on the one hand, and a resistance to the entire practice of mothering as the only important form of female occupation on the other.

The simultaneous beatification and vilification of the maternal colonizing body is, ironically, most dramatically achieved in Wollstonecraft's own issue, so to speak: her daughter, Mary Shelley, makes almost painfully clear the cultural and psychic vicissitudes of xenophobic reproduction in *Frankenstein*. Though many critics have read this novel in the interests of cultural critique, and though my reading takes those ideological issues into account, I am specifically interested in the ways that maternity functions in the xenophobic figuration of romanticism. Do maternal bodies, because they serve the interests of nation by reproducing its citizenry, also perpetuate the xenophobic elements of national identity? Do they also critically resist the reproduction of imperialism? How complicit or implicit is maternity in the production of imperialist ideology?

The problems with the maternal, the xenophobic, the colonial, and the romantic body by no means end with the advent of late romanticism. Domesticity and its discontents, education and its oracular effects equally complicate popular readings of female-authored fictional works. What Mary Shelley articulates as "female" marginalization is further complicated by Charlotte Brontë. *Villette* in particular has been privileged as the text that most thoroughly investigates the female writer as marginalized subject. Set in the typically Gothic "foreign" space, *Villette* demonstrates with breathtaking concision the ways Lucy Snowe's national affiliation to Britain, no matter how vexed by gender, is determined by xenophobia. Providing a transitional text into Victorian ideologies of gender, Brontë's work articulates romantic ideals of identity, demonstrating similar xenophobic paradigms that inform early Victorian culture.

Reading women's work without understanding how technologies of race and gender inform representation is a lot like imagining that one's desires originate from oneself. There is no "outside" space in which to place the arena of women's work; to imagine that such writing is not a product of the same kinds of ideologies informing men's work is simplistic. To imagine that such work can remain "outside" the parameters of gender is also obfuscating. There is a significant body of work done by scholars of gender studies, cultural studies, and postcolonial studies that has established the ways gender often mediates strategies of othering. What is less clearly established is the rendering of gender into a thing capable of such agency. Looking at the production of women's writing during the late eighteenth and early nineteenth century discloses the same xenophobic systems that structure imperialism in the works of male authors. The reification of gender roles in the eighteenth century may have allowed women to claim an "agency" that discouraged them from questioning the xenophobic construction of national identity. Even the most overt appeals to end slavery, cast by Ann Yearsley, Hannah More, and others, do not question the deeply embedded structures of xenophobia within the frame of Britishness. Even if she chastises British "fancy" as the underlying material "cause" of slavery in her "Poem on the Inhumanity of the Slave Trade," for example, Yearsley does not critique the system that produces a "renegade Christian" slavemaster.

Demonstrating the ways in which gender, race, class, sexuality and nationalism inform and get informed by xenophobic drives, Defoe's *Robinson Crusoe*, first published in 1719, lays the groundwork for the institutionalization of xenophobia and provides compelling evidence for the argument that romanticism may have been extension of rather than an antidote to ideologies of conquering "nature" and "other." In the next chapter I discuss how thirty-six years later, Johnson codified xenophobic drives within the parameters of lexicography.

1 Institutionalizing Xenophobia: Johnson's Project

How does language get institutionalized? Johnson's 1755 *A Dictionary of the English Language* and his *Preface* to this project address some of the strategies involved in standardizing language. Embedded in Johnson's *Preface* are ideas that reflect his understanding of language as a cultural barometer. Johnson's invectives against the loose "license" of translators who destroy the integrity of language and his desires to preserve the purity of language by using pre-Restoration writers (the "pure sources of genuine diction") as authoritative examples for his definitions together demonstrate an interest in keeping English (language) for the English. It is somewhat surprising, then, given the vehemence with which he treats these ideas, to remember that his first published novel was a translation of the seventeenth-century Portuguese Jesuit, Father Jerome Lobo's *Voyage to Abyssinia*.

The apparent conflict between the ideas about language he represented in the *Preface* (1755) and the book he published in his early years (1733) is not especially problematic: given the enormous breadth of Johnson's work, it would be surprising if his ideas about literature and language didn't alter with time. More interesting, however, is the fact that when Johnson dwelled on the putative dangers of translation in the *Preface* he was referring particularly to translators of French, even though his early translation of Father Lobo was from the French and his later version of the "Oriental tale," *Rasselas*, published only four years after the *Dictionary*, was heavily influenced by Voltaire's *Candide*. It seems, then, that for Johnson, the French are crucially implicated in a strategy of othering: their place is somewhere between the "pure sources of genuine diction" that define Englishness and the "mingled jargon" that describes the language of Indian traders. That the genre of the "Oriental tale" was probably French in origin also suggests a metonymic connection of the French to more outlandish oriental exoticism.[1]

Johnson's translation of Father Lobo and *The History of Rasselas, Prince of Abyssinia*, both written under trying circumstances,² illustrate an eighteenth-century use of the "Orient" as an effective screen onto which to project English fantasies about the exotic. This use of the "Orient," not altogether limited to the eighteenth century, may have been crucially negotiated by an infamous British francophobia. In the case of *Rasselas* (and those *Rambler* essays featuring Seged), exoticism—which had little to do with actual representations of Oriental countries—had an educational and moral edge. Although many of the French Oriental tales functioned as parables whose moral purposes were duly translated into English, for Johnson such narratives may also have been possible because, as *Rasselas*'s Pekuah says (a propos of the specters inhabiting the Pyramids), "our entrance is no violation of their privileges; we can take nothing from them, how can we offend them?"³ In other words, the function of the "Oriental tale" in England was, in part, to provide a different kind of backdrop (French/Oriental) onto which one could throw into sharp relief the moral lessons of English nationalism that would advocate cultural separation. After all, like the protagonist of Voltaire's *Candide* who concluded "Il faut cultiver notre jardin," Rasselas and his company decide to return to Abyssinia rather than take up residence elsewhere. The other simultaneously circumvents the potential threat of national and cultural miscegenation and upholds the English ideology by keeping itself at bay. Also important to the eighteenth-century sensibility was the belief that tourism was "no violation"; that the fantasy about cultural purity ("we can take nothing from them, how can we offend them?") was maintained on both ends, English and other; that the intermingling of cultural standpoints, at least in the context of travel, afforded few problems.

But, clearly, there *were* problems with this form of exchange. Rather early in the novel, Rasselas asks:

By what means . . . are the Europeans thus powerful? or why, since they can easily visit Asia and Africa for trade or conquest, cannot the Asiatics and Africans invade their coasts, plant colonies in their ports, and give laws to their natural princes? The same wind that carries them back would bring us thither. (91)

Imlac replies:

They are more powerful, sir, than we . . . because they are wiser; knowledge will always predominate over ignorance, as man governs other animals. But why their knowledge is more than ours, I know not what reason can be given, but the unsearchable will of the Supreme Being. (91)

The reasonable question Rasselas poses is dismissed by Imlac's irrational (to postcolonial readers) answer. This answer, however, is informed by the English (and European) belief that their epistemological stature is unassailable; the only kind of knowledge that can "predominate" is western. A character fashioned out of the English imagination, the "Oriental" Imlac crucially demonstrates the cultural fantasy that English imperialism was recognized by the "other" as natural.

Anxieties about the invincibility of English epistemology, however, were more forcibly articulated in Johnson's non-Orientalist writings than in the narratives that directly engaged the Orient. "Oriental tales" like *Rasselas*, the *Rambler* essays, or even his translation of Father Lobo provided his audience with an engaging if fictitious representation of the "Orient." Such a representation, however, was clearly alien to anything English. Thus Imlac's stories of his travels form more a catalogue of countries and travels than a detailed description, which in a culture that structured itself on taxonomies is hardly surprising. Readers could satisfactorily identify the lesson or story without necessarily thinking too deeply about their own relations to the different cultures being represented because what was reflected back to them was a picture of themselves. This is not to say that the representations of foreign places had no effect on English readers; rather, that they could dismiss cultural anomalies as foreign issues that had no relation to England.

Johnson's *Preface to the Dictionary* and other fictional works that explicitly address England and Englishness are different. These works do not treat their settings—London, Wales, Scotland—as mere backdrops; the settings act as politicized places that support the moral and political trajectory of the texts. The "lessons" or morals about language that Johnson represents in his *Preface to the Dictionary* are qualitatively different from those that he represents in his writings directly engaging the "Orient," but in both cases the understanding of the power and authority of English epistemology is unquestioned. It is also clear, however, that the other—the French, the Orient—signifies the vulnerability of Englishness and their susceptibility to decay, to the corruption of the defining parameters of English cultural identity.

For these reasons the following chapter on Johnson focuses on the *Preface* to the *Dictionary*, the poem *London*, and the cultural biography *Life of Savage*. These texts illustrate Johnson's definition of English culture as one produced through xenophobia. Unlike the *Encyclopaedia Britannica*, the *Oxford English Dictionary*, or various other bibliographical tomes, there are no "authors" of this reference work; rather, dictionaries are produced by such institutions as the academy and the publishing house. There is no place for individual acclaim or defamation. Perhaps because of the lack of visible and individual flair, the institution assumes a comforting solidity, a weighty sense of reliability and legitimacy that has established itself in early modern European cultures.

The exception is Johnson. His name stands out as an authorial presence in lexicographical history. The construction of the *Dictionary* is attributed exclusively to him, and yet his authorial presence, canonized as it is, has the same sort of legitimacy as that of the anonymous institutions. The ideological practices and positions embedded in his work, I will argue, are ones that are informed by xenophobia and produce the determining language for the privatized authorial space later privileged by romantic writers. Likewise, *London* also profits from a popular eighteenth-century poetic form: the imitation. The question of individual authorship is tethered to a faithful rendering of a national and cultural belief in its own incomparability. That this incomparability is embattled on the one hand by malignant Frenchified presence, and, on the other, by a vacuous and insipid Welsh pastoral motif again suggests the peculiar vulnerability of an English cultural identity that exists in an uneasy balance between xenodochy and xenophobia.

The *Life of Savage*, thematically connected to *London* because of the historical association of Thales (the poem's speaker) and Richard Savage, exemplifies a domestic conflict about the status of English authorship. Johnson uses no explicit "others" to engage a representation of the English writer; several figures, however, function as impediments to the progress of Richard Savage's literary development. These obstructions are domestic rather than foreign in origin: the troubled maternal relations that Savage invents for Johnson's delectation, and the ways in which Johnson deploys Savage's stories (Savage is also held under scrutiny, albeit sympathetically) in order to render the plight of the English author heroic. Thus Johnson's poignant biography, recording the hazards that the embattled Savage experiences (and thereby illustrating a very effective portrait of himself), demonstrates the ways in which English authorship is also contingent on gynophobia. Turning the domestic household into a troubled spot suggests that the internal national space needs to be continually and carefully policed by the rigors of a regulated masculine authorship.

"Lost" in Lexicography

"It is the fate," writes Johnson, "of those who toil at the lower employments of life to be driven by the fear of evil than attracted by the prospect of good. . . . Among these unhappy mortals is the writer of dictionaries; whom mankind have considered not as the pupil but the slave of science . . . doomed only to . . . clear obstructions from the paths through which learning and genius press forward . . . without bestowing a smile on the humble drudge that facilitates their progress" (277). These somewhat mordant words open Johnson's *Preface to the Dictionary* and betray a keen sense of the costs of undertaking this task. The *Preface* subtly addresses concerns about the status of the lexicon as a text, an institution, and a cultural index. In the opening passage of the *Preface* is not only the droll complaint of the lexicographical lackey but Johnson's absolute certainty that such drudge-work is vital to the production of knowledge. The "dream of comprehensive and universally available knowledge" is linked to the vexed relation Johnson had to the academy. If he derided academic institutions, he was also in competition with them to make accessible the notion of an encyclopedic body of knowledge.[4]

The importance of academic cultures in eighteenth-century England has been admirably discussed by critics of intellectual history and cultural studies.[5] For the purposes of my argument, I focus on Johnson's unsettled relation to the academy to spotlight his other troubled and sometimes contradictory reactions to the conditions of epistemological production. Ironically, considering the prominence of the academic institution in British intellectual culture, rejecting the structure and support of academies marks, for Johnson, a moment of nationalist investment as well as one of individual liberty. For him the "soft obscurities of retirement or . . . the shelter of academic bowers" (297) that conventionally foster the kind of work he undertakes are linked with French and Italian institutions, at least insofar as Johnson is competing with European academies to produce national lexicons. Johnson's nettled relationship with wealthy patrons of letters, from whom he suffered personal humiliation on several occasions, may inform his representation of the academy as a potentially effete space, one that thwarts individual authority and control. English conventions of patronage, dependent as they are on the claims of class, are practices which Johnson seems happy to find in decline. Certainly his *Dictionary*, produced "with little assistance of the learned, and without any patronage of the great," attests to his censure of the academy and its patrons alike.[6]

Many critics read the simultaneous events of the publication of Johnson's *Dictionary* on April 15, 1755, and the conferral of his honorary degree from Oxford—received in time to be included on the title page of the *Dictionary*—as a gesture that automatically elevated the hack writer from Grub Street to a position as one of England's intellectual authorities.[7] This reasoning, while conveniently encouraging and reinforcing notions of "virtue rewarded," for the most part ignores the powerful ideologies informing the production of knowledge in encyclopedic and lexicographical institutions. I want to consider these ideological implications. More specifically, I want to look at the production of knowledge when the contexts of race, class, gender, sexuality, and nationality are highlighted rather than effaced.

Most intellectual histories, argues Murray Cohen in his introduction to *Sensible Words*, are forms of self-validation whose main concerns seem to revolve around making "history safe for our understanding." These histories tend to obfuscate their beginnings and, according to Cohen, "start after important first steps have been forgotten or buried."[8] Cohen's metaphoric descriptions about writing histories may be a useful place to begin to uncover the ways in which certain "fundamental" shifts of paradigms may themselves be entrenched in ideological networks. Cohen explains that, in avoiding "modern limitations of terminology and discipline," he "did not expect to find confirmations of explanatory patterns that I had been taught." He remarks "in approaching the past, I expected to meet comparative strangers, not domesticated pets."[9] The use of the terms "strangers" and "domesticated pets" resonates considerably when one takes into account the conditions that have produced such phenomena. Indeed, the notion of "domesticity," invented and established by powerful cultural institutions, reifies and recontains "strangers" and "pets" in very specific places, and in different relations to power.

Another paradigm of epistemology may be necessary to uncover some of the problems with eighteenth-century lexicography. The anecdotal richness of Boswell's *Life of Johnson* furnishes splendid, humorous moments in literary history while serving as a model for biographical representation, but it may also be read as a way in which "Johnson" is made "safe" for "our" understanding. In this respect, a feminist epistemology becomes crucial to uncovering some of the dominant fictions informing both Johnson's lexicography and the body of work written about Johnson as lexicographer.

Donna Haraway has identified as a major area of feminist struggle "the canonization of language, politics, and historical narratives in publishing practices, including standard reference works." Although she is describing a "'keyword' entry for a new Marxist dictionary" in which certain words are being rewritten because "women do not appear where they should," such a practice reminds us that models for standardization have been in place in early modern British culture and that ideologies of imperialism, gender, and sexuality account for the predominance of anglophone lexicons (although directly competing with European academies that have produced their own lexicons). Haraway argues,

> The gaps and rough edges, as well as the generic form of an encyclopedia entry, should all call attention to the political and conventional processes of standardization. Probably the smooth passages are the most revealing of all; they truly paper over a very contentious field. Perhaps only I need a concrete lesson in how problematic an entry on any "keyword" must be. But I suspect my sisters and other comrades also have at times tended to simply believe what they looked up in a reference work, instead of remembering that this form of writing is one more process for inhabiting possible worlds—tentatively, hopefully, polyvocally, and finitely.[10]

Robert DeMaria's claim that Johnson employed an encyclopedic tradition of lexicography because of the "vast amount of illustrative quotation he included" functions as an example of the tautological reasoning Haraway identifies.[11] Keeping in mind Haraway's questions and cautions about works of reference, how does our understanding of Johnson's *Dictionary* shift, and how are our assumptions about the status of reference and definition destabilized? Johnson's *Preface* serves to frame the various problems of representation embedded in his lexicographical task. In doing so, it locates Johnson's political imperative to construct bourgeois British identity.

One of the compelling features about the opening of the *Preface* is the concern Johnson expresses not only for the thanklessness of the lexicographer's task, but for the barbarous state of language itself. Language, it seems, behaves not unlike an unruly child or flighty woman of fashion. He writes:

> while [language] was employed in the cultivation of every species of literature, [it] has itself been hitherto neglected; suffered to spread, under the direction of chance, into wild exuberance, resigned to the tyranny of time and fashion; and exposed to the corruptions of ignorance, and caprices of innovation. (277)

Johnson positions himself as the slave rather than the pupil of science in a history of drudgery that attends the production of knowledge. This representation imbues his labor with a bourgeois ethic that preaches toil as virtue. Yet the word "slave" seems curiously excessive in the context of Johnson's typically measured and moderate language. The use of the term calls into question the status of his definitional progress. "Time" and "fashion" form a "tyranny" to which Johnson is a "slave." Such a "tyranny," composed largely of the "corruptions of ignorance" and the "caprices of innovation," needs a steadier hand to wrest control from "accident or affectation" and steer the course of knowledge back on a progressive track. "Notwithstanding this discouragement," Johnson decides to assume the part of cultural arbiter and write "a dictionary of the English language" (277–79), placing himself, impossibly, as both slave and tyrant of scientific knowledge, or, perhaps more accurately for capitalist culture, as its owner.

His first tyrannical move as owner is to position language as something material: either as "rubbish" and "obstruction" or as "learning" and "genius." This gesture emphasizes the visceral and substantive qualities of language, endowing it with value, especially in the hands of a wise venture capitalist. Johnson's material view of language does more than act as a convenient metaphor: it uncovers a discourse of cultural materialism at work in his representation of language. It is important to consider Raymond Williams's argument for "the indissoluble connections between material production, political and cultural institutions and activity, and consciousness" when thinking through the ways in which Johnson's catalogue of language replicates a model of British bourgeois identity.[12] When we take into account the various academic institutions with which Johnson competes, and their place in determining material conditions of life, Johnson's concept of selfhood, informed by an uneasy relation between Enlightenment models of the individual and an increasing attention to the status of nation, may be read as an ideological position, a necessary fiction of a mystified lived relation about the material conditions of his life at the time: impoverished, embittered, and alone.[13]

Johnson is fated, he suggests, to serve a thankless public with his lexicographical toil. He is "doomed only to remove rubbish and clear obstructions" in the service of "learning and genius" that "press forward to conquest and glory, without bestowing a smile on the humble drudge that facilitates their progress" (277). Yet "tongues," he reminds us, "like governments have a natural tendency to degeneration; we have long preserved our constitution, let us make some struggles for our language" (296). Such reminders prompt an awareness of certain kinds of authorial power: as despised, hopeless, or invisible as lexicographical labor may be, it documents the coherence of national culture as crucially as the "constitution," an argument that would have had considerable force in eighteenth-century England.[14] Johnson's identification with such labor is troubled by his relation to academic cultures. Caught between two categories, neither a member of the intellectual elite nor a mere Grub Street hack writer, he is highly sensitive to the competing and at times conflicting desires to have his work remain unnoticed ("I have protracted my work till most of those whom I wished to please have sunk into the grave"); to serve as the price for his service to the nation ("I have devoted this book, the labor of years, to the honor of my country"); and to append his name, by the very act of writing this *Preface*, "to the reputation of English literature," remarking that the "chief glory of every people arises from its authors" (296–98). One way of accounting for such contending desires may be to see Johnson's project as a challenge to the practice of patronage and as his competition with academies. Johnson's own definition of aristocratic patronage, one that "supports with insolence and is paid with flattery,"[15] suggests a necessity for establishing an identity in which issues of propriety override the corrupt system of patronized literary production.[16] That is, Johnson eschews aristocratic aid for an implicitly bourgeois self-reliance and derides aristocratic indulgences while promoting independent temperance. Johnson's representation of language can be read as a study of culture. It reconstructs for a British audience the need to moderate potential imperial prosperity with a stabilizing bourgeois ethic. The potential of literary wealth that language offers can only be realized by the rational restraining hand of a lexicographer schooled in the arts of moderation.

The *Preface* provides an outline for the problem of representing English, and by association England, to the British. Much like an appraiser of fine gems, Johnson takes up the lexicographical burden of establishing a "settled test of purity" for language: he studiously endeavors to "collect examples and authorities from the writers before the Restoration, whose works [I] regard . . . as the pure sources of genuine diction" (289). With this explanation, Johnson places himself in the position of final literary authority. The contradictions in his writing—namely that "purity" of language incorporates not all English literature but only pre-Restoration works, specifically Elizabethan—illustrate not only his own uneasiness with the claim of a "pure" origin but also the ideological nature of his project.

Purity suggests the existence of its opposite: corruption. In his catalogue of the various forms of neglect the English language has suffered, Johnson names the "corruptions of ignorance." These corruptions take the form of "irregularities" that, in the process of "adjusting the orthography, which has been to this time unsettled and fortuitous," he has found "inherent in our tongue" (278). These "improprieties and absurdities," he writes, are "the duty of the lexicographer to correct or proscribe" (278). However, in many cases "Such defects are not errors of orthography, but spots of barbarity impressed so deep in the English language that criticism can never wash them away" (279). What I find compelling about this passage is that the issues of contamination inform Johnson's lexicographical task. On the one hand, his position as a critic has the potential to wash clean contaminating error by locating and testing pure sources of "genuine diction." On the other, the spots of barbarity indicate an otherness that, though domesticated—indeed, "inherent"—always represents a site of resistance to the contention of a seamless national language. Like the very construction of British national identity, the composition of language is impure and uneven. Indeed, it seems that there is something barbarous about language in its "natural" state; only when schooled by particular authors' hands does language represent a pure source of "genuine diction."[17]

One way to examine the way ideology operates in this context is to read "purity" in language in light of Derrida's discussion of Condillac. In his essay "Signature Event Context," Derrida writes:

The representational character of written communication—writing as a picture, reproduction, imitation of its content—will be the invariable trait of all the progress to come. The concept of *representation* is indissociable here from the concepts of *communication* and *expression*. . . . Representation regularly *supplements* presence. But this operation of supplementation . . . is not exhibited as a break in presence, but rather as a reparation and a continuous, homogeneous modification of presence in representation.[18]

Derrida's account of an ideology of representation is helpful for reading Johnson's concern with representation. Language's constitutive "impurity" is related to the function of the sign itself: in order for the sign to operate as a sign, it needs to be repeatable. The sign's necessary iterability—the fact that the sign, standing for something else, is repeatable in a variety of contexts—makes the presence of an originary moment or meaning simultaneously necessary and impossible. The sign's susceptibility to repetition, and consequent failure to coincide *entirely* with what it is supposed to represent in any instance, marks each instance of its occurrence. The "impurity" inherent in the sign is what defines it as a sign: iterability accounts for the authentic, the seamless "presence" of meaning, that is always preceded by the inauthentic.

While Derrida's account usefully complicates the ideological formation of language, marxist terms underscore its material construction. If language is "practical consciousness which is inseparable from all social material activity," as Raymond Williams affirms, if it makes visible the material consequences of ways of thinking and acting in different worlds, then Johnson's positioning of language and lexicographers is undeniably ideological.[19] From a related critical stance, Haraway cautions against assumptions of objectivity in conventional processes of standardization. Her call to read the political worlds that reference works inhabit permits us to see the impulse to circumscribe as one that is ideologically fraught. The fiction of stabilizing language that the lexicographer performs is politically linked to establishing a place for the author within the literary and academic marketplace, a place not dependent on aristocratic patronage or the tyranny of academies and yet not bound by the equally oppressive bonds of hack writing. It would seem then that the resistant "spots of barbarity," while masquerading under cover of a monolithic mother tongue, perform what can be called continual disruption.[20]

Johnson's desire to shape language by recourse to its earlier manifestations (e.g., Elizabethan works) is informed by the (im)possibility of fixing an originary moment. While Elizabethan England may have represented to Johnson and other eighteenth-century readers a nostalgic moment of enviable national coherence, Johnson himself articulates the unsettling and destabilizing work which lexicography performs even in the act of circumscribing that ostensible coherence. Johnson writes that he has

fixed Sidney's work for the boundary beyond which I make few excursions. From the authors which rose in the time of Elizabeth, a speech might be formed adequate to all the purposes of use and elegance. If the language of theology were extracted from Hooker and the translation of the Bible; the terms of natural knowledge from Bacon; the phrases of fiction from Spenser and Sidney; and the diction of common life from Shakespeare, few ideas would be lost to mankind for want of English words in which they might be expressed. (289)

But he goes on to contend that

When we see men grow old and die at a certain time one after another, from century to century, we laugh at the elixir that promises to prolong life to a thousand years; and with equal justice may the lexicographer be derided, who being able to produce no example of a nation that has preserved their words and phrases from mutability, shall imagine that his dictionary can embalm his language and preserve it from corruption and decay. (294)

Johnson establishes the impossibility of his task to confine and secure linguistic meaning and usage to a specific historical period. Elizabethan writers stand for Johnson as a powerful cultural fantasy of national coherence. This is a putatively idyllic moment of absolute (although, unlike the French, inherently just) monarchy, global exploration, and military strength. An increase in consumerism in eighteenth-century society and succeeding dependence on commercial expansion, however, threatens the logic of this cultural fantasy.

One way of analyzing the possible threats Johnson perceives to the integrity of language is to identify how language and labor come to be associated in ways other than intellectual. Johnson warns against the "folly of naturalizing useless foreigners to the injury of the natives" (283). English works are used by Johnson as examples of "genuine diction" just as lexicographical drudgery paves the way for works of "genius," or language is "employed" in the cultivation of literature. An English work ethic thus stands for a specifically English morality, positioned directly against the slothful uselessness of "foreigners." Johnson's xenophobic response to adopting foreign words that might "reduce us to babble a dialect of France," together with his desire for a "pure" Englishness, construct the *Dictionary* as an undertaking of cultural representation. Johnson notes the etymological roots of words may be from Latin or French "since at the time when we had dominions in France, we had Latin service in our churches," and "the French generally *supplied* us . . . [with] . . . terms of domestic use"; ironically, then, the British are "babbl[ing] a dialect of France" even if their appropriation of French words as a result of their "dominion" in France is an imperial one (296, italics mine).[21] Johnson seems to be willing to entertain the possibility of a French supply of language (xenodochy) while rejecting the notion that such a source of valuable material could possibly affect or alter the original structure of English (xenophobia). Interestingly, the same sort of francophobic response Johnson has toward these "useless foreigners" complements his xenophobia toward Great Britain itself. The list of Elizabethan works Johnson deems pure enough to serve as references in his *Dictionary* not only fetishizes a particular literary period but the writers he names—Sidney, Hooker, Bacon, Spenser, and Shakespeare—are all English (as opposed to British). There seems to be a certain cultural imperialism, to borrow Said's phrase, at work in Johnson's national representation: the boundaries that he "fixes" for a definitive language do not stray beyond the borders of England to Scotland or Wales.[22]

But language proves recalcitrant, even if it is the medium through which the imperialist literary products of "learning and genius" are made possible. One of its major forms of resistance is the inherent impurity of the sign that resists being "fixed" in an originary etymological moment but, rather, shifts its meaning from moment to moment. As he admits, Johnson cannot hope to change or alter language, but merely attempt to direct its movement. Faced with this verbal impotence, however, Johnson maintains a thoroughly bourgeois sensibility: "we retard what we cannot repel," he reasons, "we palliate what we cannot cure" (296). Thus he modifies his desire, his fantasy of circumscription, proscription, and authorial control, as "duty." In keeping with his representation of a work ethic, Johnson claims that "every language has likewise its improprieties and absurdities, which it is the duty of the lexicographer to correct or proscribe" (278). Language as representation is ideologically informed. In the *Preface*, it is a reflection or communication of a unified and integral cultural and national identity. Yet language is dependent on its constitutive contextual iterability that by definition is cut off from its referent, intended signification, and context of communication. Language as a means of representation, as "practical consciousness," is as "impure" as the sign, and its reflection of an integral national identity is equally flawed, changing, and contextually iterable.

Faced with this malleability, Johnson constructs an empirical model of a national language and identity that depends on the fiction that an individual can redirect the course of words and meaning. This model is one that he has uncovered while applying himself to the "perusal of *our* writers . . . noting whatever might be of use to ascertain or illustrate any word or phrase accumulated in time the materials of a dictionary," whose progress he charts according to "such rules as experience and analogy suggested to me; experience, which practice and observation were continually increasing; and analogy, which, though in some words obscure, was evident in others" (278, italics mine). Language is determined by Johnson's experience and observation: cultural identity is not discovered or revealed but proscribed and prescribed.

Another problem with Johnson's project of representing an integral culture through its language is the difference he establishes between oral and written language.[23] Containing language within the lexicographical project is made urgent by Johnson's rearticulation of the possibility of a contextual rupture. The potential for rupture is always present and partially accounts for what is disruptive about language and problematic about lexicography. Johnson's warning against babbling foreign dialects is predicated on the notion that the representation of a unified national identity through language depends on controlling and limiting its contexts—oral and written. This sort of control is as necessary as it is interminable. For Johnson, language's mobility and motility, its tendency toward capriciousness and willfulness, confirms the necessity of an authority to control its energy within the confines of the *Dictionary*.

Perhaps most striking in this conflicted account of Englishness is that Johnson assigns a feminine role to language. The fitfulness, waywardness, capriciousness, and willfulness that, according to him, constitute the various problems that vex a lexicographer's task, are now bound up with ideologies of gender, and language acts even more like a flighty woman. Gender intersects with and informs Johnson's project of cultural representation. He writes:

> I am not yet so lost in lexicography as to forget that *words are the daughters of the earth, and that things are the sons of heaven.* Language is only the instrument of science, and words are but the signs of ideas: I wish, however, that the instrument might be less apt to decay, and that signs might be permanent, like the things which they denote. (280, italics Johnson's)

This passage establishes the hierarchical priority of things over words and at the same time of sons over daughters. It is a telling instance of how gender categories overlap with the tenet that things precede words. The feminine is directly associated with a mutable language prone to decay; masculine "things" and "ideas," in contrast, of which language is "only the instrument," conform to the stability and uniformity that Johnson would recommend. Equally crucial is that the representation of the masculine as permanent and material is only established by way of the faulty, corrupted "instrument." The availability of masculine "things," that is, is guaranteed only by employing, or trafficking in, the feminine body of language. The mobility, the femininity of language makes possible a solid, unmoving, permanent masculinity within English culture.

The relationship of feminine to masculine in this passage is produced by the same wishful anxiety that characterizes Johnson's more forceful moment of sociological scapegoating, here involving Mediterranean and Indian "trafficking":

> Commerce, however necessary, however lucrative, as it depraves the manners, corrupts the language; they that have frequent intercourse with strangers, to whom they endeavor to accommodate themselves, must in time learn a mingled dialect, like the jargon that serves the traffickers on the Mediterranean and Indian coasts. This will not always be confined to the exchange, the warehouse, or the port, but will be communicated by degrees to other ranks of the people, and at last incorporated with the current speech. (294)

Here the necessary evil of commercial traffic functions as the screen onto which Johnson can project his anxieties about recontaining language within a lexicographical frame. The slippery, suspect position he has previously allotted the feminine now becomes pointedly othered; Johnson aligns "strangers" with corruption, and particularly strangers from exoticized ports of exchange like the "Mediterranean" and "Indian" coasts. The "mingled" mongrel dialect such traffickers speak, produced out of such questionable spaces as "the exchange, the warehouse, or the port," may penetrate British bourgeois propriety and be "incorporated with the current speech," thus infecting the proper language and hindering the lexicographer's search for linguistic "purity."

Johnson's conflicting representations of primary features of capitalism—his promotion of a bourgeois work ethic on the one hand and his fear of commerce on the other—suggests internal inconsistency in capitalist logic. Capitalist enterprise is at odds with the bourgeois impulse to protect national borders. That such a territorial impulse is opposed by an equally powerful desire to invite commerce in the foreign reveals the xenodochy on which xenophobia rests. For Johnson, lexicographical drudgery—a product of the bourgeois work ethic—is useful because it polices the borders of nation, here marked by language; commerce, "however necessary, however lucrative" to the power and efficacy of a national whole, is highly suspect because it "corrupts the language."

Although Johnson warns against the dangers of commerce, he is not particularly concerned with the actual disappearance of English words, or even with the emergence of a "dialect of France." It is the "mingled dialect" or mixed "jargon" emerging from those Mediterranean and Indian traffickers that worries him. This worry reveals Johnson's political imperative to construct not only an inviolable English language but also an inviolable English (bourgeois) society.[24] Johnson's anxiety about the possibility of linguistic infection seems to be class based as well as xenophobic; he fears that dialects from the Indian and Mediterranean coasts (and not France) will be "communicated by degrees to other ranks of people, and be at last incorporated within current speech." His anxiety—connected to the categories of class ("ranks"), race, gender, sexuality ("communicated")—readily shifts its focus from one to the next. These anxious shifts indicate that Johnson sees identity in terms of difference.

Foreignness is analogous to femininity in the way in which Johnson constructs an ideal of Englishness by debasement and rejection. Both the foreign and the feminine are cast out of Johnson's representation of permanence, as masculine "things" and "ideas" eventually evolve into "pure," timeless English diction. In the *Preface*, Johnson sustains his belief in a pure origin by turning and orienting English toward the past. He rids English (and England) of the "improprieties" of innovation and ignorance that are, by implication, feminine. Such improprieties and infelicities of usage are intrinsic to language, however, and are not just contingent errors or accidents that can be excluded from the definition of language.

Purity of origin, as represented in the *Preface*, lays the groundwork for Johnson's representation of English cultural and national identity. Before Johnson can cast out foreign and feminine "improprieties," however, he must identify and construct them. Johnson employs a strategy of othering—a process that creates the other in order to cast it out—by engaging in precisely the sort of traffic that he identifies as among the "lower employments of life" and associates with both the foreign and the feminine. That is, Johnson must use language itself with all its improprieties as the means by which a representation of his own position as well as Englishness is produced.

One way of accounting for the others Johnson employs on behalf of constructing an inviolable and "pure" sense of Englishness is to use Gayatri Spivak's notion of "self-consolidating" and "absolute" others. The feminine, previously aligned with those "spots of barbarism" that resist critical cleansing, function as the "self-consolidating" other: the presence of something identifiably not-English but yet able to combine with an English "self" (represented as the "genuine sources of pure diction" to which Johnson refers) and to present a unified front against the highly visible, "absolute other": the foreign.[25] Johnson's invective against the dangers of translation cohere with his cultural representation. Johnson complains that the

> great pest of speech is frequency of translation. No book was ever turned from one language into another without imparting something of its native idiom; this is the most mischievous and comprehensive innovation; single words may enter by thousands and the fabric of the tongue continue the same, but new phraseology changes much at once; it alters not the single stones of the building but the order of the columns. If an academy should be established for the cultivation of our style, which I, who can never wish to see dependence multiplied, hope the spirit of English liberty will hinder or destroy, let them, instead of compiling grammars and dictionaries, endeavor, with all their influence, to stop the license of translators, whose idleness and ignorance, if it be suffered to proceed, will reduce us to babble a dialect of France. (296)

Part of this invective is informed by Johnson's own investment as a rival lexicographer to those academies in France and Italy that were engaged in producing their own dictionaries. And certainly part of his rancor can be accounted for by the bitterness he felt toward English academic institutions, which had, in the powerfully empathetic words of Walter Jackson Bate, "for fifteen years . . . barred" him entrance for lack of a degree.[26] It is curious, however, that Johnson focuses on translation itself as a single cause for the problems he has with language (especially since he himself has profited from French translation in time of dire need). Like trafficking with Mediterranean and Indian cultures, translation functions as a kind of porous border, a membrane that, while marking out discrete languages and cultures, does not enforce these boundaries. These borders present the most difficult and antithetical problems for one whose task is to regulate and monitor the boundaries of meaning.

Johnson's representation of "ideas" and "things," linked to cultural chauvinism under the guise of rewriting a national identity, comes about by trafficking in language he has cast as feminine or feminized. Johnson's representation of a dominant, masculine, English authority relies on a foundation of language that is almost always in a state of decay. Because, as Johnson claims language is by its nature prone to change, and because language is unreliable as a fixed signifying system, the task of securing "pure" meaning becomes impossible.

According to Johnson, at the heart of language, and therefore at the heart of Englishness, is a series of unfixable others; Johnson's responses articulate a xenophobic anxiety of contamination by those others. Johnson's representation of language and culture depends a good deal on instituted difference. His construction of English national identity relies on the maneuver Edward Said discusses in *Orientalism*. With this maneuver "European culture gained in strength and identity by setting itself off against the Orient as a sort of surrogate and even underground self."[27] There are at least two levels of this othering occurring in the *Preface*; one can be read as a familiar francophobia, based on economic and imperial rivalry between France and England, and the other as a deeper, less specific, xenophobic scapegoating in which a feminized language operates as a representation of "decay" or contamination. Thus Johnson describes in *London* the importance of distinguishing "British lineaments" from an undifferentiated other.

The comparison he makes between his task and ones undertaken by the French and Italians pits the single British lexicographer against others, even if all are engaged in the same sort of drudgery usually ascribed to the "lower employments" of the masses. Johnson describes others involved in lexicographical projects as "the aggregated knowledge, and cooperating diligence of the Italian academicians" or the "embodied critics of France." While these descriptions ascribe an intellectual weight to Continental academies, the final effect is to negate such value. The "soft obscurities of retirement" and "shelter of academic bowers" convey a peculiarly effeminate and hence in the *Preface*'s terms, a repellent quality to foreign critics. In contrast, the more surly, singular and rustic English effort Johnson associates with himself produces "honor to [his] country," against the indiscrete "nations of the Continent," to whom the "palm of philology" is not yielded without a "contest" (296). In distinguishing between English and foreign efforts, Johnson's defense of national identity may be aligned with his attempts to distinguish himself from the hack writers of Grub Street. In both cases, he constructs a masculine, bourgeois English identity through the an act of othering, a process of elimination.

Once again: Johnson's notion of distinction, of aligning individualism with intellectual esteem, develops from his portrayal in the *Preface to the Dictionary* of the singularity of English intellectualism and English culture. In turn, this singularity is informed by an imperialist ideology and cultivated by the colonizing gestures underwriting the political imperative of the *Preface*. Johnson's attempt to control language derives from anxiety of contamination by the very thing he has colonized and duly incorporated into the cultural matrix, such as French "terms of domestic use." Johnson assumes a proprietary tone when he discusses his etymological research. He describes the "obscure recesses" he would "enter" and "ransack," finding the "treasures with which I expected every search into those neglected mines to *reward my labor*" (291, my italics). Such tropes not only shape his representation of imperialist culture but also assign gender to these linguistic acquisitions. Like the treasures brought back from English colonies to adorn English women, the "treasures" he pillages from literature figure language as a display-case of Western patriarchal power. Johnson seems to be guilty of the commercial trafficking in metaphorical language he deplores.[28]

Translation and trafficking lead to new inventions of "dialect," and in earlier descriptions Johnson links oral speech to moral depravity, vulgarity, and indolence. The problem with dialect is its "anomalous formulations," which "once incorporated, can never afterward be dismissed or reformed" (278). The implicit suggestion is that spoken language or dialect, as it follows class alignments, is able to infect written language in the same way that a "mingled dialect" may infect the "other ranks." Written language, figured as property that can be shaped according to Johnson's notion of culture, occupies a curiously double position here as a marker of both the stability and the instability of national and cultural identity. As an inherently capricious and wayward commodity, written language must be prevented from complying "with the corruptions of oral utterance," yet it also constitutes the "wells of English undefiled."

In Johnson's representation, the "natural" slips from one pole to the other without apparent contradiction because, as Laura Brown suggests, it represents "not the landscape of England at all but a naturalized fantasy about English culture."[29] The double position that Johnson's texts ascribe to language reflects his own double position: as a lexicographer, doomed to the "lower" employments of life; and as an intellectual authority, an authority that is, ironically, produced out of lexicographical drudgery.

What Johnson incorporates and what he casts out in the preface to his project reflect the problems implicit in cultural representation. In his invective against translation, he marks out his political ambivalence toward the other. Johnson claims that "single words may enter by the thousands and the fabric of the tongue continue the same, but new phraseology changes much at once." Individual words are more easily incorporated than whole works, whose retention of "native idiom" presents the possibility of native resistance to colonial "incorporation."[30] Johnson casts out the (distressing) oral by writing the *Dictionary*, and secures his authority by supplementing it with another's: "when it happened that any author gave a definition, I have produced his authority as a supplement to my own" (289–90).

The "spots of barbarity" or "anomalous formulations" are incorporated but not disseminated within the fabric of language: their existence, therefore, is a reminder of the foreign invasion and domestic weakness. There are, however, other instances where barbaric phrases supply "real deficiencies, such are readily adopted by the genius of our tongue, and incorporate easily with our native idioms" (289). Here Johnson's discussion of etymology once again exposes his self-conscious desire for a pure origin. The fantastic image of Englishness is not unlike his created image of others; both sets of images are constructed from powerful cultural fantasies about identity. The suggestive imagery of recesses and forgotten mines—in which Johnson "pierces deep," leaving his mark or "inquir[ing] the nature of every substance of which [he] inserted the name," with the end that this "book might be in place of all other dictionaries whether appellative or technical"—not only indicates that his project reflects imperialist acquisitiveness. It also figures the other in terms of the foreign and the feminine, positioning Johnson as the voice of patriarchal authority. Language and the foreign are therefore able to replace each other as forms of property. The other is threatening because of its difference from Johnson's representation of Englishness. The feminine is threatening because it is unreadable, and must, therefore, remain "untouched." It thus stands in for language's dirty spots that criticism cannot wash from a cultural fabric.

Robert DeMaria describes his book on Johnson as a rediscovery of the *Dictionary*'s capacity as a book. "After spending time reading a dictionary as a disguised encyclopedia," he writes, "it is possible to describe its contents—to classify and name the "galaxy of pieces of world knowledge" that the book contains."[31] Books disclose stories, and both Johnson and DeMaria seem drawn to storytelling. By his own admission, DeMaria describes how he imitates Johnson's research for the *Dictionary*, and he seems to have employed the same plot: the narrative of ideologically constructed privilege. Although DeMaria discusses Umberto Eco's demystification of a "dictionary" as a record of definition, the alternative model that Eco offers and DeMaria accepts—the encyclopedia—is just as subject to ideological investigation. Haraway's proposals for a feminist epistemology and Bhabha's and Spivak's postcolonial investigation of epistemological representation have clearly identified the ideological impetus of the encyclopedic project.

In sum, Johnson and his admirers write from within a self-contained fellowship of intellectuals that depends on promulgating ideologies of race, class, gender, and nationality to sustain itself.[32] Within eighteenth-century scholarship, Johnson studies in particular have been especially clubbish both in British and U.S. academic institutions. Epistemological paradigms that afford a history of imperialism, such as those of Bhabha, Haraway, and Spivak, complicate models of Johnson scholarship and offer new readings in cultural representation and crucial ways to formulate the politics of national identity.

Foreign Bodies

The sheer breadth of Johnson's literary engagement provides an example of the ways xenophobia informs a stabilizing signifying system that organizes and situates cultural and national identities. Johnson's *Preface* provides a manifesto of codification: the maintenance of English as a master language is most clearly performed by a continual engagement with the peripheries of meaning. That is, the stability of a word's meaning is accomplished through a constant concern with and policing of its outlying (or secondary) connotations. Other parts of Johnson's corpus, works that for the most part remain outside the canon of his literary accomplishment, uncover similar concerns with the structures of xenophobia.

In describing Johnson's work, for the *Gentleman's Magazine* during

44   Chapter 1

1738–44, Frank Brady and W. K. Wimsatt observe that "one kind of a job . . . was the compilation of biographical essays." They then list as examples of those found in the biographies the names Herman Boerhaave, Admiral Robert Blake, Sir Francis Drake, and John Philip Barretier. Following this notable catalogue, however, is the concession that

> another feature was a department of illegal, semifictitious and thinly disguised reports on the proceedings of the Houses of Parliament. . . . Johnson produced, on very slender evidence, sometimes hardly more than the names of the speakers and their topics, a series of Debates which were translated all over the Continent as the veritable words of English statesmen. (5)

Brady and Wimsatt hastily point out that "at about the time when he fully realized the extent of this 'propagation of falsehood,' he dropped the job abruptly" (5).

At issue in this passage is Johnson's practice and attitude toward historical writing. Brady and Wimsatt define Johnson's authority by the cultural weight of his biographical essays as well as by the moral weight of his rigidly regulated conscience that refused with admirable alacrity to condone such "propagation of falsehood." Yet the questionable status of historical "truth" in literary representation cannot be so quickly or easily dismissed, regardless of Johnson's professed moral view. His writings in *Gentleman's Magazine*, legitimate or otherwise, illustrate how personal, historical, cultural, and ideological issues complicate representation. The eighteenth-century project of carving out a discursive space for a "refined" public sphere dominated by a bourgeois ethic seems particularly open to such complications of authorship.[33] In the case of Johnson's corpus, questions of identity, legitimacy and illegitimacy, raised by his "hack" work on *Gentleman's Magazine*, are reproduced not only in the Parliamentary debates, in which he "authors" the words of English statesmen, but also in his more canonical works. During this period, Johnson also wrote the poem *London* (1738) and the *Life of Savage* (1744), two texts strikingly concerned with problems of writing an identity.

Johnson's "imitation" of Juvenal's Third Satire, *London*, opens up the question of poetic voice and poetic authority. Imitating an established Roman poet in order to legitimize one's own poetic endeavor defines much poetic work in the eighteenth century, despite the fact that this neoclassical practice poses problems regarding authorship. This poem's two "voices"—Thales and a nearly silent "me"—register the two "authors" of the poem:

Johnson and Juvenal.[34] The *Life of Savage* concerns the credibility of Richard Savage's romantic claim to be the "lost" son of the Countess of Macclesfield as much as it concerns legitimizing Johnson's own identity as an English writer. The question of cultural and personal identity at issue in *London* and the *Life of Savage* is linked to the question of authority and authorship that Johnson assumes in his writing. The authorial issues so clearly determining the production of Johnson's *Dictionary* and its *Preface* are foregrounded in these texts. It seems as if the *Dictionary* functions as a primer for lessons on eighteenth-century authorship, solidifying the anxieties about authorial identity insistent in his earlier work.[35] Thales's identification of "imported" politics invading an integrated English identity in *London* seems linked to Savage's and Johnson's project of articulating an identity that insures the virtues that Thales outlines as English.[36] While ventriloquizing his own anxieties and beliefs about the identity and role of the professional writer in both texts, Johnson uses a Juvenalian rancor to rewrite unrecognized merit as the romance of rustic English virtue.

The prevailing ethos of eighteenth-century British imperialism further complicates these issues. Both in the case of Johnson's biographies and in his work on the magazine, England's dominant position in relation to the Continent is unqualified. His heroes are either English or strongly associated with the British Commonwealth; his Debates are a type of con-job, intentional or not, that speaks for England with political confidence. Johnson displays a conscience and character that prompts him to quit propagating falsehood. This virtue of a morally alert conscience, peculiar to being English according to Johnson, is the subject of both *London* and the *Life of Savage*. Johnson's representation of nationalism is not merely a record of historical "fact" but is self-consciously produced out of dominant cultural ideologies.

The dominant cultural ideologies involve terms of national mythmaking that employ the racist and xenophobic strategy of creating and expelling foreign others. Gates describes this process as a Eurocentric habit of accounting for the Other's "essence" in absolute terms, in terms that "fix culturally defined differences into transcendent 'natural' categories or essences," so that they may be more easily displaced or expelled.[37] Problematizing the neatness of such a paradigm is the question of integrity: that is, the "origin" of Eurocentric essences, given this logic of comprehending difference, has to return to the European "body" in part for its definition. Laclau and Mouffe's understanding of the structures of "society" usefully complicate Gates's model:

"Society" is not a valid object of discourse. There is no single underlying principle fixing—and hence constituting—the whole field of differences. The irresoluble interiority/exteriority tension is the condition of any social practice: necessity only exists as a partial limitation of the field of contingency. It is in this terrain, where neither a total interiority nor a total exteriority is possible, that the social is constituted.[38]

Once again: "necessity only exists as a partial limitation of the field of contingency." In the context of articulation, there is no possibility of a "totality" and therefore "difference" can only be partially returned to the European body for its representation. It is what remains external to the incorporation of identity that formulates disruption for Johnson, a description he reconfigures according to already established figures of difference that rely on ideologies of gender and sexuality for their constitution. The surplus of meaning attached to these ideologies in both *London* and the *Life of Savage* may be read through the metaphors of imperialism, xenophobia, and gynophobia. Through these metaphors, Johnson mediates the crisis of authority and legitimacy in eighteenth-century neoclassicism.

Languages of expulsion, imperialism, xenophobia, gynophobia, are produced through xenodochial invitation. The by-products of these languages—the "foreign" bodies—are rendered visible through an invitation to reside in the domestic domicile. Hence, the foreign fops who "invade" London's hearth are brought there through cultural solicitation. This process produces, in turn, the necessity for introjecting a different order of meaning (Frenchifying English custom) which only results in the necessity to seek other (frequently less desirable) places of incorporation such as Cambria.

A bitter invective against urban corruption, Johnson's *London* ostensibly offers the pastoral—that is, "Cambria"—as a "happier place," one in which "once the harassed Briton found repose" (ll. 43–47), but perhaps now hesitates to find similar sanctuary. Johnson's invocation of pastoral values maps out political positions in this poem. One can loosely line up issues of morality, the natural, Englishness, and the self with the pastoral, while the city embodies moral and physical corruption, artifice, the foreign, and the other.[39] The distinctions implied between "Cambria," "Great Britain," and "England" reflect the changing boundaries of geographical and national identity. Despite the fact that it is regularly invaded by foreign bodies, London remains undeniably English while Cambria, nominally a part of the national hybrid "Great Britain," is not English, even though it is relatively unadulterated by a francophilic culture. Hence, the articulation of an urban English society is absolutely contingent on the partial return of this "foreign" pastoral.

Although the pastoral always functions as a way of positioning moral values, what complicates and perhaps even undermines the representation of those values in this poem is the division of the poetic and the authoritative voice: simple binarisms and symmetrical oppositions are not enough to account for the ambivalent representation of urban politics in this satire. Thales, the dominant voice, whom many have claimed to be the voice of Richard Savage,[40] argues for the pastoral life, not so much for its inherent virtues but for its difference from London—differences about which he is self-consciously ambivalent—while the first-person speaker remains allied with the city, even while ventriloquizing Thales's position.

> Though grief and fondness in my breast rebel,
> When injured Thales bids the town farewell
> Yet still my calmer thoughts his choice commend,
> I praise the hermit, but regret the friend,
> Resolved at length, from vice and London far,
>   To breathe in distant fields a purer air. (ll. 1–6)

The problem of fixing a place in the poem for the speaker in part reflects Johnson's own political ambivalence toward London: on the one hand, the city is where "malice, rapine, accident conspire. / And now a rabble rages, now a fire" (14–15), and, on the other, it is the "seat that gave Eliza birth" (23). What troubles the speaker is not so much the conventional diatribe against moral corruption, signified in part by his disapproval of the popular social phenomenon of the masquerade, but a confusion of proper class alignments that these social events create and even celebrate. In her work on the masquerade, Terry Castle argues that such gatherings were "transformed . . . into a public event, a diversion of the 'Town'—accessible, like Vauxhall or the theater or the opera, to anyone with aspirations after fashionability."[41] The dangers of accessibility are reflected in the dangers of immoderation: such excess falls into the pattern of regulating the grotesque body in order to keep the public arena clean and free from contaminating agents.[42] The masquerade also opens up another more insidious sort of accessibility: the accessibility of "Englishness"—and the cultural and political weight of that national identity—to the faceless hordes of foreigners, apparently anxious to mask their difference by this cloak of "respectability." In this poem, the city itself functions as a masquerade, available to endless numbers of frenchified fops whose social success suggests that the assumption of British identity is a masquerade too easily mastered. Thales cannot simply dismiss the city, however: he turns back to address it. The city is equally compelling both as an embodiment of loathsomeness and desirability, and as the site of such contradictory passions, must be regulated and contextualized within an institution of refinement, the Juvenalian satire.[43] Yet the process of refinement is one that is dangerously undertaken, especially in its proximity to the francophilic affectations. While urban cultural life gaily revolves around the temptations of the masquerade, "true" refinement depends on a certain amount of surly rustic distance from such activity to unmask the pretenders to British identity.

Johnson places the city in direct contrast to a pastoral that is apparently "fixed" as

> Some pleasing bank where verdant osiers play,
> Some peaceful vale with nature's paintings gay;
> Where once the harassed Briton found repose,
> And safe in poverty defied his foes. (45–48)

Even as the speaker satirizes the pastoral's supposed merits in his reference to poverty and to hunger in the lines "There none are swept by sudden fate away, / But all whom hunger spares, with age decay," the pastoral nevertheless remains open for appropriation by the English poetic imagination. It is in Cambria and not England that a recuperation from the ill effects of the city will occur, an historically suitable place for withdrawal and reparation, as "once" the "harassed Briton" found respite there from a Saxon invasion. The pastoral functions as a sort of other in this poem: a place whose qualities can best be described by what they can offer the "true" Briton, and yet a place subject to constant revision by poetic convention. Thus the protean position of the pastoral changes as the boundaries and needs of "England" change; an "England" that is renamed and geographically realigned as "Great Britain." Cambria is represented as the desirable territory that welcomes the "partial" return of an English cultural subjectivity, a subjectivity that has constructed this territory from othered bits of itself.

The threat of invasion from which Cambria provides sanctuary is not from a Teutonic or Saxon culture this time but, rather, a Frenchified one, noted for its effeminacy. This troubled gender and sexual instability link up to form a dangerous and threatening counter to fixed binary oppositions of class, race, and culture, allowing for all sorts of possibilities of political and erotic intrigue: "They first invade your table, then your breast; / Explore your secrets with insidious art, / Watch the weak hour, and ransack all the heart"

(152–55). The "needy villains" populating *London* are portrayed variously as parasites, imitators, fops, and as effeminate men. "With eager thirst" they "suck in the dregs of each corrupted state," and, thanks to them, the British warrior "dwindles" to a frenchified "beau" (95–104). It is difficult here not to imagine the exchange of fluids as somehow crucially connected with the anatomy of identity, and part of the anxiety here has to do with identifying what counts as a gendered stability. Johnson's images focus on different representations of loss, the most resonant of which is the loss of political potency: the warrior is replaced by a mannikin, active displays of military force by an "empty show." Masculine integrity is invaded not only by the insidious and disruptive figure of the feminine but also by an alternate model of masculinity that raises all sorts of specters of sexual instability.

The potential confusion of native English and foreign recurs in the problem of differentiating between Thales and "me," and the scapegoat onto which Johnson projects this anxiety is the feminized foreign body: after a long list of examples of urban evil, Johnson concludes with "*here* a female aetheist talks you dead" (15–19, italics mine). With this exception, Johnson never specifically refers to women in this poem; yet he evokes the problem of stabilizing gender within a linguistic and nationalist matrix in the form of the foreign, effeminate man: Italianate "warbling eunuchs" filling an impotent English politics. Imagined loss, fetishized as it is on the operatic figure whose penchant for high drama only underscores Thales's anxiety about the integrity of his own melodrama and the coherence of his own body, spills over into a bittersweet entertainment. As such:

> Their air, their dress, their politics import;
> Obsequious, artful, voluble, and gay,
> On Britain's fond credulity they prey.
> No gainful trade their industry can 'scape,
> They sing, they dance, clean shoes, or cure a clap. (110–14)

while, as for English politicians (such as Walpole),

> Here let those reign, whom promises can incite
> To vote a patriot black, a courtier white;
> Explain their country's dear-bought rights away,
> And plead for pirates in the face of day. (51–54)

Again, the threat to England is the threat of loss: loss of political power that is figured as the loss of sexual potency. Harassing and perhaps replacing the Briton are "others" who "sap the principles" or "taint the heart," infecting England's "purer air" with "slavish tenets" produced by a francophilic culture. Envisaging a world turned upside down, Johnson reverses the relationship between colonizer and colonized, figuring London as a "common shore of Paris and of Rome," and England—particularly England under a pacific political sway—as both "of France the mimic and of Spain the prey."[44] Yet this inversion, far from simply expressing the horrors of disrupted social and cultural conventions, may act as an apotropaic effect, a reassuring device. The fact that the terms, though reversed, remain intact suggests that all one has to do to mitigate the unpleasant results is reverse the inversion.[45] In this sense Cambria functions like the feminized other whose reclamation or appropriation will reaffirm England's "natural" right to rule, and, more importantly, will restabilize gender roles according to dominant ideological definitions.

Crucially at issue in *London* is the problem of the masquerade, of England masquerading as and being masked by Continental culture, of the self masquerading as the other, and the feminine appearing as the masculine. Johnson indulges in his own masquerade as well: the British author masking the site of an uneasy authorial identity by invoking the face of the foreign. He puts a feminine face and a sexually deviant body on the frame of a foreigner, erasing both the possibility of confusing Thales and the speaker with foreign "men" as well as countering any suggestion of homoeroticism. Johnson cements bonds between men—that is, between Thales and the speaker—by participating in effeminate traffic. He thematizes foreignness while using foreign others as poetic currency, as if to take part in the exchange of these bodies reconfirms his bond with the imaginary Thales and consolidates his position as the final authoritative, if lone, voice.[46] The poem continually shifts between the task of distinguishing between self and other (Thales and speaker) and distinguishing between English and foreign. How does one "hope the British lineaments to trace" when

>They venture on the mimic's art,
>Who play from morn to night a borrowed part,
>Practiced their master's notions to embrace,
>Repeat his maxims, and reflect his face.   (134–37)

The timely intervention of an authorial presence only unmasks the ways in which national identity is produced by entertaining other possibilities. Staged for the consumption of a putatively gullible public and denounced by the voice of poetic truth (which must resort to another act of mimicry—the imitation—in order to achieve any kind of legitimacy in the literary marketplace), Thales is only left with the option to place his loyalties elsewhere.

Johnson's anxious, three-tiered representation—gynophobic, homophobic, xenophobic—clearly positions a "rustic" virtue against the seamless "supple Gaul," whose "softer smiles" and "subtler art" suggest the figure of an unnatural male. This anxiety is mitigated, however, by a reassuringly autonomous and integral national identity: the foreign body guarantees the difference between English "rustic grandeur" and foreign "empty show." The deployment of sexual difference in this poem occurs within the homosocial relationship which is also a problematically "British" relationship, yoking Britishness with masculinity. The foreign and the feminine together perform the functions of guaranteeing nationally, personally, and sexually distinct identities as well as providing a body onto which the transgressive elements of the city—corruption, masquerade, and effeminacy—are projected.

As the producer of these constructions of national and sexual identities, Johnson himself is, in a sense, as transgressive as the foreign bodies he represents. The stability of Englishness is supported by a dialectal relation between a tolerable but deficient Wales and a vilified France; in turn, this shifting relation consolidates in order to keep more othered bodies at bay, for example, the ones with whom Indian traffickers may come in contact. In recording English sentiment, Johnson only ostensibly conceals his complicity with the other when he recuperates a romantic past when

> fair justice then, without constraint adored,
> Held high the steady scale, but dropped the sword . . .
> Blessed Age! but ah! how different from our own.   (250–54)

Thales has been historically associated with Richard Savage, and *London*, although written before Johnson knew Savage, with Savage's bitter social satire. The same issues of self-representation and the construction of national identity in *London* intersect with Johnson's representation of gender in the *Life of Savage*.

Contracting Identity

In *The Achievement of Samuel Johnson,* Walter Jackson Bate describes Johnson's friendship with Richard Savage in the following way:

Johnson trudged the streets, lived on the poorest food, and became intimately acquainted with the large, floating body of the London poor. With Richard Savage, a colorful but minor writer, who claimed to be the illegitimate son of the Countess of Macclesfield, Johnson sometimes walked the London streets all night because neither had enough to pay for lodging, not even a "night cellar."[47]

Bates's rendition of Johnson's life on the London streets mirrors Johnson's account of Savage:

In this manner were passed those days and those nights which nature had enabled him to have employed in elevated speculations, useful studies, or pleasing conversations. On a bulk, in a cellar, or in a glass-house among thieves and beggars, was to be found the author of *The Wanderer*, the man of exalted sentiments, extensive views, and curious observations; the man whose remarks on life might have assisted the statesman, whose ideas of virtue might have enlightened the moralist, whose eloquence might have influenced senates, and whose delicacy might have polished courts. (605)

Bate echoes Johnson's sense of the irony of Savage's position:

And not the least among the almost grotesque incongruities of these years is the unforgettable picture of Johnson dining at the home of the publisher of *The Gentleman's Magazine*, eating behind a screen because his clothes were too shabby, and yet for two years writing Parliamentary debates that included speeches supposed to be by England's foremost statesmen.[48]

I bring these passages together not only to display their striking similarity of tone, nostalgia (in both Johnson and Bate, the perception of bygone days is quite acute), and sense of irony, but also to illustrate the intersection between the ostensibly biographical project and self-representation. Bate reproduces Johnson's aims and strategies for validating a figure to the authority of culture (Savage) in validating a figure of cultural authority (Johnson). Bate's text, like Johnson's, strives to create cultural authority and a legitimate identity for the professional writer against a background of privation and squalor. Legitimation that is constructed self-consciously must be reasserted insistently in this text. The opposing nature of the authority of high culture and the Grub Street ethos of suspect professional writing might otherwise appear too clearly. It seems odd that Bate, an established, widely recognized authority on Johnson would let slip such anxieties; *The Achievement of Samuel Johnson* was an early book, but even his later biography on Johnson, when Bate had become something of an institution himself, betrays an anxiety about authorial legitimacy. Like language, authorship needs the kind of continual policing that Johnson found so necessary to his *Dictionary*.[49]

In the following discussion of Johnson's *Life of Savage*, arguably one of the most vexed chapters in his *Lives of the Poets*, I want to tease out the politics of maintaining authorial identity; specifically, I would like to examine the apparatus upon which such epistemological endeavors rest. Although Johnson focuses almost exclusively on his gynophobic representations of class and little of the francophobia or xenophobia characterizing both the *Preface to the Dictionary* and *London* is apparent in this text, this curious *Life* provides a useful way of reading the ways in which domesticity is historically structured according to xenophobia.

Johnson adds his life of Savage to those "volumes" that have been written about "heroes of literary . . . history." Johnson's "mournful narrative" is a list of woes based on problems of mistaken identity and unrecognizability, both of which derive from matters of class, property, and propriety. The passages from the *Life of Savage* and *The Achievement of Samuel Johnson* focus on the incongruity of shabby appearances and refined sensibilities, an incongruity itself dependent on class differences. Johnson is not only "screened" or partitioned off from reputable society, but he is confounded with part of the "large, floating body of London's poor." Savage lives among "thieves and beggars," his purported identity as the illegitimate son of the Countess of Macclesfield so masked by poverty that he is mistaken for a thief and a murderer by his own "mother."

One of the major sources of class ambiguity in relation to personal identity in the *Life of Savage* is the association of "low" places with "high" discourse. Glass-houses, night cellars, coffee-houses, taverns, and streets, primarily designated as gathering places for low life in this text, become sites from which "high" cultural discourses issue—Savage's and Johnson's—in particular. Places produce their own protocols of language and codify their own social identities. The discourse of the drawing room obeys a different convention from the discourse of the tavern. In the *Life of Savage* such relationships between place and discourse are inverted, yet such inversion furnishes the most concrete evidence for the manifest destiny of existing class hierarchies.[50]

Johnson's treatment of Savage as a biographical subject does more than reveal the unhappy irony of Savage's inverted circumstances, the putative high life and grinding poverty, cultivated sentiments and a squalid scene of writing. Johnson's assessments of the life of Savage reflects a larger class anxiety both about his own ambiguous position as a writer and about the task of representing England to the English. Because it focuses on a specifically English writer working within the English literary canon (represented most cogently by the self-consciously titled *Lives of the Poets*), the *Life of Savage* functions in part as an index to a cultural and national identity. Richard Savage's humble authorial aspirations are thwarted by a murky maternal threat whose form itself is often represented as monstrous or hardly human. The individual authorial subject may be vulnerable to foreign intrusion masked by gender, just as foreign bodies enter English spaces by "imitating" the characteristics of English aristocracy in the poem *London*. The Countess of Macclesfield's maternal role in Savage's life, therefore, cannot be anything other than an aberration.[51]

The "high" and the "low" in class terms become powerfully confused in the *Life of Savage*. Johnson's representation of Savage depends on the depiction of the Countess of Macclesfield, the monster in the text. Savage is inextricably bound to the "low" despite his putative mother's title and class superiority, and despite his authorial aspirations. Both Savage and the Countess of Macclesfield elicit bourgeois responses of horror and fascination. The monstrosity of the mother's relation to the son and of the son's deliberate self-sabotage complement and comment on one another, crossing boundaries of class and propriety in the process. What these monsters demonstrate, then, are the dangers of an unregulated life. But it is the maternal transgression that is meant to be read as particularly horrific because it is "unnatural." Whereas Savage can occupy a number of different social positions at once (like Johnson himself) without risking too much damage to himself because he is protected by nation and gender, the same cannot be said of "others." The Countess of Macclesfield is clearly able to negotiate in the masculine world of class and commerce: speculating on the South Sea bubble, attempting to pack Savage off to the American plantations as an indentured servant. She rejects Savage's claims to be her illegitimate son; she is monstrous, incapable of satisfying women's "natural" maternal impulses. Domestic arrangements, then, far from being considered incidental and unimportant to authorship, are clearly powerful and therefore dangerous.

It may seem strange that the *Life of Savage*, the catalogue of a tawdry and somewhat vaudevillian life and death, should figure prominently in Johnson's conception of "high" culture, represented by his placement of it next to Pope and Swift in the *Lives of the Poets*. The seeming incongruity between Savage's work and his unfortunate life is excused by Johnson on the grounds of "misfortunes" that "claim a degree of compassion not always due the unhappy, as they were often the consequences of the crimes of others rather than [Savage's] own" (561–62). The *Life of Savage* is not only compelling for its representation of one writer's cultural integrity but also for the Johnsonian self-representation it betrays. Part of Johnson's contradictory feelings of repugnance toward and fascination with "low" life in *London* can be accounted for as displaced identification. And part of that identification may rest in the models of national identity, written in xenophobic representation, that are contingent on an entertainment of marginalia within a domestic fold. If the *Life of Savage* as a biographical text reflects an imperative to instruct society on the dangers of mistaken (class) identity and unnatural motherhood, the autobiography underwriting the narrative complicates that function. Here again, however, as in the case of *London*, identity-making is produced by the express invitation of a mediating third term: gender. Anticipating Rousseau's arguments that linked proper patriotic initiation with proper mothering, Johnson's invectives against Savage's putative mother accuse her first and foremost for having failed her maternal role properly to furnish strong citizenry, leaving the vulnerable author to struggle as best he can. What this invective implies, however, is that the indomitable position of English authorship—and, if we recall the conversation Rasselas has with Imlac, Western epistemology—is curiously dependent on disenfranchised figures like the mother.

The place for the other in this narrative is most frequently occupied by the criminal mother, whose first crime was the adulterous union that produced Savage. Johnson blames the uncertainty of Savage's social position on the Countess of Macclesfield. Displacing the ambivalence with which he usually represents the lower class onto the feminized other, Johnson writes:

But whatever her motives, no sooner was her son born than she discovered a resolution of disowning him. . . . Such was the beginning of the life of Richard Savage: born with a legal claim to honour and to riches, he was in two months illegitimated by the parliament, and disowned by his mother, doomed to poverty and obscurity, and launched upon the ocean of life only that he might be swallowed by its quicksands or dashed upon its rocks. (563)

In Johnson's as in Savage's own account, the question of the father's name never arises, despite the fact that it is not clear whether Savage's father is the Earl of Macclesfield or the Earl Rivers. As a titled woman, the mother is vested with the power of the father's name. The task of conferring a name, therefore, is contingent upon her. Such a scenario is not new; what is different—and hence disruptive to an established continuum of property inheritance—is the fact that the name with which she endows her son is not the name of the father. Savage's entrance into the symbolic is therefore bound to be a hysterical one: placed in his mother's unscrupulous hands is the power of assigning him a birthright, class, and accompanying credentials, all of which she refuses him. Savage's own inscriptions—both his published fictional work, most tellingly, *The Author To Be Let* and *The Wanderer*, and the kinds of fantastic romantic histories he invents for himself—endlessly and obsessively reiterates his crisis with mastering the symbolic order.[52]

Savage's alienated identity is quite literally coupled with his mother's absence: because his mother rejects him, he must assume the name of his nurse, which he later changes.[53] His "actual" origins are, to say the least, uncertain. In *The Artificial Bastard*,[54] Clarence Tracy suggests several possibilities, all of which imply some sort of romantic construction on Savage's part: "It is tempting to conclude that Savage, whoever he really was, first learned about the legend [of the unknown whereabouts of the Countess of Macclesfield's second son] . . . when he would have been about fifteen years of age, and decided to take the role of the missing hero for himself."[55] Savage's claims to be the "natural" son of Lady Macclesfield and the Earl Rivers, claims supported by Johnson's narrative, authorize the artificial construction of familial identity. Savage's promise is blighted first and foremost by his lack of family. So much importance is placed on familial identity in Johnson's text that it is clearly overdetermined—that is, it bears the weight of class and cultural identity as well. Lady Macclesfield's centrality in Johnson's and Savage's family romance demonstrates the ways in which the definition of cultural identity crucially depends on other matters such as gender, race, sexuality, and nationality.

This particular mother, although she holds the key to Savage's proper Englishness, violates the code of English bourgeois propriety and property with which Johnson is so preoccupied and so positions herself as utterly foreign to English protocol. In Johnson's text, her moral corruption associates her with contamination and disease, effectively casting her out of the possible redemption sanctioned by her class, race, sexuality, and nationality.[56] She therefore functions effectively as a foreign body, the subject of xenophobic survey. Johnson describes her variously as a person able to "infect" others with cruelty and to be "infected" with the "general madness of the South Sea traffic"; he questions whether such a mother could "exist in human form," placing her very status as a human being in question, not unlike the arguments about the relationship between subjectivity, citizenry, and black slavery.[57] Her character provides a site for the contradictory representations that Stallybrass and White identify with the politics of transgression. She is an embodiment of all kinds of transgressive behavior—adultery, illegitimate birth, unnatural (nonmaternal) mothering. Despite her connection to the low, she is nevertheless undeniably in a position of power and control both in class terms and in relation to her progeny. She thus becomes in Johnson's discourse a figure of multiple monstrosities, possessing an impeccably upper class position and yet subverting rules and violating codes of propriety, giving credibility to the bourgeois notion that impropriety is as much connected to the upper as to the lower classes. She is an example of what Stallybrass and White recognize as figural inversion. Such a semiotic inversion, while reordering pairs, does not change the terms themselves. Lady Macclesfield is a powerful woman in the *Life of Savage*; she is able to control Savage's social situation and consequently violate a code of behavior that is highly gendered. But Johnson's specific representation of her is a conservative one that merely reaffirms the "natural" necessity of masculine authority, a necessity he also sees fit to deploy in the *Preface* to the *Dictionary*. The terms in which Johnson describes this ritualized inversion of class stability and propriety ensure their respective inviolability as well as their inevitable replacement.

The reversal of terms is not untroubled by anxieties of adulteration: the fear of contamination of one by the other, the polite by the plebeian, the high by the low. The *Life of Savage* and *London* express this fear by an insistence on female monstrosity.[58] The powerful mother replaces the lower classes, the "rabble" in Johnson's earlier phrase, as the despised other. Johnson's other readily shifts from class opposite to gender opposite and back again, and the implicit contradiction—that the woman is upper class and not lower, yet still monstrous—only suggests how much cultural identity depends on such contradictions.

Lady Macclesfield also transgresses the social and economic boundary belonging to her titled status; if her identity depends on the "subtler art" of aligning herself with moneyed and titled men, it is she who emerges as the powerful economic figure and not her husbands and lovers. She is thus able, under cover of someone else's name, to rob Savage of his "rightful" title and name as Richard Savage, the fourth Earl Rivers:

While the Earl of Macclesfield was prosecuting [their divorce], his wife was ... delivered of a son; and the Earl Rivers, by appearing to consider him as his own, left none any reason to doubt the sincerity of his declaration, for he was godfather and gave him his own name which was by his direction inserted in the register of St. Andrew's parish in Holton. . . .[N]o sooner was her son born than she . . . removed him from her sight by committing him to the care of a poor woman, whom she directed to educate him as her own, and enjoined never to inform him of his true parents. . . . [H]e was called by the name of his nurse, without the least intimation that he had claim to any other. (562)

The question of legitimacy, illustrated here by the various institutions signifying legality—the Church, the state, the father—depends upon masculine honor, not feminine agency. Yet Lady Macclesfield's trespasses perpetrated by her undeniably powerful agency disrupt gender boundaries set by Johnson's authorship. She controls her money and her domestic arrangements and in doing so, deprives her son of his "natural" right to title. She also erases the boundaries of "natural" motherhood by withholding knowledge that should be most natural—who the mother, if not the father, is—and tries to "rid herself from the danger of being at any time made known to him, by sending him secretly to the American plantations" (564). Such a scheme testifies to her "unnatural" capacity to engage in the traffic of a human being.

The maintenance of English nationalism—and British imperialism—depends on the proper alignment of commodified bodies. That is, commercial traffic in commodities that included human beings was necessary to the expansion of a British economy. A sense of national well-being relied on the more removed services of authorship. Johnson's representation of the confusion of authorship with the social inversions of commerce, gender, and class in the *Life of Savage* demonstrates his anxieties about proper regulation, but more tellingly betrays a profound anxiety about the status of authorship itself. He writes:

But all his assiduity and tenderness were without effect, for he could neither soften her heart nor open her hand, and was reduced to the utmost miseries of want while he was endeavouring to awaken the affection of a mother: he was therefore obliged to seek some other means of support, and, having no profession, became by necessity an author. (565)

Savage's place as the subject of the illustrious *Lives of the Poets* comes about, it would seem, only by maternal rejection. Johnson's own authorial aspirations may well be projected in this curious account of Savage's choice; clearly, the privations of Grub Street and the squalor of hack writing are embedded in Johnson's representation. But also embedded here is the disturbing suggestion that authorship is contingent on maternal rejection and maternal monstrosity.

Lady Macclesfield's corruption is intensified by her alignment with other women such as prostitutes and bawds. Her impropriety, especially in contrast to ladies like Mrs. Oldfield, Lady Mason or the Countess of Hertford, is most evident during Savage's trial for the murder of James Sinclair:

Mr. Savage had now no hopes of life but for the mercy of the Crown, which was very earnestly solicited by his friends, and which, with whatever difficulty the story may obtain belief, was obstructed only by his mother.... Thus had Savage perished by the evidence of a bawd, a strumpet, and his mother, had not justice and compassion procured him an advocate of rank too great to be rejected unheard, and of virtue too eminent to be heard without being believed. (576)

The "lowness" of the incident leading to Savage's trial is suggested by many things: the coffee-house, the dubious characters of Robinson and Gregory, the lateness of the hour, the presence of strumpets and bawds in opposition to the virtuous advocate. Johnson mentions the strumpets and bawds only in the context of the trial, almost as if to dissociate them from Savage except as obstructions to justice being done on his behalf. Lastly, the fight itself, during which James Sinclair is killed, marks the scene as "low"—romantic not as a duel of honor but a garish error. Johnson's reason for describing this "calamity" is ostensibly to use its tawdriness as a backdrop for Savage's unalloyed virtue. But this backdrop brings into the foreground the crucial contradiction of loathing and desire with which Johnson invests his representation of London life. Whereas Savage's virtue remains relatively unscathed during his trial and he behaves with "great firmness and equality of mind," confirming the "esteem of those who before admired him for his abilities," his acquittal does not signal a favorable change of fortune but, rather, the reverse.

The scapegoat in Johnson's version of this trial is the complicated assortment of feminized figures that together function as some sort of perverted hybrid: the prostitute, the bawd, and the mother who constitute the witnesses to Sinclair's murder. If the "only" obstruction to Savage's acquittal is the mother, then the bawd and strumpet may be read as aspects of the mother: the more apparent versions of female sexuality. Stallybrass and White argue that "any transgression of the high-low domain creates a grotesque hybrid right at the social threshold, a neither/nor creature, neither up nor down, which repels and fascinates ... and which guards, like the hydra, the pathways and meeting-places between high and low."[59] This "grotesque hybrid" is clearly gendered in the *Life of Savage*. Lady Macclesfield stands as the barrier between and the signifier of both high and low. Her strength is expressed by her transgression: not a natural mother, not a proper lady, she represents the feminine deliberately transgressing the boundaries set by a patriarchal precedent, becoming a monstrous version of herself.

Arguments concerning cultural hybridity, however, inevitably raise the kinds of paradigms Homi Bhabha identifies. If, as he argues, subversive mimicry is the distinguishing effect of colonialist power and its representations, are there ways in which such a model could usefully complicate this hybrid moment in Johnson's text? It seems as if Johnson's (and Savage's) obsessional desire with Lady Macclesfield may signify her absolute capacity for subversive mimicry, in much the same way that subaltern resistance embeds and codes itself within a master language.[60] Given Laclau and Mouffe's understanding of the terrain of the social that I raised earlier, clearly her incomplete exclusion or inclusion within Johnson's social text identifies her as the critically overdetermined figure providing the site for the social. "Society" as Johnson has it "never manage[s] to be fully fixed," a notion that attests to the instability of professional author.[61]

It is useful to turn to other models of subjectivity to discuss overdetermination. Psychoanalytic paradigms help account for the powerful fantasies often reproduced across cultural contexts. Johnson's gynophobic representation of the grotesque body as the maternal body is cast in xenophobic language. Such xenophobia, however, necessarily invites the monstrous body to inhabit the text: Savage's portrait can only be drawn in relation to the Countess of Macclesfield's. The practices of abjection, encoded in these texts as the horrifying maternal/effeminate body, inevitably recall Kristeva's account of the subject's first attempt at separating itself from the pre-Oedipal "mother" as expulsion, nausea, and horror.[62] The expulsion and retention of the abject, resonant with Laclau and Mouffe's asserting the impossibility of reducing the social to the interiority of a fixed system of differences, reveals the complications inherent in Johnson's representation of identity as the contradictory relations of low and high. Lady Macclesfield's political status in the *Life of Savage* is versatile: on the one hand she is titled and propertied; on the other, she joins the polluted company of bawds and strumpets, sharing their "low" morality. Because of her connection with the low and her role as the body onto which Johnson projects horror and nausea, she functions both as a scapegoat and as a way of situating the "I." That is, she provides a way in which the subject (Johnson/Savage) can guarantee its singularity and identity—that which is expelled is not me.

Similarly, the primary and secondary subjects of "I" and Thales, respectively, are constituted by Johnson's anxiety about Frenchified fops. Their role in *London* as the collective body demonstrating urban transgression curtails sexually and nationally intact identities for properly male and properly British subjects. Johnson's abjecting practices are clearly autobiographical, marked most visibly by his self-identical representation of Savage. These practices also account for the somewhat fantastic relation to the historical "truth" of representation, figured earlier by his Parliamentary speeches and read in the *Life of Savage* as the family romance.

Kristeva writes:

Before calling itself "death," the libido undergoes first a threat to its omnipotence—one that makes the existence of an *other* for the *self* appear problematic. Freud seems to suggest that it is not Eros but narcissistic primacy that sparks and perhaps dominates psychic life; he thus sets up fancy at the basis of one's relationship to reality.[63]

The triangle of self, other, and mother in the *Life of Savage* plays out several important relations between subjects. The mother acts not only as a natural given or a textual metaphor but as a means through which social formations are read. Kristeva and Freud suggest that what endorses representation is fantasy or "fancy": self-representation depends on eliciting the purged faces of mother and other.

Among the sexually transgressive forms of femininity in the texts—fops, bawds, strumpets, unnatural mothers—we might locate another maternal figure who functions as a social "hybrid," standing within the division created by class difference: the nursemaid. Because she substitutes for the abjected mother, she is abjected herself. The only difference between mother and maid is that the latter is defined almost entirely by economic exchange (though Johnson's model of maternity suggests that such an exchange is also what defines Mother Macclesfield).

Maternity triangulates into three representations of the feminine: the monstrous but powerful mother, the nurse, and the good but weak mother. Lady Mason (one of the last) tries to relieve Savage's situation by agreeing to "transact with the nurse, pay for her care," and she "directed him to be placed at a small grammar school . . . where he was called by the name of his nurse, without the least intimation that he had claim to any other" (563). Thus the mediating nurse negotiates blood relations (the family) and class relations (the family hiring a lower class surrogate "mother"). Savage's body becomes a site of similar ambiguity: a mark of transgression constituted by his illegitimacy and the uncertainty of his name. The wet-nurse provides a name as well as nourishment; with her milk Savage ingests a social place. She is also the motherlike body, however, from which disease issues, most notably as the low social rank which obscures Savage's "rightful" entitlement to high birth, no matter how illegitimate.[64] In the family romance, mother figures fantasmatically substitute for one another; when one fails, the other takes over. The nurse's role in the *Life of Savage* dwindles in significance beside Lady Macclesfield's, but both are intimately connected with Savage and provide sites for overdetermined abjection.

The nurse serves as an intermediary figure between Savage and his mother. Her body literally comes between them, while the economic transaction by which her position is defined establishes her as a sort of conduit between the high and the low. Her body also comes to signify a kind of abjection that is later transferred to the mother's body: not only is she completely written out of the triangle (to be later replaced by other forms of feminine economic transgression—prostitutes and bawds), but as a surrogate mother her body is located in an ambiguous and intermediary state, and its transgression, although domesticated in the form of paid labor, is confirmed by her movement between classes.

This complex position the nurse occupies resembles that of Freud's nurse, as described by Stallybrass and White. Investigating Freud's case histories, they argue that "at one level, the disappearance of the nurse seems to correspond with an attempt by Freud to rewrite unconscious desires in closer conformity to the endogamous rules of the bourgeoisie. Paradoxically, to desire one's mother, despite the incestuous implications, is more acceptable than to desire a hired help."[65] If we read the *Life of Savage* as a Freudian case history, the nurse disappears from the text only to be replaced by a more desirable mother.

Somewhere between shedding the nurse's name and inserting himself in the Macclesfield romance, Savage is "so touched with the discovery of his real mother" that it becomes his practice to "walk in the dark evenings . . . in hopes of seeing her as she might come by accident to the window" (565). This practice touches off another "accident" of mistaken identity and undefined desire when Savage, finding the door open "by accident," enters Lady Macclesfield's chamber, only to be driven out as the "villain who had forced himself upon [her]" (565). The coincidence of "accidents," the unhindered passage, and the final blockage together suggest a symbolic reconstruction of an Oedipal scenario in which the father is effaced and illegitimacy, previously shed by means of the nurse, resurfaces in the threat of incest. Such an incident marks a repetition of the mother's rejection of her son and provides a further occasion for a textualization or rewriting of it.

These impulses or drives to reinscribe oneself in the symbolic order subscribe to the fantasy that it is somehow possible—and certainly preferable, in the case of Johnson's representation of Savage—to give birth to oneself. Such drives on Johnson's part also demonstrate the extent to which his literary representation, contingent on a sense of class, gender, and national sensibility, is equally driven by psychosubjectivity. Thus Johnson provides an early prototype for a romantic model of inward, solitary, self-reflective authorship that positions him, perhaps, as an Oedipal figure for romantic writers like De Quincey. Indeed, De Quincey's later reflections on his *Confessions* raise the specter of Johnson in relation to the question of his own authorial success:

Dr. Johnson, upon some occasion, which I have forgotten, is represented by his biographers as accounting for an undeserving person's success in these terms: "Why, I suppose that *his* nonsense suited *their* nonsense." Can *that* be the humiliating solution of my own colloquial success at this time in Carnarvonshire inns? . . . No matter: won in whatsoever way, success *is* success: and even nonsense, if it is to be victorious nonsense . . . must involve a deeper art or more effective secret of power than is easily attained.[66]

De Quincey's invocation and resistance to Johnson's remark demonstrates a romantic opposition and dependence on eighteenth-century authorial legacies that provided powerfully Oedipal models.

Like Savage and the speaker of *London*, Johnson remains subject and voyeur of other bodies. His writing secures a place for him within British literary historiography, yet questions of his contamination continually and self-consciously vex this position. Johnson attempts to insert himself into a narrative of high culture and high life: to find a way out of the poverty and disease informing his material and psychic circumstance. Yet, as a writer living on Grub Street while fashioning the respectable lives of eminent poets, he slides from one position to the other, from hack writer to cultural authority in the same way that Savage and Lady Macclesfield are able to obfuscate virtue and vice, high life and low life. It would seem that Johnson invests in the fortunes of Thales and Thales's others, of Savage and Savage's others, and of his own misfortunes only to engage in a purgatory affect—to reclaim a space rightfully, though problematically, his: "I have protracted my work till most of those whom I wished to please have sunk into the grave, and success and miscarriage are empty sounds: I therefore dismiss it with frigid tranquillity, having little to fear or hope from censure or from praise" (298).

2   De Quincey and the Topography of Romantic Desire

Until the second half of the eighteenth century, and the enormous expansion and consolidation of British power in India, the tiger seems to have stood, in the British imagination, for something especially ferocious but not very *specifically* so: its ferocity differed in degree but not in quality from that of other exotic animals.

—Barrell, *The Infection of Thomas De Quincey*, 49

With indiscriminate fury he tears in pieces every animal around him; and, while thus intent on satisfying the malignity of his nature, hardly, however famished, does he find the time to appease the cravings of his appetite. . . . Would that this thirst for his own blood the tiger gratified to an excess! Would that, by destroying them at their birth, he could extinguish the whole race of monsters which he produces!

—Buffon, *The Natural History of Animals, Vegetables, and Minerals*, 382

What immortal hand or eye,
Dare frame thy fearful symmetry?

—Blake, *The Tyger*

"There Would This Monster Make a Man"

Johnson's restoration of authorial space to its proper place is forged by purging the "impurities" he perceives in language. *London*, for example, articulates with considerable poignancy the problems Johnson identifies with cultural representation. Even while fashioning a space for authorship, Johnson is highly aware of the boundaries that define such spaces and the ways in which these boundaries are hopelessly politicized. Johnson's use of organizing oppositions like the exotic/external, the urban/rural, and the domestic/internal are not as clearly mapped out as might be expected in an Enlightenment milieu nor are they quite as binary. Rather, the interface between these ostensibly discrete positions reflects a romantic conflation of the exotic with the domestic. Johnson's *Preface to the Dictionary* spells out the anxieties of inscribing an exclusionary sensibility in very definite terms. Johnson's London is the heart of English life; his *London* represents an obsessive return to the city despite ventriloquized rhetorical invectives against it and poetic apostrophes to the pastoral. In the *Life of Savage* it is clear that Johnson's authorial personae are more concerned with the renewing possibilities of city life (despite the fact that it is a highly urban situation—the drunken brawl in a tavern—that effectively destroys Savage) than with the dubious benefits a forced exile into an enervating pastoral might yield. Yet, as all these texts make clear, London's very vitality is curiously susceptible to radical invasion and major damage by foreign bodies. The *Life of Savage* demonstrates how equally vulnerable the putatively disembodied and powerful authorial voice is to material forces. In particular, sexual and maternal feminine figures erupt throughout the text and impose bodily infections on masculine authorial discourse and, in the process, expose the fragility of a Cartesian structure of epistemology.[1]

Johnson is able to represent the conflicting aspects of an English internal self—its simultaneous imperviousness and susceptibility to alien influence—by invoking certain eighteenth-century embodiments of externality. But the fact, that Johnson can refer to the British self as an internally coherent subjectivity at all attests to a historical shifting of aesthetic accounts of identity from the Enlightenment to romanticism. In fact, Johnson implies that a privatized sense of self is necessary to defend Britain from French enervation, as the poem *London* makes abundantly clear. This poem textualizes a model of the coherent internal self that bears witness, judges, and sometimes condemns the external affects of national sensibility. If, however, his cultural injunctions are publically aired in the accepted eighteenth-century fashion, Johnson's own sense of an internal psychic self is plagued by the vissicitudes of the unconscious.

Johnson's abstract conceptions of the self are never divorced from the material circumstances of their production, and in this way Johnson displays his predominantly eighteenth-century sensibility. Those circumstances change quite dramatically when romantic models of difference and identity challenge Enlightenment ones. Johnson's representation of the internal self embattled by the trials that plague national well-being is markedly different from the romantic embrace of those very same hazards of change in order to define a sense of self. Such changes, disrupting the continuity of intellectual life, take shape for Johnson most emphatically as misfortunes: Thales's hasty retreat to a Welsh hinterland, Savage's unfortunate change of material circumstances, Johnson's own depressed situation resulting from his lexicographical labors, and even the uninspired return to Abyssinia that Rasselas and his companions finally decide upon, based upon Voltaire's model. These changes of fortune bring about a monstrous reshaping of the original life: Thales's malcontent, Savage's demise, Johnson's gloom, and Rasselas's ennui. Despite Johnson's anachronistic representations of the power of the psyche and its irregularities, his eighteenth-century faith in the restorative capacities of order, moderation, and regularity dominate his discourse. Johnson's monsters remain at bay, their tenacious hold over his sanity are kept just out of reach by the severe discipline of his writing.[2]

The late eighteenth-century interest in the wild and the irregular, by contrast, is something that shapes or defines romantic representation. Wordsworth's apostrophe to the river Derwent, for example, in the *Prelude* welcomes the river's unexpected meanderings that for him signify radical changes in the course of his imaginative development; he greets them as "shapeless eagerness."[3] The more outlandish instances of transfiguration he describes are also hailed with a confident sense that their immensity will inevitably yield something crucial to his poetic development. Book Seven's description of Smithfield and Book Nine's representation of "revolutionary power" as the "hubbub wild" both approach these radical shifts in the poet's life with some trepidation but also with the secure knowledge that change can only benefit the poetic temperament. Perhaps, however, Wordsworth has more in common with Johnson than we think. Wordsworth recalls these wild moments that often focus on representations of monstrosity in a time of relative stability and tames them within the parameters of his discourse. The relation between the immediate experience of disruption and its later tranquil recollection suggests an eighteenth-century regulation implicit in the poetics of the Lake District circle. Even Coleridge's most famously eccentric poem, *Kubla Khan*, is a remembrance mediated by memory; the invocation of the damsel with a dulcimer functions as the domesticated figure that represents, for Coleridge, the way in which a wilder romantic topography might take shape within the confines of an English (re)collection.

Unlike these prominent early romantic writers, Thomas De Quincey's musings about his own imaginative development, set in the Lake District, never really achieve such grandeur in either geographical or poetic scope. Rather, it seems as if forgotten or repressed images from imperial outposts return to take root in his writing, almost against his will, and populate his domestic stronghold with their exotica. I say almost against his will because, if

De Quincey displays a curious lack of agency in relation to these exotic monsters (he has, after all, conjured them in the first place), he also plainly welcomes them, even into the most recessive (if mundane) domestic spaces: the kitchen and nursery.

The difference between Wordsworth's and De Quincey's relation to these exotic forms is the degree to which they are introjected within the perimeters that define English domesticity. For Wordsworth, the procession of strange faces in Book Seven's London only enables him to read the face of the Blind Beggar as personally prophetic. For De Quincey, the faces of the Malay that continually haunt his Lake District abode increasingly dismantle his own autobiographical coherence.

Such exotic images representing Britain's imperial outposts—the Malay, the crocodile, the tiger—are invariably monstrous, not especially comforting for De Quincey because his writing doesn't have the same powers of regulation that Wordsworth, Johnson, Coleridge, and even Blake exhibit. Rather, the endless proliferation of De Quincey's stories about monsters signifies a deep anxiety to get the story right: a desire to emulate the authoritative discourse of the Lake District intellectuals, while maintaining his own difference from them (particularly Coleridge).

In this chapter I argue that the differences between eighteenth- and nineteenth-century notions of the self are manifested by the various cultural meanings of monsters. More specifically, De Quincey's marginal relationship to the Lake District prominence Wordsworth and Coleridge wielded in the literary world may demonstrate the ways in which the larger structures of romanticism may well rely on the abject in order to sustain their strong poetic identity.[4] Thus the relationship between the monstrously self-abjected writer (De Quincey) and the master romantic poet (Wordsworth) provides a model for understanding romantic identity as tied more closely to Enlightenment models of self-identity.

Renewed critical interest in De Quincey's work, particularly *Confessions of an English Opium Eater*, establishes this text as one that deploys Western-created notions about the Orient in order to represent a coherent English subjectivity based on national identity.[5] However, the ways in which such subjectivities are called into being differs according to different historical contestations and constructions of identity. In early eighteenth-century texts, we read representations of subjectivity such as Defoe's *Robinson Crusoe* in relation to the externally exotic; in De Quincey's "Oriental" narrative we may locate otherness in its consolidation within fantasies of a coherent notion of the "self." His *Confessions* are an exceedingly convoluted representation of the self, produced by a kind of trade in opium, not in opposition to the exotic but, rather, in relation to the introjection of otherness. De Quincey's representation of "Asia" tends to conflate geographical difference into a monolithic account of the "Orient," despite his attestations to specific detail. What this may suggest is the murky area "Asia" occupies in the English cultural unconscious: a place where imperial political strategies of subordination and domination rotate between success and failure, compliance and resistance, and therefore intensify their demonization.

De Quincey describes such a trumped-up "Asia" in the following notorious passage from his original 1822 *Confessions*:

The Malay has been a fearful enemy for months. I have been every night, through his means, transported into Asiatic scenes. . . . I have often thought that if I were compelled to forego England, and live in China, and among Chinese manners and modes of life and scenery, I should go mad. . . . Southern Asia, in general, is the seat of awful images and associations. . . . In China, over and above what it has in common with the rest of Southern Asia, I am terrified by the modes of life, by the manners, and the barrier of utter abhorrence. . . . All this . . . the reader must enter into before he can comprehend the unimaginable horror which these dreams of Oriental imagery . . . impressed upon me. Under the connecting feeling of tropical heat . . . I brought all creatures . . . that are found in all tropical regions, and assembled them in . . . Indostan. From kindred feelings, I soon brought Egypt all her gods under the same law. I was stared at, hooted at, grinned at, chattered at, by monkeys.[6]

De Quincey's passionate representation of all things "Oriental"—of which the "Asian" remains a distinctly powerful and resistant image—needs to be brought under the "same law." I would argue that law may be clearly identified as the law of the British empire, which recognizes, up to this point, difference as mobilized by race. In this case, as Leask has argued, "race" is embodied by the "Malay," who negotiates De Quincey's relation to "Asia" as something marked as differently colored. Race may also be mobilized by other ideological practices that exploit xenophobia for their articulation. De Quincey's fantastic representation of oriental artifacts in the context of his horrific dream in fact seems informed by the British nineteenth-century compulsion for archival collections of exotic *objets*; here the monkeys stand in metonymical relation to emerging scientific discourses of paleontology and primatology, whose historical status, according to Haraway, has "depended on the social relations of extractive colonialism and neo-colonialism."[7]

Particularly relevant to the construction of identity are the cases of various cultural monsters that at one time or another are either expelled or embraced by domesticity. What counts as difference in the eighteenth-century household—such as the one Crusoe replicates on his island—is readily identifiable as something not coherent with the rest of that household's inmates. Hence the monstrous hybrid cats (so different from the ones he brings from the ship) have to be killed.[8] In De Quincey's household, this difference, while still perceived as monstrous and therefore problematic, is somehow both welcomed and woven into the domestic fabric even if it is also feared. His monsters are materializations of xenodochial desire that determine aesthetic representation, particularly of the self, especially given the relative newness of autobiography as a literary genre in the 1820s.[9]

If "natural history is nothing more than the nomination of the visible," as Foucault argues, then it may seem that "unnatural" history (perhaps what we could also term human history) may be similarly connected to the invisible: the mythic accounts of things we can't see.[10] Crossover creatures (in the sense that they are both real and fantastic animals) such as tigers and crocodiles mark the edges of a naturalized imperial conquest and the liminal spaces of fantasy; they function as both material creatures and monsters. They justify imperial mastery to domestic culture because they are synonymous with danger. They give material shape to abstract fears about boundaries, about what lies beyond, and about the increasingly destabilized position with which England had to contend in the face of its continual accrual of colonial territories.

Both the accounts heading this chapter that Buffon and Barrell give of the enduring place of privileged violence that tigers occupied at the apex of British imperialism describe with varying degrees of relish the tiger's famed ferocity. For De Quincey, particularly, this ferocity became a metaphor for signifying the enormous complexities his opium habit presented to his professional scholarship. Like Blake, whose attempts to "frame" the "dread" posed by tigerish behaviors finally took shape as a "symmetry" or a balance between the material and monstrous, De Quincey may have disciplined his own oriental phobias into a more comforting domestic scenario: one that tigers and other exotic animals invaded with regularity, but whose potentially disruptive and threatening conjurings could be safely attributed to the ingestion of a powerful drug.[11] By all accounts, however, tigers and crocodiles were also naturalized within a taxonomy that granted a logical space for such monstrous eruptions. Monsters in the shape of tigers or crocodiles, performing as both mythical and natural beings, had the effect of naturalizing the ideological dimension of imperial fantasy: turning the invisible, unnatural spaces existing at the outposts of imperial territory into something with a definitive shape, something that could be brought home, so to speak, in order to give physical dimensions to an abstract understanding of "colony."

To read De Quincey's opium habit in this light is to recognize addiction itself as a domesticating habit: it denatures tigerish ferocity and recontextualizes the whole scope of "an obscure and imaginary oriental ferocity" within the security of the British household. As Barrell points out, the most infamous tigerish persona—Tipu, Sultan of Mysore (whose name is Kanarese for "tiger")—"from the early 1790s and for more than thirty years after his death in 1799 . . . became 'firmly embedded in . . . nursery folklore' as the oriental tiger the British loved to hate."[12] Tipu enters and populates the fictions of domesticity at its most vulnerable point: the nursery. Like nursery food—whose discrete outlines get pureed beyond recognition in order to promote consumption and digestion—and even more crucially like maternal milk (a likeness to which De Quincey was particularly sensitive), opium and its attendant potential for invoking oriental fantasy and horror have a curiously *familial* place in De Quincey's household.[13]

De Quincey's drugged state also mimics and reproduces the experience of the oceanic of Freud—the blurring of the edges of the ego, the separate self—the prototype of which is infancy, when the baby can't tell the difference between formal structures like inside/outside or self/other/mother.[14] The formal structures of De Quincey's narrative break down as the *Confessions* near their conclusion. The boundaries defining his autobiography have been continually interrupted by the Malay (now magically metastasized into a frightening proliferation of Malays), and it is to "motives external to myself" that De Quincey attributes any kind of authorial success in concluding his narrative of "unreasonable length." Barbara Johnson has argued that autobiography enacts the fantasy that one can give "birth" to oneself; De Quincey's oceanic state, produced through the consumption of opium, effectively stages a continual return to the Imaginary or pre-symbolic state.[15] He writes:

it may be as painful to be born again as to die: I think it probable: and, during the whole period of diminishing the opium, I had the torments of a man passing out of one mode of existence into another. The issue was not death but a sort of physical regeneration: and I may add, that ever since, at intervals, I have had a restoration of more than youthful spirits. (115)

Rather than demonstrating the ways in which otherness is productively internalized by the discipline of writing—as we see in Johnson, Blake or Wordsworth—De Quincey's writing is itself othered. Thus De Quincey's "renegade" authorship may more closely articulate the characteristics we associate with romanticism than do the writers who have come to embody that literary period.

Barrell's references to the third and fourth Mysore wars between 1790 and 1799 locate the origins of popular British associations of tigers with the orient. He mentions Tipu's obsession with tigers in relation to the British obsession with Tipu:

> In 1800 a panorama by Robert Ker Porter of the storming of Seringapatam, at which Tipu was killed, was exhibited in London. A play about Tipu was staged at Covent Garden in 1791, and the following year two more plays about him were put on at Astley's. Tipu's death inspired a fourth play, performed at Covent Garden in 1799. In 1823 there was a fifth, when *Tipoo Sahib, or the Storming of Seringapatam* was produced at the Royal Coburg Theatre . . . a version of this play was marketed for use in toy theatres.[16]

The several stagings of Tipu's defeat certainly seem to suggest not only an enthusiasm for this display of British valor but also a latent anxiety about the contest between British and Indian imperial might. Barrell argues that the connection between tigers and oriental ferocity deepened in the mid-nineteenth century. For De Quincey, seeing such toys as the near-life-sized tiger mauling an East India Company guard, originally commissioned by Tipu and brought to the India House in London as war booty in order to exhibit the British conquest, probably furnished material for many fantasies about tigerish violence. The fact that this mechanized beast was a toy and that dramas about Tipu's defeat eventually found their way into the "toy theater" suggest the profound incorporation of tigers into the domestic British fold.[17] Blake's own representation of a "tyger," the illumination accompanying the 1794 poem (which was probably drawn between 1792 and 1798), also strikingly resembles a toy. Belying the magnificence of the "distant deeps or skies" in which "burn the fire of thine eyes," this overgrown housecat's expression can only be described as congenial: eyes wide open, smiling an invitation to an invisible (and unsuspecting) "interlocutor."

Whether or not Blake, De Quincey, or the various artists who staged the Tipu dramas had first-hand knowledge of tigers, their renditions of these fabled creatures reflect a happy domesticity rather than a terrifying ferocity. (Even Delacroix' and other romantic painters' representations of tigers are oddly inconsistent with their famed immensity—they are generally rendered smaller than life, more cat-like, more domestic.) Thus these monsters were not unfamiliar to British households; their double-duty as creatures that defied and defined imperial boundaries was successfully introjected within the domestic fold. For De Quincey, it is arguable that these creatures might indeed have been far more familiar and familial to him than his legitimate household. His wife, Margaret Simpson, and his children, none of whom are ever named in the original *Confessions*, even while his more shady shared domesticity with Ann, the prostitute of Oxford Street, and the young, perhaps illegitimately conceived, girl of the lawyer Brunell's Greek Street residence with whom De Quincey shared a surreptitious existence, are discussed in quite a bit of detail. One reason for his uneasiness in naming these members too explicitly or discussing his relations with them in too much detail may have had to do with the venereal disease Leask suggests that he probably contracted from his traffic in prostitutes—not all his relations were as purified as those he had with Ann.[18] Such a transmission of infection generated by his peripatetic straying attests to his problematic suitability to traditional familial ties. However, another intriguing insinuation is that these ties are contingent on the communication of disease—that the structural relations that formulate familial or national domesticity can only be implemented through trafficking in foreign bodies that are themselves the arbiters of infection.

As creatures feared, loathed, and desired, "exotics" occupy a good deal of cultural space. Do they function as peripheral creatures, ones that serve to locate the parameters and perimeters of what constitutes imperial historiography? It seems that in the case of De Quincey, these "boundary creatures," to borrow Donna Haraway's term, negotiate the various kinds of positions De Quincey arbitrates with addiction and writing. Haraway suggests that such creatures

have a destabilizing place in the great Western evolutionary, technological, and biological narratives. These boundary creatures are, literally, *monsters*, a word that shares more than its root with the word, to *demonstrate*. Monsters signify. . . . The power-differentiated and highly contested modes of being of these monsters may be signs of possible worlds—and they are surely signs of worlds for which we are responsible.[19]

Monsters destabilize and demonstrate the limits of cultural capacity. For this reason, however, they also function equally to stabilize cultural positions in "evolutionary, technological, and biological narratives" and can, therefore, operate as "signs" of the "worlds" for which "we are responsible." In this sense, the boundary creatures not only define the perimeters of national formations—for example, as tigers do the edges of the British empire—but also signify the parameters of domestic cultural consciousness: for example, the status Tipu's tigers have in the British nursery. De Quincey's romantic writing invokes western-created monsters in order to signal the expanse and limits of imperial territorialization. They are invented at the edges of known spaces and then brought home to roost, so to speak, within the defining boundaries of domesticity. They cannot exist as external phenomena alone; rather, as products of xenophobia, their signifying faculties can only be fully articulated the moment they are returned home (although they are also always at home, the outside that makes possible the inside, the supplement).

The monsters of De Quincey's creation all have histories of meaning. But, such forms of monstrosity are not always as visible as their exoticized external forms may suggest. Finding a crocodile, a tiger, or even a Malay wandering about the Lake District would certainly demonstrate the far-flung reaches of imperial Britain brought home; finding one's children in the nursery would not. De Quincey manifests how the faces of his offspring (though not necessarily children themselves, as is the case of the hunger-bitten girl of Greek Street or Kate Wordsworth) perform as signifiers of introjected cultural monstrosity. That is, his indulgence in xenophobic fantasies define him as a cultural monster himself, and various forms of his issue—wife, children, writing—are thus similarly infected. De Quincey's xenophobia crucially disarticulates foreign territory in order to rearticulate imperial terms for the domestic consumption of the foreign.

Close readings of some familiar passages from the *Confessions* can reveal the ways in which the xenophobia that defined Enlightenment notions of external and internal, exotic and domestic, public and familial in relation to authorship, is at work in nineteenth-century romantic authorship. Although I examine similarities in these discourses, ultimately I want to investigate a crucial difference De Quincey's authorship makes to xenophobia and the construction of British psychosubjectivity.

Fixing the Orient, Orienting the Fix

De Quincey's romantic conception of "individual" is produced by the material effects of identities—imperial, national, sexual, gendered—in the process of writing a life. Like Crusoe in his journal or Johnson in his lexicography, De Quincey is determined to define a specific authorial territory of his own, and chooses himself as the subject for such writerly exploration.[20] Critically unlike Crusoe, however, is De Quincey's obsession with the incorporation and integration of exoticism within the framework of his self-representation. While foreignness is so clearly marked for Crusoe (and for Defoe) as difference, represented by the skins and coats of national identification, for De Quincey those props take on a different meaning, one that seems ineluctably connected with the emergence of national psychosubjectivity. Eighteenth-century strategies of coping with the other were characterized by incorporation; romantic subjectivities, on the other hand, were a more complicated matter of introjection.[21] Crusoe's understanding of difference is something that negotiates bodily (cannibals are different; I am not a cannibal) and psychic frontiers as external (I have taken a former cannibal [Friday] into the heart of my household, but such is my belief in my subjectivity that this is not entirely problematic). By contrast, De Quincey is continually seeking out ways in which he can occupy or lose himself in the place of the other. He not so much internalizes otherness as projects himself into the places where he perceives that otherness exists. Deliberately marginalizing himself, for example, to the Lake District Circle or seeking out the company of prostitutes like Ann, he is able to subsume himself in his later fantasies of "cancerous kisses" by "crocodiles" while lying "confounded amongst reeds and Nilotic mud." His *Confessions* not only help us to read the effects of introjection but even more critically to observe how these effects are materialized.

Perhaps a useful way of understanding the material effects of introjection is to examine the ways in which other critics, contemporary and otherwise, have treated the relation between opium eating and De Quincey's autobiographical project. Contemporary critics' responses to De Quincey's frank discussion of his addiction were enthusiastic; they admired his dreams which were "quoted extensively and admired as magnificent descriptive setpieces."[22] Predictably, their interest in De Quincey's opium use was primarily in its effects on him, and especially on his moral temperament. More recent critics have also tended to focus on the effects of opium upon De Quincey's writing, although not necessarily from a moral standpoint. Instead, scholars like John Barrell, Nigel Leask, Charles Rzepka, and Saree Makdisi, among others, have discussed the political and psychoanalytical ramifications of De Quincey's consumption, reading a relation between his obdurate and continuous use of opium eating and larger questions of cultural identity: subjective, economic, and imperial. My own contribution to this substantial and compelling discourse is (as I've argued with Johnson) to read xenophobia—the psychological hinge between imperialism and nationalism—as a crucial drive defining De Quincey's addiction and authorship, but also to uncover the profound and dramatic relations between xenophobia and domesticity.

One way to begin such an analysis is to think about the various meanings of addiction itself. The first meaning of "addict" the *Oxford English Dictionary* provides is "formally made over or bound (to another); attached by restraint or obligation; obliged, bound, devoted, consecrated"; the second addresses the more familiar meaning (in our culture) of being "attached by one's own inclination, self-addicted to a practice." The first meaning of its past tense is "delivered over by, or as if by, judicial sentence." These particular definitions seem at odds with the ways in which we have come to understand addiction as a state in which one is compelled beyond reasonable or formal limits (like the law) to act in particular ways. In fact, most narratives about addiction, historical and contemporary, recount a lack of formality in the consumption of addictive substance. That is, the point of writing these autobiographies at all is to represent the failure of formal limits to one's consumption—at least as long as one doesn't take into account the fact that inscribing anything in language constitutes, according to Lacan's formulation of language as the symbolic order, a juridical formality.

It is because of that exception, however, that I want to argue that De Quincey's xenophobia determines a connection between addiction and autobiography.[23] De Quincey's confessional text is compelling not only because of the self-consciousness with which he disciplines the record of his addiction but because of his equally compelling desire to be formally acknowledged as a scholar. Initially, he writes his *Confessions* in order to answer the following questions: (1) "How came any reasonable being to subject himself to such a yoke of misery, voluntarily . . . and knowingly to fetter himself with such a sevenfold chain?"; (2) how to "furnish a key to some parts of that tremendous scenery which afterward peopled [his] dreams"; and (3) how to "creat[e] . . . a personal sort of confessing subject . . . which cannot fail to render the confessions themselves more interesting" (33). Such a focus on egotism—his understanding that his very addiction provides him with a type of academic mastery (albeit one that is not necessarily sanctioned)—combined with the illusion of authenticity accompanying autobiographical narratives, characterizes this genre as peculiarly romantic: focused on the inward, solitary, and somewhat subversive autobiographical voice. Yet De Quincey is also highly conscious of his status as a cultural spokesman. His compulsion to demarcate the English opium-eater from, as he writes, "any Turk, of all that ever entered the Paradise of opium-eaters" together with his wish to offer explanations for the reasons he has foreign bodies populating his opiated dreams renders his personal portrait of English addiction a national and cultural one.

De Quincey's fascination with xenophobic representations of "orientalism" undermines the putative stability of British national identity in general, but even more pointedly of an English one, as Barrell, Leask and others have suggested. Part of what informs British xenophobia in the age of romanticism is a desire to fall into the foreign, to invite the other to occupy spaces deep within the domestic folds. Thus stories—true ones, if we are to believe the genre—of Malays wandering around the Lake District, or visions of Judean cities projected upon sublime British mountain landscapes erupt with some frequency in De Quincey's *Confessions*.

What seems to solidify the connection between self-portraiture and addiction is De Quincey's consumption of opium: eating the explicitly material exotic fruits of oriental origin transmutes into an abstraction: autobiography. Autobiographies of addiction like De Quincey's thus simultaneously occupy the registers of the real and symbolic. De Quincey writes in his prefatory apology:

If opium-eating be a sensual pleasure, and if I am bound to confess that I have indulged in it to an excess, not yet *recorded* of any other man, it is no less true, that I have struggled against this fascinating enthralment with a religious zeal, and have, at length, accomplished what I have never yet heard attributed to any other man—have untwisted, almost to its final links, the accursed chain that fettered me. (2)

To be "bound" to "confess" for De Quincey rehearses the first meaning of addiction the *Oxford English Dictionary* gives ("formally made over or bound to another"); the formality of this binding is manifested in writing, specifically, in self-authorship. Žižek suggests, a propos of Lacan's definition of the symbolic, that the "symbolic order is precisely such a formal order which supplements and/or disrupts the dual relationship of 'external' factual reality and 'internal' subjective experience."[24] The factual reality of opium supplements the subjectivity of De Quincey's confession, which in turn produces another, illusory factuality: the "authenticity" of autobiography. In another sense, the external material reality of opium supplements the abstract internal subjectivity of De Quincey's confession, and together they produce an example of "authentic" (autobiographical) British imperial authorship. The drug provides a material way in which De Quincey can access his more abstract investigation of subjectivity, while it also provides the excuse for his autobiographical narrative in which he discusses at length his scholastic relation to the Lake District poets. In spite of his attraction to the drug and its attendant effects, De Quincey remains in staunch support of Englishness. De Quincey's writing may make sense of English xenophobia: addicted to the spoils of imperial conquest and yet compelled to denigrate the sources of such spoils. Thus addiction as restraint or obligation and writing as the form in which such an obligation takes shape are mutually constitutive drives.

De Quincey's "enthralment" to the sensual pleasures of opium-eating—a word that has yet another etymological root in bondage and slavery—places him as the subject of servitude that needs, link by link, to be undone through his first formal obligation: the record of his confession. If we refer to the questions he hopes to answer by writing *The Confessions*, the sevenfold chain with which he knowingly fetters himself and the self-conscious creation of the confessing subject define this "enthralment" as something more than a drug addiction. Although writing is meant to unchain him from the opiated bonds, it seems as if writing—or, more specifically, autobiographical and confessional writing—itself becomes addictive. Writing therefore has a twofold part in the "sevenfold chain": it is both the disease and the cure. De Quincey's writing distinguishes him as an intellectual and also exposes him as a problem. De Quincey adds in a footnote to the passage I just quoted: "Not yet *recorded*, I say: for there is one celebrated man of the present day, who, if all be true which is reported of him, has greatly exceeded me in quantity" (2).

That man is of course Coleridge, and De Quincey's deliberate emphasis on the "record" of his autobiographical confession in order to identify the "quantity" of addiction makes crucial the proximity of addiction and self-representation.25 Although De Quincey claims that writing these confessions becomes the way he undoes the "accursed chain which fettered" him, to fulfill his contract completely and to formally finish the autobiographical narrative is as impossible to him as absolutely cutting himself off from opium and its effects. After all, he untwists that chain only "*almost* to its final links," thus leaving himself room for endless comments, appendices, sequels, and revisions to his *Confessions*.

De Quincey's mention of Coleridge in the footnote may also signify another formal obligation and another form of servitude and bondage: that of family (first meaning from the Latin *familia*, household, *famulus*, servant). Charles Rzepka outlines De Quincey's anxious desire to be included in the Lake District circle of William and Dorothy Wordsworth, Coleridge, and Southey (and later others) as well as his equally compelling desire not to be included:

Like the Malay who visited Dove Cottage in 1816, De Quincey had himself come "alone and devious from afar" to pay homage to his literary "idol," not once but twice. . . . De Quincey's youthful trepidation before his "idol" was also firmly rooted in a profound sense of his financial helplessness and dependency at the time. As he himself acknowledges, it was not until legally coming into his inheritance at the age of twenty-one and acquiring immediate control over his father's bequest that De Quincey felt truly man enough to venture an appearance on the doorstep of Dove Cottage.[26]

De Quincey's "deviousness"—his feelings of financial and perhaps authorial inadequacies—expresses his ambivalence about this circle, a desire to remain just outside it as a way of resisting familial bondage. Typically, De Quincey refrains from naming members of his family in his texts, referring to them in generic terms (such as the "boy" in his description of his son's death in *Suspiria de Profundis*) or deferring their mention by naming someone else much more explicitly. The fact that he also relegates Coleridge to similar anonymity (at least in original *Confessions*, although, as Nigel Leask has argued, the entire text is written with Coleridge very much at the forefront of his thought) may suggest an uneasily familial relation to the Lake District fellowship of poets in whose circle he so desperately wanted to be included. At the very least, his continual references to Coleridge in the *Confessions*, the protracted *Comments on the Confessions* (1821–55), and his 1856 revisions of the *Confessions* suggest an authorial rivalry for expertise in opium-consumption. De Quincey writes:

I may presume from the circumstance that Mr. Coleridge experienced the very same sensations, in the same situation, throughout his literary life, and has often noticed it to me with surprise and vexation. The sensation was that of powerful disgust with . . . his powers of composition. . . . Reverting to my own case, which was pretty nearly the same as his, there was, however, this difference—that, at times, when I had . . . armed myself by a sudden increase of opium for a few days running, I recovered . . . a remarkable glow of jovial spirits. In some such artificial respites . . . I wrote the greater part of the Opium Confessions. (125–26)

But what is the nature of this rivalry? The second part of De Quincey's addiction is the need for scholarly notice and, in particular, the need for Wordsworth's approbation.[27]

De Quincey embarks on a project to put a paternal face onto his self-representation. However, this process is quite complicated, and his motives are often in conflict with one another. His primary motive seems to be related to becoming Wordsworth's "son": getting included within the Lake District school (which he did in 1807) that was characterized by "a love of nature; simplicity in subject matter and style; the celebration of emotional and imaginative power rather than moral pedagogy or reasoned argument; and an antiurban and anti-commercial basis."[28] Even if De Quincey seeks to make more visible the "real" authorial father of his narrative in order to make material what was a disembodied concept, the figure of the father has to remain disembodied if it is to perform as the voice of cultural authority. De Quincey's paternal attachment to Wordsworth glosses the inadequacy of De Quincey's own dead father (whose impotence seems most dramatically displayed by his anonymous authorship).[29] The flawed father's successors, De Quincey's teachers (Edward Spencer and Charles Lawson at the Manchester Grammar School in particular) succeed in teaching De Quincey Greek, a language that signifies classical education but that also affords him little material use. De Quincey's attachment to Wordsworth is metonymical: he speaks Wordsworth's language and loves Wordsworth's child.[30]

To decline a "fellowship with the great family of man" seems to propel De Quincey's desire to write his *Confessions*. That his wish is expressed "in the affecting language of Mr. Wordsworth" suggests that out of a vast cultural gene pool, De Quincey chooses, as Rzepka and others have argued, the smaller, more exclusive fellowship of Lake District poets for his "family"(29). Mr. Wordsworth's language in this instance also reinvents the moment, for De Quincey, of his entering into language, culture, and subjecthood as a moment within his control.[31] A self-consciously constructed identity—"from my birth I was made an intellectual creature: and intellectual in the highest sense my pursuits and pleasures have been, even from my school-boy days" (30)—De Quincey's fantasies about fathers conveniently picture them as both model and scapegoat. De Quincey's own father seems to have abandoned him: he dies in 1793 when De Quincey is eight, leaving him to the surrogate parenting of his mother and other guardians. In De Quincey's narrative, they clearly appear as substitutes for the dead father, their varying degrees of aptitude in teaching the young De Quincey express his ambivalence about the abandonment he experienced with the death of his father. Thus De Quincey embarks on a mission to reconstruct his relation to the ideal father of his own making. According to his narrative, he

was very early distinguished for my classical attainments, especially for my knowledge of Greek. At thirteen, I wrote Greek with ease; and at fifteen my command of that language was so great, that I not only composed Greek verses in lyric metres, but could converse in Greek fluently, and without embarrassment. . . . "That boy," said one of my masters, pointing the attention of a stranger to me "'that boy could harangue an Athenian mob better than you or I could address an English one." (35)

De Quincey's compulsion to convey his mastery of Greek suggests another moment of family romance; he is in full control of his reentry into the symbolic, and yet the language he masters, while signifying the crucial mark of a classical English education, is also one that does him no material good. At best he can "harangue" an imaginary Athenian mob—one that has been reconstructed according to English fantasies about what counted as a "Athenian mob"—at worst he has conversations that no one understands.[32] Part of this compulsion has to do with his desire to be included in the rarified circle of Lake District poets—to be enfolded, like Coleridge, within the reassuring embrace of Wordsworth's authorial protection; the other part, as I've suggested, is vexed by his reluctance to be incorporated by them.[33] De Quincey's *Confessions*, then, may be read as a metonym of this desire: a way of inscribing a biological face (Wordsworth's) onto the cultural body of the writer, as others have argued, but also of finally resisting the full implications of what that inscription might mean. After all, De Quincey persistently alludes to the increasing disintegration of his autobiographical memoirs without resorting to any kind of superimposed coherence that an imitation of Wordsworth might have furnished.

De Quincey is careful, however, to give his readers a reality "check from any erroneous conclusions." He is, he assures us, the "son of a plain English merchant . . . strongly attached to literary pursuits. "Indeed," he adds parenthetically, that his father "was himself, anonymously, an author" (61). While reminding us of his biological parentage, inoculating himself against any charge of superficial snobbery, De Quincey replaces his father's authorial anonymity (a signifier, perhaps, of other forms of inadequacy) with the authorial prowess of a published, literary father: Wordsworth.

He represents his mother as "still more highly gifted," describing her writing in elaborate detail and concluding with the ways her letters "exhibit as much strong and masculine sense, delivered in pure 'mother English', racy and fresh with idiomatic graces as any in our language" (61–62).[34] Although he rarely mentions his mother in the 1822 text, his 1856 revision discusses her place within his familial consciousness in much greater detail. For example, he writes in the 1856 *Confessions* a propos of his decision to leave the Manchester Grammar School:

Under my present circumstances, I saw that the very motives of love and honour, which would have inclined the scale so powerfully in favour of the northern lakes, were exactly those which drew most heavily in the other direction. . . . And just at that moment suddenly unveiled itself another powerful motive against taking the northern direction— viz., consideration for my mother—which made my heart recoil from giving her too great a shock. (172)

De Quincey's predilection for offering himself opposing choices is manifested with breathtaking concision in this important revisionary moment. His powerful inclination ("love and honour") to pursue romantic intellectual company ("the northern lakes") can only be articulated by choosing its hysterical counterpart: choosing to visit the more destabilizing domestic domain of the mother. It is difficult not to be reminded of a similar choice that De Quincey constructs for himself around the very same issue in the 1821 *Confessions* when he favors the Oriental scene, crowned by the reappearance of Ann, in favor of the sublime mountain landscape.

This maternal domestic stronghold—the Priory—is complicated by its close association with oriental monstrosity. "Not one minute had I waited," De Quincey writes, describing his anticipation of meeting his sister in the gardens of the Priory, "when in glided amongst the ruins—not my fair sister, but my bronzed Bengal uncle! A Bengal tiger would not have more have startled me" (179).[35] This tigerish uncle and De Quincey's mother "regarded each other as sole reliques of a household living once living together in memorable harmony" (180). De Quincey's domestic origin (one that he persists in imitating) is remarkable primarily for its monstrosity: not simply because of the murky association with the tiger and imperial monsters manifested by his uncle, but also because of the household's dependence on the mother's injunctions. While his uncle, "whose Indian munificence ran riot upon all occasion, would gladly have had a far larger allowance made to me," his mother "interfered with a decisive rigour that in my own heart I could not disapprove," leaving De Quincey to walk "amongst Welsh mountains . . . upon a slender allowance of a guinea-a-week" (180). The excessive expenditure practiced by the Bengal uncle is kept in check by the British mother's more restraining hand. Such control, however, far from having the effect of teaching moderation and control (what Johnson would advocate as a national characteristic), perversely stimulates De Quincey's excessive behavior despite (or because of) his attestations to Englishness. The pangs of hunger he experiences are stayed or even deferred by an overconsumption of opium. His gastric distress, initiated by maternal withholding, leads to the psychic torment produced, indirectly, by "Indian munificence."

These forms of malaise are not independently experienced; rather, the lack of maternal nutriment (in this case, the cold maternal disregard for the physical conditions of De Quincey's well-being) as well as the chimeric promise of exotic largess together produce De Quincey's compensatory overconsumption of opiate. Caught in an economy of familial and imperial relations (mother/uncle—but not father), De Quincey's entrance into the intellectual life of Lake District poets is vexed from the start. The exquisite sensibility that prevents De Quincey from "even tolerat[ing] the prospect of Wordsworth's hearing [his] name first of all associated with some case of pecuniary embarrassment," is swept aside by "another powerful motive against taking the northern direction," one that "suddenly unveil[s]" itself to him, "viz., consideration for my mother—which made my heart recoil from giving her too great a shock" (171–72). Despite his desire to claim fellowship with the paternal authorship Wordsworth represents to De Quincey, then, he is bound to his mother's language. His mother tongue (English) is the language that continues to wield authority even though his reputation as a classical scholar is grounded in his familiarity with foreign languages, particularly Greek. Such knowledge, as I suggested earlier, only serves him the dubious mastery of haranguing nonexistent Athenian mobs or speaking nonsensical phrases to bemused Malays.

In contrast to Wordsworth's claim to literary authority, demonstrated by the reshaping of poetic language attributed to him (and to romanticism), De Quincey self-consciously puts his authorial project at a severe remove; his *Confessions* are, as Leask has argued, at once "impersonal, 'preternatural,' pharmaceutical, rather than autobiographical, natural or spiritual," or a domestication of "this exotic 'hero'": opium. Even the revised 1856 text that "removed [the English opium-eater] from the troubling no-man's land of the elegant case-history or pathology settled comfortably into the genre of literary autobiography" is one that establishes a different, somewhat more suspect form of romantic representation, one that is "delightful but now . . . more autobiographic."[36] For De Quincey "opium eating [is] a sensual pleasure, . . . and I am bound to confess that I have indulged in it to an excess, not yet *recorded* of any other man."[37] De Quincey's multi-tiered narrative apparently eschews the literary for the scientific ("I here present you . . . the record of a . . . period in my life . . . that will . . . prove, not merely interesting, but, in a considerable degree, useful and instructive"), despite his desires to be recognized literarily (29). Such a choice, however, demonstrates his remarkable nose for the political ramifications of poetics, as Leask and other have pointed out. Donna Haraway suggests:

Throughout the early period of the industrial revolution, a particularly important development of the theory of the body politic linked the natural and political economy on multiple levels. Adam Smith's theory of the market and the division of labour as keystones of future capitalist economic thought, with Thomas Malthus's supposed law of the relation of population and resources, together symbolize the junction of natural forces and economic progress in the formative years of capitalist industrialism.[38]

De Quincey's ambivalence regarding political economy would certainly have placed him in the middle of such debates. On the one hand, he subscribed to Ricardo's principles of political economy and deplored the notion of unlawful capitalist profit; on the other, he believed in the natural right of the aristocracy and expressed a Malthusian fear of teeming foreign masses. His scientific interest is a way of providing a frame for romantic poetics. He is aware of the aesthetic possibilities of scientific discourse—as were many writers of this period—but he uses scientific discourse to draw a politicized representation of himself.[39] However, despite his arguments for another kind of aesthetic formulation, De Quincey is subject to dominant aesthetic pronouncements and is, therefore, not entirely or unproblematically included within the "primary" circle of romantic writers, then or now. Unlike the projects that his real or imaginary father authored—the anonymous productions his father wrote, the poetic language Wordsworth fathered—De Quincey's language was read (by Coleridge, among others) as hopelessly bound to his narrative of confession—that is, aligned to the sensual, to the body, to the mother, and to the domestic.[40]

The accusations De Quincey levels at Rousseau seem curiously a propos to his own confessional endeavor: a "spurious and defective sensibility of the French" affects any reading of his work. His invocation of both Augustine and Rousseau may work as a form of inoculation and maintenance against the dangerous effects of the other that Leask and Barrell have discussed. De Quincey's deliberate invocation of the French may, however, also work as an example of using a self-consolidating other in order to erase the discrete authorial presence he creates for himself. The French embody a xenodochial position from which De Quincey can inscribe himself. Expressly inviting the "gratuitous self-humiliation" characterizing French confession—or "that part of the German" similarly infected—De Quincey's corrective offers an excuse for a discourse continually contaminated by his xenophobic self-representation.

Some crucial and telling descriptions of his familial household, particularly ones that place monsters and children in close proximity with one another, help illustrate the inevitability of the domestic—and cultural—bondage De Quincey experienced. He describes his hideous opium dreams as follows:

Into these dreams only, it was . . . that any circumstances of physical horror entered. All before had been moral and spiritual terrors. But here the main agents were ugly birds, or snakes, or crocodiles. . . . The cursed crocodile became to me the object of more horror than almost all the rest. I was compelled to live with him . . . for centuries. I escaped sometimes, and found myself in Chinese houses, with cane tables, &tc. All the feet of the tables, sofas, &tc. soon became instinct with life: the abominable head of the crocodile, and his leering eyes, looked out at me, multiplied into a thousand repetitions: and I stood loathing and fascinated. (110)

Shortly afterward, De Quincey awakes:

And so often did this hideous reptile haunt my dreams, that many times the very same dream was broken up in the very same way: I heard gentle voices speaking to me (I hear every thing when I am sleeping) and I instantly awoke: it was broad noon; and my children were standing . . . at my bed-side; come to show me their coloured shoes, or new frocks, or to let me see them dressed for going out. . . . [S]o awful was the transition from the damned crocodile, and the other unutterable monsters and abortions of my dreams, to the sight of the innocent *human* natures and of infancy, that, in the mighty and sudden revulsion of mind, I wept, and could not forbear it. (110)

While his children seem important to his recovery from the crocodile dreams, De Quincey does not actually equate the sight of his children with recuperation. Narrative coherence is not marked by the intrusion of his children whose material bodies he has presumably fathered.[41] Rather, he has to make room for the presence of his children within the coherence of his dream. The dreams alone maintain narrative integrity; the way they are "broken up"—the "very same way"—is monolithic, perhaps suggesting that originality and creativity are continuously subject to a monstrous interruption and dispersal by the intervening and censoring faces of "innocence." De Quincey's children, metonymically arranged to stand in for the "damned crocodile and other unutterable monsters," present themselves as monsters of sorts. They are the figures that intrude upon his fantasies of authorial integrity with the sights and sites of the banal: "coloured shoes," "new frocks," or going-out dress. This last item—perhaps less an item and more a condition—may signify the problem De Quincey has with being "out," unprotected by the fantastic effects of opium, mediated only by the paraphernalia of everyday life. In fact, the disparity between dreaming and waking calls into question the status of knowledge.

De Quincey by his own admission "knows"—("hears every thing")—the waking voices to be external to his fantasy, and yet, upon waking, has to recast those known (that is, known as innocent) voices as monstrous in order to perpetuate his fantasy of authorial control. Later, in one of his appendices to the *Confessions*, he writes: "so powerful was my feeling . . . of some long, never-ending separation from my family, that at length . . . I was obliged to relinquish my daily walks in Hyde Park and Kensington Gardens, from the misery of seeing children in multitudes, that too forcibly recalled my own" (124). The conventional reading of this moving passage is to understand De Quincey's reticence as an overwhelming desire to see his children. In the context of his problematized relation with his family, it seems more appropriate to imagine the double meaning of "recall"—to conjure and remove—as articulating his desires to be rid of familial reminders.

As I suggested earlier, the nursery is a vexed site, vulnerable to invasion by nurses and mothers repeating folklore featuring monstrosity (Tipu's tiger, Savage's mother, Johnson's own wet-nurse). Perhaps a way of accounting for De Quincey's "sudden revulsion of mind" when he views his children's faces is the fact that all his interiors are peopled with monsters. Even the furniture of everyday life is fashioned after the crocodile. De Quincey focuses on the suddenness of the transition from one object of contemplation (the "abominable head of the crocodile") to another (his children's faces) that causes him to weep. It is as if *his* children, issuing from *his* contaminated body, are like the "unutterable monsters and abortions of [his] dreams." His body is incurably linked to the body of the mother, the body of the prostitute (disease), the marked other—the conglomerate of the Malay, China, Egypt, and Indostan; together they intrude upon his autobiographical writings, effectively infecting his body and preventing any legitimate authorial or paternal issue. Linked to the maternal body, De Quincey cannot even produce what his mother obviously could: his children are abortions, unnatural births embodying "unnatural" knowledge. Such unnatural knowledge is sustained by certain material realities: the illegitimate birth of his first child (1816), his fear of the possibility of his wife Margaret Simpson's venereal infection perpetrated by his earlier traffic in prostitutes, and the trope of dead sisters that continually march across his text, signifying his own impotence (to protect them from death, to protect himself from being subsumed into the melancholia their deaths generate).

Wordsworth's child, however, is a different story. Not only is she the progeny of a far more renowned literary conception, she has no physical body. Unlike the unmistakably material bodies of De Quincey's children, his wife, and even his dead sisters (described in the lurid terms of their ruined corpses), Kate Wordsworth is sublimated. Her name stands in more direct association with a recovery narrative, even if De Quincey eventually rejects its recuperative possibilities. De Quincey's representation of Kate Wordsworth is protected by an elaborate romantic showcase.[42] She becomes one of the two alternative models of subjectivity he offers himself in the dream that effectively closes *The Confessions*. Here the "well-known scene" outside Dove Cottage appears in a pastoral pose: "cattle tranquilly reposing upon the verdant graves, and particularly round about the grave of a child whom I had tenderly loved . . . [it was] a little before sun-rise in the same summer, when that child had died . . . I said aloud to myself . . . I will walk abroad . . . I shall be unhappy no longer" (111). The child is enshrined within a Wordsworthian pastoral scenario that presents delicious possibilities of "resurrection" for De Quincey. The grave is "verdant," the "sun-rise" inspires hope, even the animals—the domesticated cattle that signify agricultural bounty—are tranquil, completely unlike the horrifyingly enervating "unutterable" creatures of De Quincey's opiated fantasies. But Kate Wordsworth herself is dead and sublimated into nothing more threatening than a pastoral scenario.

Curiously, knowledge again comes into question; De Quincey's off-hand mention of that "well-known scene" suggests that the archetypical romantic site—Dove Cottage and its environs—is common knowledge to his readers. De Quincey has earlier in his *Preliminary Confessions* extolled the position of the opium eater as (natural) philosopher: "For amongst the conditions which he deemed indispensable to the sustaining of any claim to the title of philosopher, is not merely the possession of a superb intellect in its *analytic* functions . . . but also such a constitution of the *moral* faculties" (33–34). To "know" the requirements to be a philosopher—natural or otherwise—is a problem: who can know what constitutes knowledge? Lacan addresses this serious epistemological rift: "The notion that to be a philosopher means being interested in what everyone else is interested in *without knowing it* has the interesting peculiarity that its pertinence does not imply that it can be verified. For it can be put to the test only by everyone becoming a philosopher" (italics mine).[43] De Quincey's "knowledge" of the conditions of philosophy, then, displays the opposite. He can't know such conditions but can know what is wanting in those conditions: what is missing, what needs to be supplied, what needs to be excised. He can, therefore, produce such opinions as "our English poets have possessed [the faculties of the philosopher] in the highest degree,—and Scottish professors in the lowest" with far more authority than Wordsworth, because Wordsworth, as master—as philosopher—can't know to want. De Quincey, on the other hand, is far too aware of the conditions defining his intellectual life; he is the hysteric who supplements the master signifier, the other on whom the master relies in order to articulate the discourse that establishes mastery in the first place.[44] The assumption of the reader's recognition of this Wordsworthian scene as a romantic one exemplifies De Quincey's foreclosure of the master. His assumption suggests that the apparatus on which the recognition of the romantic location rests is entirely dependent on another kind of knowledge: a recognition of its opposite—the oriental city staining the horizon, for example. Like Lacan's master, who according to popular consent has a one-to-one correspondence with truth, romantic dominance doesn't know that it is wanting because it doesn't know to want. The scene of popular romanticism De Quincey resists can only be supported by someone who has no entrance to the club. Interestingly, De Quincey's resistance to the Wordsworth club also extended to the erotic choices he made. Eschewing the expectations the Wordsworths had for his marriage to Dorothy Wordsworth and striking up an affair with a local farmer's daughter (Margaret Simpson), with whom he had an illegitimate son almost a year before they married, De Quincey virtually guaranteed the severance of his relations with the Wordsworths even though they were near neighbors. Thus he carried on a "far different" scene of writing vis-à-vis the legitimated Wordsworthian literary production.

In "Subversion of the Subject and Dialectic of Desire," Lacan asks "who is speaking" and responds with "the right way to reply to the question . . . when it is the subject of the unconscious that is at issue. For this reply cannot come from that subject if he does not know what he is saying, or even if he is speaking."[45] De Quincey himself demonstrates the "rightness" of this reply within the same dream. Hardly has he reached the garden gate after his (romantic) decision to "walk abroad" among hills so "high" they "stretch away to heaven" so that "old griefs shall be forgotten" and he will "be unhappy no longer" when "immediately I saw upon the left a scene far different" (111). It is an Oriental vision ("at a vast distance were visible, as a stain upon the horizon, the domes and cupolas of a great city") where he sees Ann the prostitute from his former peripatetic days framed by Judean palms, and, "in the twinkling of an eye, I was far away from mountains, and by lamp-light in Oxford-street, walking again with Ann" (112).[46] The fact that this scene, unlike the previous one, is "immediate" suggests that such exotic locales, putatively informed by a xenophobic desire, may be part of a xenodochial invitation. De Quincey the hysteric is entirely capable of recognizing the ways in which dominant romantic discourse is mediated.[47]

His choice, then, for the exotic trappings that define an English (un)consciousness—the slide he makes from Ann framed by Judean palms to the lamp-lit streets of London—articulates an important moment for romantic representation. The choice De Quincey makes, favoring this "far different" scene over its pastoral counterpart, is interesting in several respects. It suggests, first of all, that De Quincey's sympathies lie with the murky underpinnings of the characteristics defining high romanticism. For De Quincey, the Judean city, visible only as a "stain upon the horizon," exudes far more romantic resonance than the comparative cleanliness of Alpine visions ("the air is cool and still . . . the forest-glades are as quiet as the churchyard; and, with the dew, I can wash the fever from my forehead, and then I shall be unhappy no longer"). That this "stain" is the catalyst for his equally stained memory of the prostitute Ann, rushing back to him with such force, also points to his choice of the prostitute over Wordsworth's daughter as the only possible one he could make. As if recognizing that his place in the Lake District circle is that of the hysteric that supports their visionary company, De Quincey deliberately decides against the rejuvenating possibilities of romantic discourse and adopts instead the seedier version Oxford-street offers.

De Quincey's achievement of even a flawed romantic ideal is, by his own account, wrested from him in the moment of its materialization, and he is doomed to tread the same path repeatedly. The body of the prostitute unmistakably associates De Quincey with the contaminating body of the maternal feminine (a subject I elaborate on in the following chapters). But we cannot forget that De Quincey's account is notoriously unreliable: what does his choice of romantic exile imply? Can we read this choice as part of the vexed relation of subjectivity between the master and the hysteric?

By now it should be clear that, while the father in question assumes a conveniently fluid position in De Quincey's paternal fantasies, the mother has a rather more complicated position. De Quincey describes his early acquaintance with hunger more allusively in the original *Confessions* than the detail he supplies in the later revisions:

> It was not for the purpose of creating pleasure, but of mitigating pain in the severest degree, that I first began to use opium as an article of daily diet. In the twenty-eighth year of my age, a most painful affection of my stomach, which I had first experienced about ten years before, attacked me in great strength. This affection had originally been caused by extremities of hunger, suffered in my boyish days. (35)

One may read these "extremities of hunger" produced by his motherless narrative as somehow responsible for his addiction. De Quincey goes on to describe the vicissitudes of his fortunes that land him in London, homeless, friendless and penniless, with nothing but opium and the company of the prostitute, Ann, to stave off complete despair. Here, he pauses to enshrine Ann in a burlesque of Wordsworth's poetic language:

> Oh! youthful benefactress! how often in succeeding years, standing in solitary places, and thinking of thee with grief of heart and perfect love, how often have I wished that, as in ancient times the curse of a father was believed to have supernatural power given to it from above to chase—to way-lay—to overtake—to pursue thee into the central darkness of a London brothel. (52)

As the father, Wordsworth's curse incites De Quincey to "chase," "way-lay," "overtake," and "pursue" romantic poetics to its end in a brothel—a fit place for unfruitful production, the "abortions" of his dreams. Such a chase and such an end suggest that for De Quincey, the emptiness of Wordsworth's language can only be filled with hysterical discourse, and thus he blocks any integrated sense of romantic consciousness. Indeed, it seems as if the only concrete thing the "affecting language of Mr. Wordsworth" has accomplished thus far in either version of his narrative has been to lead him to the druggist who first furnishes him with opium. De Quincey writes: "My road homewards lay through Oxford-street; and near 'the *stately* Pantheon" (as Mr. Wordsworth has obligingly called it) I saw a druggist's shop" (70).[48] Thus begins the "second birth of [his] sufferings." Part Two of the *Confessions* apostrophizes Oxford-street as "stony-hearted stepmother! thou that listenest to the sighs of orphans, and drinkest the tears of children" (67). The lack of nutriment De Quincey claims as his childhood affliction, the substitute he makes of opium, and the fantasies about Oxford-street together make the mother's absence a curious presence. She causes bodily discomfort, and is replaced by the suitably diabolical figure of the stepmother who, contrary to maternal logic, drinks the nutriment provided by the bodies of her stepchildren.[49]

Yet the mother also offers a kind of succor. Such sustenance is most clearly given by Ann when she nourishes De Quincey back to consciousness with a glass of wine after a fainting spell. More complicated, however, is the support provided by Oxford-street herself; De Quincey's obsessive return to her bosom furnishes for him a place for articulating his "confessing subject" (33). Such a place—as far removed from the Lake District as possible—is where the framework of De Quincey's contribution to romantic discourse takes shape. But to prefer Oxford-street to Dove Cottage is too dramatic a shift for De Quincey to make without mediation; Ann's body—purified by De Quincey's narrative—glosses the brute reality of this preference, this instance of xenodochial pleasure. It is Ann who furnishes the aesthetic pleasures of Oxford-street and mitigates the monstrosity of its step-maternity, yet she too is abjected. Despite her good intentions she is in some displaced way responsible for De Quincey's collapse: "Suddenly, as we sat, I grew much worse: I had been leaning my head against her bosom; and all at once I sank from her arms and fell backwards on the steps" (51).

The identity of the mother, far from having the same signifying possibilities as an insubstantive father, is inescapably bound to the material (similar to the way De Quincey is inescapably bound to his *Confessions*). In relation to De Quincey, Ann's position as a prostitute binds him, corporeally, with the illicit.[50] She is his agent of contamination just as surely as opium is. While the search for mythical fathers presents romantic possibilities, the mother is more often than not a hindering presence. De Quincey's connection to the mother's corporeal identity is too hideous even to contemplate without losing consciousness. Perhaps, then, his careless forgetfulness in noting her surname and subsequently losing her is not altogether accidental.[51] He closes his eulogy to Ann with the following hope: "I now wish to see her no longer; but think of her, more gladly, as one long since laid in the grave; in the grave, I would hope, of a Magdalene taken away, before injuries and cruelty had blotted out and transfigured her ingenuous nature, or the brutalities of ruffians had completed the ruin they begun" (65). Ann's buried body, lying in its Magdalene-like state, is the one relic of childhood De Quincey pockets as a kind of literary talisman against the fearful prospects the Malay threatens (Barrell suggests the conflation of Ann with his dead sister Elizabeth, lying in state before the ruination of autopsy). This gesture is highly resonant of Wordsworth: in Book Nine of the *Prelude*, the one relic Wordsworth manages to salvage from the ruin of his ideals of the French Revolution—a ruin perpetrated by brutal ruffians like Robespierre—is a memory of Le Brun's Magdalene, streaming tears.

> I sate in the open sun
> And from the rubbish gathered up a stone
> And pocketed the relick in the guise
> Of an enthusiast; yet, in honest truth . . .
> I looked for something which I could not find . . .
> For 'tis most certain that the utmost force
> Of all these various objects which may shew . . .
> Less moved me, gave me less delight, than did
> A single picture merely, hunted out
> Among other sights, the Magdalene of le Brun,
> A beauty exquisitely wrought—fair face
> And rueful, with its ever-flowing tears. (*Prelude* 1805, Book Nine, ll. 66–80)

Ann's body is buried by Wordsworth's "affecting language" but, like the return of the repressed, is exhumed by De Quincey's narrative.

The feminine/maternal body works in conjunction with another foreign body that infects and affects De Quincey's narrative. "One day," De Quincey writes in one of the most memorable moments of the *Confessions*, "a Malay knocked at my door. What business a Malay could have to transact amongst English mountains, I cannot conjecture." What business, indeed: perhaps, as Leask has argued, to furnish De Quincey with a display of his powers of classical languages in front of the English servant-girl. De Quincey "addressed him in some lines from the *Iliad*; considering that, of such languages I possessed, Greek, in point of longitude came geographically nearest to an Oriental one" (91).

I will address the problem of language in this passage later, but I want here to make more explicit the ways De Quincey assigns color to race in precisely the ways he assigns body to gender. He writes: "In a cottage kitchen, but panelled on the wall with dark wood that from age and rubbing resembled oak, and looking more like a rustic hall of entrance than a kitchen, stood the Malay—his turban and loose trowsers of dingy white relieved upon the dark panelling" (90). With the exception of his "trowsers" and turban, the Malay is virtually indistinguishable from the wall paneling in the cottage kitchen. De Quincey's comment on the way in which the dark paneling of the kitchen comes to "resemble oak" seems incidental at first, until we later hear of his comparison of the Malay to "mahogany."

In the context of this comparison, oak and mahogany become more than simple distinctions between woods: they are significant cultural signposts to De Quincey's anxieties about borders and boundaries. Dove Cottage's kitchen is not paneled by oak, only by wood that by "age" and "rubbing" now *"resemble[s]"* oak. This resemblance resonates the cultural importance of timber in the seventeenth and eighteenth centuries. Timber became a signifier of British imperial power (as both military and commercial ships were made primarily of oak), but it also may have been associated with imperial anxiety over deforestation and the loss of timber.⁵² The association between timber and national self-identity took a specific form: oak.⁵³ In the case of De Quincey's description, the cottage wall's resemblance to oak suggests that the "real" thing can only be marked by what is not real: thus the political power that oak wields is only sustained through what cannot be oak: the mahogany De Quincey uses to describe the Malay's skin—"the sallow and bilious skin of the Malay, enamelled or veneered with mahogany" (91). The fact that this particular cottage is Dove Cottage thus visibly contests, for De Quincey, the popular belief in the exclusivity of Lake District poets.⁵⁴

It is only by his dress that De Quincey can identify the Malay as other: his skin is coherent with the walls of the cottage. His racial difference must then be invented, as it is by De Quincey's xenophobia. But this difference is not simply demonstrated by the contrast the Malay makes with English inhabitants. This Malay, a production of a powerful opiated fantasy about cultural difference, stands in stark relation to Englishness only when placed against English children: the servant girl, Barbara Lewthwaite, who answers the Malay's knock, and the young boy who creeps in afterward. While her "exquisite fairness" provides her with a "native spirit of mountain intrepidity" that contrasts with the Malay's "slavish gestures," once again De Quincey places children and monsters in close proximity with one another, and such a proximity may suggest a profound likeness a difference between these disparate categories rather than. Their linguistic impasse places Lewthwaite and the Malay in an exquisite balance: "his attainments in English were exactly of the same extent as hers in Malay, there seemed to be an impassable gulf fixed between all communication of ideas, if either party had happened to possess any" (90). De Quincey's qualifier turns the meaning of this tableau vivant into something more complicated than a racial face-off. Lewthwaite's apparent emptiness of ideas places her on a level with the "tiger-cat"'s lack of intellectual activity; the young child can do nothing more than gaze upward at the "confounding" turban, and moreover remains "half-hidden by the ferocious looking Malay" (90–91). The article of dress, the turban, with which De Quincey demonstrates his savvy for identifying (with) oriental *objets*, confounds the children: it is the particular item that perplexes Lewthwaite, sending her in a fluster to summon her master, and it is what the young boy "gaze[s] upward at," transfixed by the "fiery eyes beneath [the turban]" (91). The children are confounded (mingled so as to make it impossible to distinguish the separate elements) with the "tiger-cat"'s vestments (not the cat himself): as for Crusoe, difference is manufactured by coats and skins. De Quincey's intervention crucially separates out an epistemological difference between himself—not the children—and the opium-eating other. Not unlike the scene I discussed earlier where De Quincey's children become the hindrances to the ultimate jouissance of his oriental nightmares, here the children are conflated with oriental monsters, making De Quincey's presence critical to the recovery of the scene for English use. Such uses most probably took shape as ones in which the difference of race was essentialized and naturalized.

Aside from xenophobic references to the Malay as non-European, prominently represented by his inhuman invulnerability to a potent drug (De Quincey offers him enough opium to kill "three dragoons and their horses," for which he feels "some alarm . . . but what could be done?"), what is striking about this scene is the way in which the Malay becomes incorporated into the veneer of domesticity. The cottage kitchen, against the walls of which the Malay becomes invisible, resembles less a kitchen and more the "rustic hall of entrance." Since this is Dove Cottage, we might read the scenario as one in which a foreign body stands at the point of entry to the site of romanticism. The Malay interrupts De Quincey's life and consequently reconfigures it ("This Malay has been a fearful enemy for months" 108); he functions as a projection of De Quincey's own inability to integrate into the writerly world of the Lake District poets.[55] We may, therefore, read the foreign body as De Quincey's: desiring fellowship with the Lake District poets and yet also deliberately undermining the potential that fellowship offers (90–91).

This same Malay returns as his "fearful enemy, one that brings "other Malays with him worse than himself" to haunt De Quincey's dreamlife, and "every night, through his means, [De Quincey is] transported into Asiatic scenes" (108). The various horrors of being "confounded with all unutterable slimy things, amongst reeds and Nilotic mud," figured by the presence of the very brownness of the Malay, present to De Quincey the possibilities of being physically marked by opium and culturally marked by the same difference that enamels and veneers the Malay (109). That such a marking is necessary to romantic and intellectual discourse may have been equally horrifying to De Quincey.

De Quincey's romantic autobiographical confessions are especially susceptible to psychoanalytic reading which conventionally situates a discourse within the realm of the personal or the individual. What is striking about the *Confessions* is that De Quincey's self-consciousness moves away from the kind of interior, solitary reflection characterizing romantic discourse and toward an understanding of writing as a cultural practice. The body of culture that he chooses to represent in fact later comes to assume the form of the body of his family: the familial trope is a recuperative one for him, but one that is entirely divorced from any "real" or even chronological circumstance. To have no father is liberating. To have no father, as De Quincey demonstrates, opens up an entire cultural gene pool for his perusal and disposal: to pick and choose his fantasies, both ideal and monstrous, about paternity and cultural legitimacy and, conversely, about illegitimacy, both familial and cultural.

3 Mothered Identities: Facing the Nation in the Works of Mary Wollstonecraft

> As the addressee of every demand, the mother occupies the place of alterity. Her replete body, the receptacle and guarantor of demands, takes the place of all narcissistic, hence imaginary, effects and gratifications; she is, in other words, the phallus. The discovery of castration, however, detaches the subject from his dependence on the mother, and the perception of this lack makes the phallic function a symbolic function—*the* symbolic function. This is a decisive moment fraught with consequences: the subject, finding his identity in the symbolic, *separates* from his fusion with the mother, *confines* his *jouissance* to the genital and transfers semiotic motility on to the symbolic order.
>
> —Julia Kristeva, *Revolution in Poetic Language*

At the end of the last chapter I suggested that the boundaries defining romantic authorial subjectivity are contingent on an uneasy domesticity that balances homeopathic xenodochy with the purging effects of xenophobia. How does gender affect this balance? Perhaps it may be more accurate to argue that romantic subjectivity is reproduced within a national frame, and that the act of reproduction itself as a specifically gendered activity secures cultural continuity in contexts where imperial morphologies are continually shifting. Gender, therefore, is decisive to the propagation of ideological structures. But what specific contributions do feminine bodies make to the shaping of imperial identity? For Mary Wollstonecraft, dining at Joseph Johnson's table—consuming perhaps some of the more radical and dominant intellectual positions of the day—the popular disavowal of women's intellectual and political capacities in favor of their exquisite sensibility helped shape her *Vindication* that in turn reshaped the configurations of political writing at that time. More interesting to this study of xenophobia, however, is how gender stabilizes the imperial understanding of British national identity. Wollstonecraft coopted the subordinated positions women occupied in Britain in order to dramatize her political positions. Yet her calls for a type of feminist essentialism may well have served the interests of imperial Britain first and foremost. To relegate the feminine to specific realms of representation—for example, to the foreign or to the domestic—is to ignore and obfuscate the ways gender is mobilized to secure dominant ideological positions.[1] While Wollstonecraft denounced educational discourses that molded the overly sensible woman, her xenophobic rhetoric also braced the ideological structures framing constructions of the feminine that depended on the very discourses she sought to decry. Thus gender is formulated out of competing drives of xenophobia and xenodochy: in the case of Wollstonecraft, the feminine is a chiasmus in which the invitation of foreign figures (like Rousseau) to help restore women to citizenry competes, simultaneously, with eschewing and abjecting their presence. The invitation of a specifically French figure, Rousseau, repeats another kind of triangular relation between British, Francophone, and "Eastern" cultures and locales.[2] Wollstonecraft's use of Rousseau was, however, quite vexed; on the one hand, his devotion to liberty inspired her writing of *A Vindication*, on the other, she strongly resisted his account of innate infantile female sexuality. Like Johnson and De Quincey, Wollstonecraft also finds it necessary to invoke the fantasy of French sensuality and moral depravity in order to negotiate with the more outlandish "Orient."

Acting according to the logic of the supplement, gender supplies the lack implicit in the first term of articulation. Mary Wollstonecraft represents British ideas of female education as flawed, in need of a necessary supplement in order to enrich or replace them. In this instance of "supplement," I am referring to Derrida's formulation in which he contends that its twofold signification is slippery and dangerous. As the professed suppliant to the first term, it can also supplant. It is the thing that "adds itself," it is "a surplus, a plenitude enriching another plenitude, the *fullest measure* of presence." Yet this thing also "adds only to replace. It intervenes or insinuates itself *in-the-place-of*; if it fills, it is as if one fills a void."[3] Situated as the uneasy, unstable arbiter of imperial morphology in representations of British national identity, gender may work against the hegemony that drives these representations. Clearly, paying attention to the material conditions of ideological production—of gender and race and class and nation—usefully demystifies the imperial body. But if read as a supplement, gender can also work in conjunction with xenophobia in order to solidify a secured national front. When Wollstonecraft writes on the vicissitudes of education, she is principally articulating an idea of nation that depends on the gendered supplement—in this case, the feminine—for its existence. Her notion of nation is one that depends on xenophobia just as surely as De Quincey's or Johnson's ideas.

The coherent shape of British imperial identity is produced independently of the political codes that govern its colonial bodies and therefore acts differently as well. This shape—one that summons the might of imperial weight for its authority—inevitably rests on supporting cultural fantasies about the internal as well as external coherence of the mother country. However, such coherence is not organic to the emergence of nationhood; this coherence is not some natural, progressive result of an escalating sense of national identity that develops coincidentally with the increase of colonies. Rather, it only comes about as a result of deterritorializing the domestic. In the following chapter I wish to look at how gender operates as the crucial metaphor for accomplishing such deterritorialization.

Upon the "maternal bosom the minds of nations reposes; their manners, prejudices, and virtues,—in a word, the civilization of the human race all depend upon maternal influence" writes Louis Aimé Martin in 1840. Margaret Homans opens her chapter on maternity and authorship with this particular quote as a way of introducing the ways in which women in early Victorian England engaged in cultural production by embracing motherhood as a vocation, as well as by participating in signifying practices that may be read as simultaneously reproductive and literary.[4] It seems, however, that propped up against the notion of motherhood—naturalized and sustained, as it were, by the accommodating breast—is the concept of "nation." This relation in itself is nothing new; Rousseau expostulates at length on the "civilizing" presence of the woman of sensibility in *Émile* seventy years or so before Martin's *The Education of Mothers of Families*. What seems a more absorbing issue is the way in which ideologies of nation and of motherhood continue to be reproduced in close connection to one another, both in eighteenth- and nineteenth-century formulations about women's identities and in more contemporary feminist theories about identity politics.

The 1790s proved to be a highly vexed period for Britain, especially in the context of the revolution in France and an emerging politics of the Enlightenment. During this period, the construction of subjectivity in relation to national affiliation provided a foundation upon which notions of a universalizeable manhood were being invented, notions Martin disseminates later in the nineteenth century. The problem this subjectivity posed to women, however, was qualitatively different; in most of western Europe and North America, women were "formally excluded from exercising political rights, and in England and Wales the restrictions on them were harsher in some respects than elsewhere." Even if a renewed emphasis on functional differences between men and women of the sort that Rousseau proposed in *Émile* helped stay the potential threat the enfranchisement of women posed to upwardly mobile British men, events like the Taunton march in Somerset in June of 1814, and, more critically, the Duchess of Devonshire's political campaigns for her son in 1784, indicated that middle-class women's roles may have been shifting, perhaps because of the violent retaliations they precipitated.[5] Mary Wollstonecraft's revolutionary feminist manifesto, *A Vindication of the Rights of Woman*, then, was hardly produced in a political vacuum.

Donna Landry's assessment of the *Vindication*'s cultural impact as an "impure idealization," however, suggests that the "radical" moves made toward enfranchising women were vastly overrated, even if there seemed to be some ideological space for the woman patriot. Not even "the revolutionary potential of British social movements of the 1780s and 1790s could be said to represent an historical rupture, and the revolutionary potential of these years was itself ruthlessly suppressed by arms as well as the persuasive arts."[6] Reading Wollstonecraft in this context might cause us to reevaluate our assumptions about historical representations of the feminine. On the one hand Wollstonecraft is engaged in an ideological maneuver around questions of identity, and, in some cases, it may be argued that she is constructing a foundation upon which to base the political subjecthood of women. It may, however, also be crucial to take into account the structural continuities of ideological underpinnings—of nationalism, imperialism, xenophobia, political identity—informing constructions and reconstructions of identity. The deep ambivalences writers like Ann Yearsley and Hannah More expressed toward Wollstonecraft's bourgeois radicalism may also suggest other disturbing social and cultural ideological continua that insured for British women different sorts of accommodations to the revolution in France even if such accommodations eventually sorted themselves out.[7]

One might usefully turn to recent formulations about identity to help uncover some of the problematic positions facing the construction of a place for "women" in the context of citizenry and nationhood at the close of the eighteenth century. Judith Butler, for example, suggests that the foundationalist reasoning of identity politics tends to assume that "identity must first be in place in order for political interests to be elaborated, and, subsequently, political action to be taken."[8] Preconceived formations of identity have dominated many of the ways in which we have addressed questions about nation and culture, especially in relation to authorship in the eighteenth and nineteenth centuries. Such foundationalist assumptions about national and cultural identity perform the task of constructing a privileged and valorized space for authorship without necessarily accounting for the powerful ideologies underwriting these assumptions.

Taking into account the problems foundationalist assumptions about national identities pose, scholars like Benedict Anderson have formulated models of nationalism that demonstrate the ways in which they are ideologically constructed as imagined communities. Assumptions about nationality that get naturalized as a transcendent entity complete with biological characteristics are, in fact, produced by ideologies of "community."[9] Preconceived formations of identity have also dominated many of the ways in which we have thought about "women": how we have recovered women's texts, women's voices, women's work, and women's various negotiations with being agents, resistant subjects, objects, figures, representations, and victims. The invocation of a feminist "we," according to Butler, "denies the internal complexity and indeterminacy of the term and constitutes itself only through the exclusion of some part of the constituency that it simultaneously seeks to represent."[10]

Are there ways in which the questions of foundationalism vis-à-vis identity may be asked of Wollstonecraft's representations of "women" in her corpus? What sort of relationships between investigations into her political and historical contexts and more postmodern interrogations of identity might be usefully uncovered? My interest here is to reassess the ways Wollstonecraft establishes a ground for representing "women" with these questions in mind. I am particularly concerned with the reproduction of national subjectivity in the context of a female "vocation" of mothering; and what a "vocation" would imply for women in Britain, uncitizened and disenfranchised, whose position in English culture was increasingly dependent on a "natural" identification with motherhood. Specifically, I want to investigate the ideologies that produce certain popular conjectures about identities: the notion that "women" are inevitably linked to mothering, whether or not they actually perform this function, and the idea that nationality is something everyone can "have."

In the interests of deterritorializing the domestic, perhaps ideologies of mothering and nation had to be produced in order to furnish other models of identity that accounted for colonial and imperial expansion. Cast as "creatures" (I borrow Wollstonecraft's use of the term to refer to women in *Vindi-*

cation) incarcerated by ideologies of reproduction, women supplied immediate prototypes for colonization: feeding on the body of the mother, nourished and taught to emulate the parental precedents of citizenry, surely children were effective blueprints for colonies. Clearly, however, the maternal body cannot fully represent the model of imperial power: the name of the father endows this body with authority, investing the reproductive body politic with discursive (material) power. What's interesting are the holes left by domestic alterity; like De Quincey's vexed household, routinely invaded by exotic creatures, the very model of colonial power leaves the domestic interior curiously vulnerable to invasion. Ingesting the life-milk of its mother country as well as supplying the life-blood for its commerce, colonies in fact operate as both mother and child, ironically leaving the mother country bereft of material sources of power, though its epistemological authority may remain unchallenged. It seems incumbent to the dominant imperial ideology, then, to reinvest the domestic country with the power of "mother." Swollen with the weakness of its own maternal metaphors, imperial identity can only establish itself by an invitation to foreign insinuation, a solicitation of supplemental "creatures" (not unlike De Quincey's tigers or Malays) to supply a seamless perception of nation.

In the case of Mary Wollstonecraft, we must bear in mind Gayatri Spivak's contention that it "should not be possible to read nineteenth-century British fiction without remembering that imperialism . . . was a crucial part of the cultural representation of England to the English," despite attempts of her contemporaries to label her as French and anti-patriotic.[11] Eighteenth- and nineteenth-century British literature is preoccupied with maintaining a discrete sense of self as culturally English and imperially British. These formations of national and imperial identity within Britain often seem to depend on representations of the foreign and the feminine: as I've suggested, however, such pairings, deployed by the language of xenophobia, may be engaged in a xenodochial system of othering that creates, invites, and then excoriates the foreign body in order to maintain a putatively "native" national coherence. What happens when we consider Mary Wollstonecraft's political exhortations in particular with attention to motherhood and nationhood? Does the fact that she "pay[s] particular attention to those in the middle class, because they appear to be the most natural state" pose problems to audiences, historical and contemporary, and suggest the fact that interlocking discourses or race, class, gender, sexuality, and nationality are appropriated in the service of hegemony?

"Fact"

Mary Wollstonecraft stands as an emblem of feminist thought in the emerging canon of feminist representation. As a writer concerned with female equality, Wollstonecraft centered her agenda on the rejection of sensibility, a rejection which has engaged the attention of scholars like Marilyn Butler, Mary Jacobus, and Mary Poovey, who have problematized this notion. Some of the implicit issues of nationalism in her work, however, have remained relatively untouched. More recently, the focus on Wollstonecraft has shifted to other questions about identity, and scholars such as Moira Ferguson have connected Wollstonecraft's work for women in England with crucial metaphors of enslavement and the discourse of colonialism. Donna Landry's work has established even more crucially the connections between class, race, and sexuality, in the context of an emerging discourse of nationalism.[12] I would like to propose a different reading of the presence of colonialist language in Wollstonecraft's work. If we turn to the histories of dominant ideologies and examine how they inform cultural production, how are we to read—and problematize—the "radical" departure from eighteenth-century notions of "women" in Wollstonecraft's writing?[13] Wollstonecraft has long been regarded as a feminist thinker who scrutinized the conditions of women's lives more critically than previous writers, and often heralded as one of the "first feminists"; her writings pose peculiar problems for a materialist analysis of her corpus. If she has been recovered and reclaimed as speaking about women's oppression, and if she has been coopted by an undifferentiated feminism to perform the very necessary work of making women's voices heard and women's work recognized, is there a way in which the counternarrative of dominant ideologies is also articulated in her writing? What happens when we apply the same investigation of ideologies of nationalism and imperialism, of xenophobia and political identity, that materialist feminists have conducted within their own field to the overtly feminist work of Wollstonecraft? For example, there are disturbing differences between sentiment and its representation that ventriloquize the insidiousness of such ideologies. These differences may suggest that one has to think through the issues of women's oppression as an *articulation* of various interlocking discourses, particularly of maternity and nationalism.

The modern historian Linda Colley's treatment of eighteenth-century British patriotism might be helpful in uncovering some of the conflicting ideologies of national and gender identity operating in Wollstonecraft's texts. Colley discusses the relationship between the "welfare of Great Britain"—a welfare that increasingly depends on both imperialist expansion and an enduring sense of national identification—and the "cult of a prolific maternity" that was favored enthusiastically by those who believed (before the 1800 census) that the population of Great Britain was in decline, and by "those who simply wanted more live births so that the nation might better compete in terms of cannon-fodder with France."[14] Colley also goes on to spell out some of the anxieties about keeping this *British* maternity prolific, arguing that an increase in urbanization foregrounded, for moralists, an anxiety about the impact on female manners and behavior; women might, writes Colley in a moment of irony, "come into contact with new and disreputable ideas. They might, like Sheridan's Lydia Languish, read unwholesome novels, or still worse, write them. . . . They might, free from the supervision of husbands and fathers, encounter men. They might cease to be virtuous."[15] Embedded in this anxiety about female virtue is the fantasy of a capricious, fitful, inconstant, and therefore volatile female "nature" that must be restrained and managed within the confines of *national* and *patriotic* duty. Not unlike the patriotic proscriptive lexicography with which Johnson disciplined a wayward feminized language, the female body must look to the stabilizing discourses about education and morals, reproduction and patriotism, produced on the whole by men.

Thus, Colley suggests, the particular concern for fertility and maternity

> increased along with the scale of European warfare, as witnessed by the spate of maternity hospitals established for the benefit of the poor in London and elsewhere. . . . Encouraging women to breed, urging the benefits of maternal breast-feeding over wet-nursing, rescuing foundlings and orphans, all of these causes became increasingly attractive to British legislators, pundits and charitable bodies in the second half of the eighteenth century.[16]

Of course maternity is a slippery category that functions differently in different political contexts. In the case Colley discusses, women's bodies and women's labor—specifically, women's capacity to produce offspring—are commodified in order to represent a physically palpable and morally healthy British "nation" and to regulate the feminine body. Women's bodies also become appropriate metaphors for Britain's imperial relation to its colonies. The idea of a "mother" country bearing colonial offspring, a maternal figure presumably prone to the same feminine waywardness as female virtue, suggests that there is something unstable about the construction of the imperial body itself, something not altogether dependable. Thus, as it is necessary for feminine virtue to submit to the more stabilizing capacities of masculine knowledge, so maternity, ennobled and endowed by patriotic rhetoric, becomes a way of securing the feminine body to the service of nation.

However, in other contexts maternity is the site of contamination and disease. In some Romantic accounts, for example, De Quincey's, the maternal proliferation of (other) races is both horrific and threatening to the integrity of the English (male) individual. De Quincey's account of domestic maternity (waking to find the "abortions" of his dreams materialized as his children, surrounding his bed), as I have argued, is extraordinarily vexed by a masculine discomfort with the confines of domesticated space; such uneasiness may well get displaced onto the body of the mother. Fraught as she is by her porous capacities to birth and nurse, the feminine figure cannot have the same ideological constancy as her masculine counterpart. The imperial "mother" country, therefore, may also signify problems of instability of national identity on the home front.

There seem to be ways in which Colley's accounts of ideologies of British maternity in relation to patriotism inform, ironically, Wollstonecraft's representational projects, especially the moral lessons about reading. In *A Vindication of the Rights of Woman*, Wollstonecraft constructs an English woman by implication. She argues, among other things, for the intellectual autonomy of women, claiming that given a chance at an equal education, women would match men in achievement. Her analysis of the oppressed social conditions for women cuts across apparent hierarchies of class although not, apparently, across lines of race and ethnicity. Even if she compares the plight of women as chattel to the plight of black slaves, these comparisons represent different forms of commodification. In the case of women, their cultural difference from black slaves is marked by the very fact of the analogy. Such an analogy suggests that the polemical issue of slavery, the horrors of which were vividly dramatized by Yearsley and More among others, may nevertheless retain vestiges of its historical presence in English discourse. Clearly anti-slavery sentiment prevailed in the latter half of the eighteenth century; but earlier commercial interests in and approval of the slave trade, culminating, perhaps in the British introduction of slavery to their colonies in North America and the Caribbean West Indies stubbornly persist as an ideological frame for the term. The presence of slaves in English daily life was qualitatively different from black slavery in the United States, although, as Gretchen Gerzina has compellingly argued, there had been a significant black population in London since the sixteenth century. Their presence in everyday (mostly aristocratic) life was perceived as "fashion accessories," which, as Gerzina argues, had the effect of increasing their numbers. The popular association of brute labor with slavery, however, was not immediately perceived to be enacted in England.[17] Rather, this idea was deployed to the colonies. Such deployment—or even projection—ostensibly limited the polluting affects of this trade to the outer limits of the empire. However, commodities brought home (like sugar and tobacco) and eagerly consumed were the distilled products of a filthy commercial practice. Wollstonecraft's use of "slave" as a term describing the position of British women is overdetermined and may be contaminated by the vexed history of the products slavery makes available to women—leisure, fashion, even education. As De Quincey amply demonstrates, the ingestion of one such product—opium—repopulates the domestic scene with monsters of alterity.

Wollstonecraft's use, in fact, of the amalgamation of Orientalist metaphors with which to compare the plight of English women, manifests the problems with her deployment of codes of racial difference. Her indiscriminate references to Eastern alterity take shape as "Chinese bands" that torture the "limbs and faculties" of women, the "seraglio" that makes "necessary" the "art" of feigning a "sickly delicacy" for that Oriental "epicure" who "must have his palate tickled," her contention that "Mahometanism" produces the authoritative model for women's subordination, and all spell out the ways in which a prevailing imperialist ideology informs cultural representation, whether or not they are articulating the subject position of the socially marginalized.[18]

Wollstonecraft's Introduction describes her "profound conviction that the neglected education of my fellow-creatures is the grand source of misery I deplore; and that women, in particular, are rendered weak and wretched by a variety of concurring causes" (7). As with "flowers which are planted in too rich a soil," so a "false system of education" has reduced "the civilized women of the present century" to model themselves after "alluring mistresses than affectionate wives and rational mothers." Wollstonecraft concludes that "books of instruction, written by men of genius" enfeeble the women to whom they are addressed: in the "true style of Mahometanism, [women] are treated as a kind of subordinate beings [*sic*], and not as part of the human species." We may conclude that the implied danger in such acts of reading by "*civilized*" women is that they will be implicated in a dehumanizing Mahometan system.

She calls up the example of the differences between a man and a woman journeying, the former "in general, with the end in view" while the latter is in particular concerned with being a "figure on a new scene; when, to use an apt

French turn of expression, she is going to produce a sensation." Sensationalism, sensibility, and the tendency for women to be creatures of sensation originate, according to Wollstonecraft, from "novels, music, poetry, and gallantry." Yet the opening lines of the *Vindication* juxtapose two different concepts of what it means to read, creating opposing openings to her project. Directly before her invective against women's education and its enervating effects on their characters, Wollstonecraft writes:

After considering the historic page, and viewing the living world with anxious solicitude, the melancholy emotions of sorrowful indignation have oppressed my spirits, and I have sighed when obliged to confess that either Nature has made a great difference between man and man, or that civilization which has hitherto taken place in the world has been very partial. (7)

Even while offering a logical and effective way to begin to overturn women's oppression, Wollstonecraft's opening sentence "seems to turn history into sentimental spectacle, and the author herself into its spectator rather than an agent of reformation," as Charlotte Sussman has pointed out. Such a fissure between two paradigms of reading—"the sentimental imperative to turn the world into an affecting page, and the empirical sense of texts as storehouses of information"—addresses the conflict of dominant ideologies in Wollstonecraft's project.[19] Wollstonecraft argues that women's characters are

thus formed in the mould of folly during the time they are acquiring accomplishments, the only improvement they are excited, by their station in society, to acquire. This overstretched sensibility naturally relaxes the other powers of the mind, and prevents intellect from attaining that sovereignty which it ought to attain to render a rational creature useful to others, and content with its own station.

It seems difficult *not* to compare her advice with that of the very eighteenth-century male writers against whom she argues: moralists who worry that middle-class wives and daughters might, like Sheridan's Lydia Languish, read "unwholesome novels" and therefore be contaminated by detrimental and unhealthy ideas (a sentiment that is not confined to the eighteenth century by any means).[20] Also interesting about this conflict, however, is the fact that Wollstonecraft's prescription for a healthy diet of rigorous education, devoid of potentially enervating novels and French sensationalism, curiously and problematically parallels the eighteenth-century patriotic fervor to better the lots of British mothers for the good of a national whole.

Even more complicated, especially given the potentially xenophobic allusion to French sensation and to French women, is Wollstonecraft's admittedly vexed and problematically executed relation to Rousseau's representation of the physical, intellectual, emotional and functional differences between men and women in his *Émile*.[21] Wollstonecraft's understanding of the capacity for Rousseau's arguments to eradicate the difference between public and private life that he is so careful to set up also ironically privileges his notion of separate spheres of activity for men and women. Her painstaking construction of the contributions of the family in *Vindication* announces this difference: "if children are to be educated to understand the principle of patriotism," she argues, "then their mother must be a patriot as well." Only if women are to "to acquire a rational affection for their country," could they be useful in their sphere, the home.[22] Rousseauian ideals of femininity imagine them within the domesticated space, exercising a "gentle and improving sway over her husband," and influencing the next generation in a similarly indirect and subordinate manner, in which children would presumably ingest a national identity and sense of public-spirited duty along with their milk during a moment of patriotic breast-feeding.

Kristeva's formulation of the mother as decathected object may be a useful way of reading and negotiating Wollstonecraft's contentious accounts of femininity. It is at the point of the discovery of castration that the mother's body ceases to signify, for the child, the absolute function it has previously assumed, and therefore becomes the body that mediates symbolic law organizing social relations. It is also the discovery of castration that signifies, ironically, the semiotic construction of identity for the child. The implications this may have for models of larger identities—by which I mean ideological subjectivities—are manifold.[23] Earlier I contended that the whole model of imperial power rested on the fantasy of domestic cultural coherence: the fantastic position the phallic mother occupies before the crucial discovery and the fantastic position she occupies after this discovery has registered as arbiter of symbolic law. It seems that the authority that imperial power wields is contingent on the "discovery" of deeply divisive fissures on the terrain of the domestic: the deterritorialization of the home front. Hence the cultural metonymic association of the maternal with the national: the flawed body of the mother mediates between the symbolic presence of imperial (symbolic) law and the colonies that must be integrated into this register of ideological subjectivity.

And so Wollstonecraft finds herself mediating as well between different ideological registers. However conflicted Wollstonecraft's relationship to Rousseau may be in the *Vindication*—on the one hand she identifies the urgency for uncovering the ideologies that allocate women their social position and cultural definition (specified by Rousseau), but on the other she repeats his exclusionary (male) practices that have defined women—it is also clear that she identifies with other dominant ideologies of patriotism, imperialism, and xenophobia in her representation. Such identifications are even more explicitly demonstrated in her fiction which provides an even more powerfully fertile field for cultural fantasy.

"Fiction"

A Vindication of the Rights of Woman is a philosophical treatise that urges "civilized" English women to take political control of their place in culture. Of course, embedded within the term "civilized" is an established role for women, even if technically uncitizened, that capitalizes on differences produced and sustained by imperial culture. What difference does fiction make? Anna Wilson suggests that many critics "treat the space of the psyche as if it were outside history."[24] The question Wilson asks that bears repeating is why novels and their language are politically suspect? Both Wollstonecraft's novels, *Mary* and *Maria, or The Wrongs of Woman*, although in many way entirely different projects, implicitly represent national identity values in the context of women's capacity for "mothering," even if the characters do not necessarily embody a monolithic account of Wollstonecraft's philosophy (even if one could represent Wollstonecraft's positions as such).

Turning to *Mary*, Wollstonecraft's first novel, we read a story about the representation of women that depends on formulations of nationalism, although we may also read a problematized relation to mothering. If *Mary* is, as Janet Todd has pointed out, a late work of sensibility and "an early effort at the creation of an alienated intellectual woman," a position that Wollstonecraft attempts to radically revise with her *Vindication* and her later novel *Maria*, it is worth noting the structural and ideological continuities informing all three of these works.[25] In her "Advertisement" to *Mary*, Wollstonecraft claims that the novel will not be a delineation of either a "Clarissa" or a "Sophie"—both of which are masculine definitions of the feminine ideal—but rather will forge another kind of representation of the mind of a woman. Yet *Mary* is complicated by the problems of political, gender, sexual, and national identity that also complicate Wollstonecraft's representation of women in other texts.

Although Mary is not a mother, and does to a certain extent practice alternative sexual and domestic arrangements, the itinerant position in which she finds herself is framed by motherlike activity. She is continually escaping from her husband, attempting to form alternative domestic arrangements with her friend Ann: an "extreme dislike took root in her mind; the sound of his name made her turn sick; but she forgot all, listening to Ann's cough, and supporting her languid frame. She would then catch her to her bosom with convulsive eagerness, as if to save her from sinking into an opening grave" (16). Here it seems quite clear that Mary, despite her transgression from the position of "wife," reassumes a maternal role as nurse to Ann. Even if her friendship to Ann "resemble[s] a passion," the potential for erotic involvement with her is rewritten as motherly solicitude. Replacing Ann's mother, Mary proves far more sympathetic than Ann's nurse "who was entirely engrossed by the desire of amusing her" (15). Mary takes care of her friend until her death, and then assumes other kinds of charitable rescue-work encouraged by eighteenth-century British culture to live up to the patriotic motto "increase of children a nation's strength."[26]

As if demonstrating the ways in which mothering is connected to dominant ideologies of nationalism and political identity, Mary and Ann's alternative domestic household in Lisbon is destined to fail: after all, Ann dies abroad, and Mary is left alone to cope with her failure as a substitute mother. As the domestic coherence in un-English countries is suspect and prone to a sort of decay, so alternative familial arrangements along lines of gender seem to fall prey to the same propensity. However, it seems that the failure of foreign domesticity performs another crucial task in the service of repatriating Mary to her mother country. In effect, the kinds of oppressive social laws—materialized and metabolized by her friend Ann's sickly constitution—that prod Mary to flee England in the first place, restore her to her proper place. Mary's mother's indolent francophilia suggests (not unlike Johnson's representation of fops in *London*) that the "contamination" produced by frenchified novels, mannerisms, in short, the whole cult of sensibility, within the confines of the domestic household is another compelling example of a failed "foreign" domesticity. (And although Mary's father's immoderate consumption—of hunting, meals, and eager employment of his *droit de seigneur*—is the most palpable proof of his unsuitable parenting, it is clear that the mother is mostly to blame for the "slave of compassion" she has unwittingly raised.)

On the Continent, Mary's wandering is ostensibly bleak—she is a lone woman among foreigners. Her wandering is placed against the rightful place of house and home she eventually finds back in England. Two women by themselves cannot constitute a coherent household; they need to be invested with the authority of the father, represented in this text not only by the sympathetic male but also by the authority of religious and national identity. Even if Mary attempts to reinvent the roles of mother/daughter according to the rules of English domesticity, she must resort to the "affection" of her countryman to save her very life:

Two days passed away without any particular conversation; Henry, trying to be indifferent . . . was more assiduous than ever . . . his spirits were calmly low . . . what was that world to him that Mary did not inhabit; she lived not for him. . . . He was mistaken; his affection was her only support; without this dear prop she had sunk into the grave of her lost—long-loved friend;—his attention snatched her from despair. Inscrutable are the ways of Heaven! (34)

This particular position is made all the more acute during a storm that occurs when she crosses the ocean to return to England:

One of the sailors, happening to say to another, "that he believed the world was going to be at an end"; this observation led her into a new train of thoughts: some of Handel's sublime compositions occurred to her, and she sung them to the grand accompaniment. [T]he Lord God Omnipotent reigned, and would reign for ever, and ever!—Why then did she fear the sorrows that were passing away, when she knew that He would bind up the brokenhearted, and receive those who came out of great tribulation. . . . the Lord Omnipotent will reign, and He will wipe the tearful eye, and support the trembling heart—yet a little while He hideth his face, and the dun shades of sorrow, and the thick clouds of folly separate us from our God; but when the glad dawn of an eternal day breaks, we shall know even as we are known. . . . After writing, serenely she delivered her soul into the hands of the Father of Spirits; and slept in peace. (37–38)

Mary considers first Handel and then Corinthians (1 Corinthians 13: 12) in this dense passage. If we attend to the national institution Handel had become in Hanoverian Britain, the fact that the language of the *Messiah* transmitted the idea of Britain as Israel, with the veiled allusion to George II in the Hallelujah chorus, we may read what enables and comforts Mary is a reaffirmation of the continuity of her *national* identity rewritten—and naturalized—as religious affiliation.[27]

Her ordained place is in England, even if she encounters a bewildering world once she reaches the shores of Great Britain. At first Mary attempts to minister to the needy multitudes. Horrified by the poverty she sees in England, her recent alien wandering made all the more poignant by the fact that she has returned to her native land, she supports and sustains a family: "She visited them every day, and procured them every comfort; contrary to her expectation, the woman began to recover"(41). Yet Mary herself contracts the "fever," which has made the woman ill in the first place, and which makes "alarming progress" because of her want of "a tender nurse" (41). It takes Henry to procure for her a "natural" place in the domestic world: her own experiments with formulating alternative domestic arrangements only meet with complete failure. Henry, of course, has returned to England because his "*native* air may work wonders, and besides, [his] *mother* is a tender nurse" (45; italics mine). In the end, Mary's new position as the adopted daughter of her would-be lover's mother (and not her husband from whom she is permanently estranged) stabilizes her. Henry's mother announces:

I come to request you to spend not only this day, but a week or two with me.—Why should I conceal any thing from you? Last night my child made his mother his confident, and, in the anguish of his heart, requested me to be thy friend—when I shall be childless.... If I am to lose the support of my age, and again be a widow—may I call her "Child whom my Henry wishes me to adopt?" (50)

Such a realignment of the positions of mother and daughter, when made according to the wishes of the masculine voice of authority, and not by the transgressive wishes of the transient woman, have such a rehabilitating effect that the novel ends with Mary engaged in relatively happy and useful work: she establishes manufactories, throws her estate into small farms, visits the sick, supports the old, and educates the young, her "gleam of joy" being constituted primarily by the fact that she is "hastening to that world *where there is neither marrying*, nor giving in marriage" (53). On the one hand Wollstonecraft addresses the unnaturalness of the definition of women's positions as wives, mothers, or daughters; on the other she uses that very definition as a solution for Mary's dilemmas.

Turning to *Maria*—Wollstonecraft's last and unfinished novel, which functions in some ways as an "answer to the sentimental but sexually frightened *Mary* and in other ways as a continuation of *A Vindication of the Rights of Woman*—we may also read the ambivalence with which Wollstonecraft articulates the part of the Rousseauian ideal that confers political power on the woman, with the materiality of women's oppression. *Maria* opens with alternating images of imprisonment and maternity: her sorrows, products of a torturing "maternal apprehension," seem to "be pictured on the walls of her prison, magnified by the state of mind in which they were viewed" (61). Yet this compelling comparison between the alternating institutions of incarceration, domestic and otherwise, conflicts with the image of maternity on which Wollstonecraft focuses:

Her infant's image was continually floating on Maria's sight, and the first smile of intelligence remembered, as none but a mother, an unhappy mother, can conceive. She heard her half speaking half cooing, and felt the little twinkling fingers on her burning bosom—a bosom bursting with the nutriment for which this cherished child might now be pining in vain. From a stranger she could indeed receive the maternal ailment, Maria was grieved at the thought—but who would watch her with a mother's tenderness, a mother's self-denial? (61)

Maria's imaginative recall of her daughter's image is bound up with her body: she feels, even as she imagines, the "twinkling fingers on her burning bosom," while the breast itself, uncomfortably full, is a reminder of the absence and loss of her child's material presence. The conflict between Maria's feeling and sensibility and her intellectual acknowledgment of the ways she has been immured collapses in this representation of motherhood. Maria's problem is that she has no place to fill; she is cut off from her motherhood, and yet the fact that the biological connection between mother and child is unquestioned, unproblematized—indeed, emphasized—literally leaving the woman with no place but a prison, ventriloquizes the oppressive dictates of eighteenth-century definitions of "women." One can also locate this fissure in the books Maria reads. Reading and feeling are especially conflicted:

Earnestly as Maria endeavoured to soothe, by reading, the anguish of her wounded mind, her thoughts would often wander from the subject she was led to discuss, and tears of maternal tenderness obscured the reasoning page. She descanted on "the ills which flesh is heir to," with bitterness, when the recollection of her babe was revived by a tale of fictitious woe, that bore any resemblance to her own; and her imagination was continually employed, to conjure up and embody the various phantoms of misery, which folly and vice had let loose on the world. The loss of her babe was the tender string; against other cruel remembrances she laboured to steel her bosom. (65)

One is reminded of the opening of *Vindication*, where sentimental and empirical imperatives war against each other. Here the "reasoning page" gives way to Maria's unabashedly sentimental recollections of her baby. However, one also may read Maria's position as a *mother* as one that profoundly affects her position as a *reader*. Maria reads Dryden's *Fables*, Milton's *Paradise Lost*, and Rousseau's *Héloïse*—books given to her by Henry Darnford—all of which she likens to "a mine of treasure" (68). Here the materiality of these books, figured by their potential as "treasure," reproduces the materiality of her baby's presence. In some ways, the transfer Maria negotiates of the baby's materiality to the epistemological value of books replicates the exacerbated model of colonial relations. Robbed of the material capacities of control (which are now situated in the far-flung metonyms of imperial Britain), the mother country's authoritative coherence is now demonstrated by epistemology.

Upon reading the Dryden, Maria notices "some marginal notes . . . written with force and taste" and containing "various observations on the present state of society and government, with a comparative view of the politics of Europe and America. These remarks were written with a degree of generous warmth, when alluding to the enslaved state of the labouring majority, perfectly in unison with Maria's mode of thinking" (68). The notes, of course, are Darnford's, and are a result of his travels in America, during which he concludes, among other things, that he is "heartily weary of the land of liberty and vulgar aristocracy," especially of American women, in whom he finds a "want of taste and ease . . . that renders them, in spite of their roses and lilies, far inferior to our European charmers" (75–76). The metaphors of enslavement, produced by colonialist discourse and employed in behalf of class (by Darnford) and of gender and class (by Maria), turn into the language of incarceration for Maria. While the use of the terms of colonial slavery certainly corresponds with her own situation as she self-consciously recognizes, in the end she returns to Rousseau's ideas of femininity, domesticity, and maternity. After the disappointment of not seeing Darnford that evening—who at this point represents the possibility of illicit love—and feeling "the disappointment more severely than she was willing to believe, she flew to Rousseau, as her only refuge from the idea of [Darnford]" (71). Rather than providing a moment of empowerment generated by engaging with the "reasoning page," the act of reading puts Maria in an infantilized position, recalling the way in which reading only calls up the presence of her baby. Maria's eager perusal of the *Fables*, *Paradise Lost*, and *Héloïse* then simultaneously offer her an intellectual freedom and a corporeal prison.

Wollstonecraft's ambivalence about Maria's position is also represented by the novel's conclusion; bereft of the "true" benefits of motherhood, unable to assume any clear social identity because she is deprived of the privilege of breast-feeding, Maria's daughter is doomed to die. In the memoir Maria writes to her daughter, she makes an allusion to the "extraordinary partiality" her own mother had for her eldest brother, the only child her mother had suckled, while Maria herself has a "great affection" for the nurse who has suckled her. We can read this maternal narrative as a displaced narrative of breast-feeding.[28] Like the ways in which the act of reading conjures up images of her baby, so the writing of the memoir similarly invokes an image of motherly solicitude—her "many observations" which "flow from [her] heart, which only a mother—a mother schooled in misery, could make" (94). Yet because of the way in which biological connections to motherhood are privileged, this narrative cannot restore the mother's function: Maria's daughter dies. In this memoir Maria writes:

As my mind grew calmer, the visions of Italy again returned with their former glow of colouring; and I resolved on quitting the kingdom for a time, in search of the cheerfulness, that naturally results from a change of scene, unless we carry the barbed arrow with us, and only see what we feel. (133)

Maria's "barbed arrow" may be read as the barb of an oppressive national, political, and cultural identity; in Maria's case anatomy *is* destiny. Having torn herself free from the confines of her existence as a "woman," relinquishing her marital ties, she is also forced to leave behind her natural and cultural progeny: "I had thought of *remaining in England, till I weaned my child,* but . . . I had soon reason to wish to hasten my departure" (134; italics mine). As a result, her improperly nourished child dies, and the escape to what would have been the Italian haven from cultural oppression turns into the prison of the English madhouse:

My God, with what a light heart did I set out for Dover!—It was not my country, but my cares I was leaving behind . . . I was already in the snare—I never reached the packet—I never saw thee more. . . . All I know is that [the maid] must have quitted the chaise, shameless wretch! and taken (from my breast) my babe with her. How could a creature in a female form see me caress thee, and steal thee from my arms! I must stop, stop to repress a mother's anguish; lest, in bitterness of soul, I imprecate the wrath of heaven on this tiger, who tore my only comfort from me. (134)

This invective is complicated by many issues that come together to problematize the position of mother as an essential, transcendent, biological phenomenon. Even if her life in England is oppressive, she cannot abandon her "country," but, rather, rewrites her escape abroad as one from her "cares."

Paradoxically, Maria is in a manner of speaking forever confined to the country that has invented her "madness," England, as Wollstonecraft dies—in a horrible irony, from complications of childbirth—before she can resolve the various conclusions to Maria's history.

Mothering and national identity come together in Maria's denunciation of the maid, who becomes a "tiger": a monstrous and, most importantly, exotic, non-British—specifically non-English—"creature" onto whom Maria scapegoats her failed maternity.[29] The maid, however, is also another "tiger" invading the sanctity of the domestic household and national nursery, drawing specific boundaries (perhaps like the maid in Johnson's *Life of Savage*) around the limits of domestic territory, effecting another form of a *solicited* or xenodochial deterritorialization. Her paid presence summons images of explicit invitations of the "foreign" to inhabit the exclusive nursery of domestic production.

In many ways, the problems Wollstonecraft articulates of the 1790s are ones that face women and feminists in the 1990s and beyond. Cora Kaplan argues that Wollstonecraft's

paradigm of women's psychic economy still profoundly shapes modern feminist consciousness. How often are the maternal, romantic-sexual and intellectual capacity of women presented by feminism as in competition for a fixed psychic space? Men seem to have a roomier and more accommodating psychic home, one which can, as Wordsworth and other Romantics insisted, situate all the varieties of passion and reason in creative tension.[30]

Wollstonecraft's work may be read as an attempt at establishing a foundation on which to build a political subjecthood of women, and then exploring various was in which women could subvert those roles: their positions as national subjects as well as their "vocations" as mothers. Taking into account Homi Bhabha's theory of "hybridity," however, as the primary culturally specific effect of colonialism, Wollstonecraft's allusions to colonialist discourse assume a different meaning.

If the effect of colonial power is seen to be the *production* of hybridisation rather than the hegemonic command of colonialist authority or the silent repression of native traditions, then an important change of perspective occurs. It reveals the ambivalence at the source of traditional discourses on authority and enables a form of subversion, founded on that uncertainty, that turns the discursive conditions of dominance into the grounds of intervention.[31]

Wollstonecraft's call to arms in *Vindication* and her representational models of feminine alterity in *Maria* and even *Mary* suggest to readers a form of political resistance. Yet if we consider the notion of subversive mimicry in relation to Wollstonecraft's corpus in a different way, an "important change of perspective" occurs. May one subvert a visibly politicized discourse to uncover disturbing alliances with other hegemonic discursive models of nationality, race, xenophobia, and imperialism?

Postmodern readings of identities problematize and politicize their status in authorship. Wollstonecraft criticism has focused by and large on her position as feminist, her concerns with sensibility and mothering, but important changes of perspective may need to start with a reconsideration of those very problems not as privileged, unproblematic categories but as formulations that need to be debated. It is in these interests that gender discloses the uneasy faculties of imperial power, an anxious fact resting on the fiction of discursive authority, troubled by the destabilizing effects of material reproduction. It is also in these interests that psychoanalytic models need to be rethought in the context of materialist analysis. To assume that the psyche has no history is to presuppose the tenets of romanticism—ones that privilege the internal space of psychosubjectivity—are equally outside any historical, ideological jurisdiction. Psychoanalysis addresses the ways in which psychosubjectivity is historically shaped precisely by examining how discourses determine its production. In the case of Wollstonecraft, such shaping reproduces its own monsters: demonstrating the inevitable conflict between competing ideological standpoints. In the case of Wollstonecraft, her own reproduction, her maternal issue, Mary Shelley, may further situate gender and xenophobia in the discourse of romanticism. But more binding than a simple connection between mother and daughter are the ideological connections between women writers. Charlotte Brontë, the champion of feminist recovery, may well be complicit with similar interests to secure the domesticated space for the posterity of romanticism. In the next chapter I examine the vicissitudes of domestic households from late romanticism to early Victorianism by examining two "case histories": *Frankenstein* and *Villette*.

4 Fair Exotics: Two Case Histories *in* Frankenstein *and* Villette

> Food loathing is perhaps the most elementary and most archaic form of abjection. When the eyes see or the lips touch that skin on the surface of milk—harmless, thin as a sheet of cigarette paper, pitiful as a nail-paring—I experience a gagging sensation and, still farther down, spasms in the stomach, the belly . . . *nausea* makes me balk at that milk cream, separates me from the mother and father who proffer it. 'I' want none of that element, sign of their desire; 'I' do not want to listen, 'I' do not assimilate it, 'I' expel it. But since the food is not an 'other' for 'me,' whom am only in their desire, I expel *myself*, I spit *myself* out, I abject *myself* within the same motion through which 'I' claim to establish myself.
>
> —Julia Kristeva, *Powers of Horror*

In this chapter I continue to examine the problems gender poses to ideological configurations of romantic identity by examining two novels. Shelley's *Frankenstein* and Brontë's *Villette* are narratives that mark the perimeters of feminine domesticity as national affiliation. Both novels demonstrate to varying degrees the ways in which the trajectory of romanticism is domestic. As in the case of De Quincey, Shelley and Brontë coopt foreign ideas of exoticism in order to enrich the native larder; however, unlike De Quincey, they also situate representations of romanticism outside the cultural confines of imperial England.

The extent to which nationalism functions as a domesticating shield, protecting the mutability of feminine identification from irrevocably falling into the foreign, is arbitrated on foreign soil—at least soil that the cultural imaginary has fashioned as alien. But questions of how that shield gets established as a shield as well of the relationship between nationalism and domesticity continue to vex romantics through early Victorian representations of the foreign vis-à-vis an anglicized household. Unlike Crusoe's negotiations with alternative island commerce, both *Frankenstein* and *Villette* imagine domesticity as the final site for national propagation. Early Victorian mediations of national identification station Englishness as an unmistakably coherent entity to be pitted against its colonial brethren; romantic desires to incorporate the exotic, however, complicate imperial injunctions for national purity.

Monstrosity's Issue

"Like the flowers that are planted in too rich a soil," writes Mary Wollstonecraft, "strength and usefulness are sacrificed to beauty; and the flaunting leaves, after having pleased a fastidious eye, fade, disregarded on the stalk, long before the season when they ought to have arrived at maturity."[1] So Wollstonecraft begins her vindication, clearing the ground for a more fruitful discussion of the "rights of woman." Mobilizing aspects of women's work as an arena of women's power, she sought to undo myths about sensibility that enervated and debilitated women rather than sharpened their capacities for feeling. Twenty-four years later Mary Shelley appropriates Wollstonecraft's metaphors to describe a very different scenario—the idealized relation between Caroline Beaufort and her husband, Alphonse Frankenstein: "Every thing was made to yield to her wishes and her convenience. He strove to shelter her, as a fair exotic is sheltered by the gardener, from every rougher wind, and to surround her with all that could tend to excite pleasurable emotion in her soft and benevolent mind."[2]

The place for the feminine in these representations of domesticity is visibly contested by mother and daughter: one bemoans soil "too rich" for healthy growth, the other extols the same hothouse climate for the enriched development of a "soft and benevolent mind" (itself figured as a garden or bower). While both narratives seem polarized, they turn out to have more in common than not. Wollstonecraft and Shelley are constructing a discursive site for the active presence of women in the household. Not simply ornamental in the case of Wollstonecraft, her "fellow-creatures" have a national duty to participate in the shaping and formation of young citizens. Shelley's representation alludes to the principally delicate state of the maternal body, but she also tries to elaborate on the legitimate space for mothering.

Not surprisingly, however, both accounts already imagine the introduction of women's roles as external or eccentric to the central "ground" of domesticity. That is, Wollstonecraft's rich soil and Shelley's hothouse shelter describe the parameters of domesticated space that inevitably exclude women.

As either familiar "flowers" or less familiar "exotics," women are planted from elsewhere in order to complete the household. The very frame of British domesticity (as Wollstonecraft and Shelley represent it) depends on the deliberate solicitation of something else—flowers, exotics—from somewhere else in order to constitute itself. This frame thus depends on the same exchange between xenodochy and xenophobia (especially when we consider the fact that gynophobia often works in conjunction with xenophobia) with which I have been examining the construction of national and cultural identity. The invitation of women outside the circle of the masculine name, as in the case of Frankenstein's care of Caroline Beaufort (whose francophonic name is not accidental and may in fact replicate the Frenchified mother in Wollstonecraft's *Mary*), repeats the xenodochial invocation of the foreign in order to disarticulate the home and rearticulate this space as English through xenophobic representation.

In order to account for the origins of *Frankenstein*'s monstrosity, Shelley writes an Introduction to the 1831 edition, at her publisher's request, that apologizes for the text by outlining her own literary reputation. As the "daughter of the parents of distinguished literary celebrity" her natural proclivity to "scribble" and indulge in "waking dreams" leads, surprisingly, to a later aversion to "bringing [her]self forward in print" (5). Shelley's identification of her origins effectively tells the story of her entry into the literary world as one that demands the crucial separation of the narratives of her own composition—her scribbles and waking dreams—from the more rigid requirements of "distinguished literary celebrity." Shelley's childhood dreaming took place mostly in Scotland, according to her introduction, "on the blank and dreary northern shores of the Tay" which to her represented "the eyry of freedom, and the pleasant region where unheeded I could commune with creatures of my fancy" (5–6). Positioned at the margins of British national territory, Shelley experiences freedom from the strictures and structures of actual writing, an activity in which she claims she was "a close imitator—rather doing as others had done than putting down the suggestions of my own mind" (5). Later, at her husband's instigation, she attempts to "enrol [her]self on the page of fame" thus proving herself "worthy of [her] parentage" (6). It seems clear that Shelley's writing, as much the subject of intense scrutiny now by literary critics as it was then by her husband and his compatriots, tells a tale of authorial stunting. Certainly recent critical examination of her writing decries the ways in which Shelley was continually subject to the editing thumb of her husband.[3] By Shelley's own reckoning, first the overwhelming burden of literary parentage and later the equally weighty responsibilities of spousal fame and the "cares of a family" may have distorted her affinities for romantic imagination, leaving her capable only of (re)producing "so very hideous an idea" with any success.

By these arguments, Shelley's writing lends itself unproblematically to feminist recovery. Critical interest in both *Frankenstein* and in Shelley's introduction has developed the notion of aversion into a critique of the novel as a whole, linking Shelley's literary reticence with her autobiographical ambivalence toward sexual and textual reproduction. This novel, therefore, articulates the problems of confinement posed by patriarchal accounts of gender. Feminist recruitment of Shelley's 1831 introduction has claimed her feelings of personal monstrosity and ambivalence toward authorship as an emblematic statement of the cultural marginalization of women.[4] In one of the earlier influential articles reclaiming *Frankenstein* for feminist theory, Barbara Johnson points out that part of Shelley's ambivalence is located in her representation of literary reputation. Authorial responsibility is vested in her parents and her husband. Shelley's self-consciously literary burden seems related to Johnson's question about autobiographical projects that somehow always seem in the process of symbolically killing the mother off by telling the lie that we have given birth to ourselves. Necessary choices *between* symbiosis and separation or *between* the mother and the autonomous self are ones that Johnson critiques because they proliferate an endless chain of binary oppositions that lock receptions of autobiographies into set patterns.[5] But even in the interests of unlocking these patterns, questions about *Frankenstein* have solidified into either/or crises, thus obliterating—perhaps usefully—the questions that are left out of such rigid accounts. Questioning our receptions of *Frankenstein* as simple oppositions between "verbal text and the biography of the named subject," as does Gayatri Spivak in one of the earliest critiques of imperialism-in-feminism, tends to dismiss other ways in which the novel acts on behalf of hegemony.[6]

How does xenophobia operate in successfully foreclosing these "other ways"? Although I am not disagreeing with the numerous readings of *Frankenstein* that figure the novel as indisputably feminist, my own interest in this novel is to uncover its incipient xenophobia, especially in the context of its admission into the emerging canon of feminist work. In many ways, *Frankenstein*'s enduring popularity may have much to do with the conservative narrative of national domesticity that such xenophobic language exhibits. What kinds of "other" ideological accounts can be taking place in this novel that overtly and eloquently but not always sympathetically describe the subject position of the socially marginalized? Beginning before the beginning, before the point at which the novel proper commences, Shelley's inscription marks the frame and structure for the novel's conservative ideological strains. The infamous epigraph from Milton that Shelley chooses as a thematic refrain (*Paradise Lost* X, 743–45) has been the subject of many a critical feminist eye, especially that of Margaret Homans, who notes that in this intellectually and poetically sanctioned piece the body of the mother is not only dispensable and unnecessary but altogether circumvented[7]:

> Did I request thee, Maker, from my clay
> To mold Me man? Did I solicit thee
> From darkness to promote me?—

More often overlooked, however, is Shelley's "epigraph" of her own making—the inscription she writes to her father:

> To William Godwin
> Author of *Political Justice*, *Caleb Williams*, &tc.
> These volumes are respectfully inscribed
> By the Author

The question of origins implicit in the passage from Milton, while asking an apology for man's existence, accepts without question the absence of women in reproduction as part of a Christian mythical account of "natural" history: an account that the monster later reads as "true" history.[8] But Shelley's inscription and anonymous dedication to her father is complicit in absenting the feminine in from the scene of literary heritage. Even if Shelley was reading the work of both parents while writing *Frankenstein*, this inscription effectively forecloses the possibility of any publicly acknowledged maternal inheritance. Prior to writing *Frankenstein*, Shelley takes her books and her lover to her mother's grave and not to her father's table. Such a gesture stages for some feminists a "strangely intimate relationship between her feelings toward her dead mother, her romance with a living poet, and her own sense of vocation as reader and writer."[9] Such a gesture also suggests that Shelley is willfully choosing her mother's literary progeny over her father's; conversely, however, such a gesture may allude to the burial of Wollstonecraft's feminist hopes by the pall of conventional domesticity. Yet the inscription Shelley writes to her first major (that is published) literary work (and her most enduring one, though she can hardly have known that at the time) is a published acknowledgment of her father's authorial status.[10] Perhaps, then, her obsessive return to this grave site stages the willful burial of her own vocation by the poetic ambitions of her husband-to-be. Perhaps her choice of the Miltonic epigraph functions more persuasively as a personal epitaph.

Shelley's personal choices of domestic arrangements hardly bear out such reasoning. Her imaginings, however, in her more fanciful literary representations (her "refuge") attest to the dreams of domestic harmony and national identification informed by patriarchal precedents.[11]

"I am by birth a Genevese," announces Frankenstein to Walton with a confidence not entirely coincident with his circumstances, "and my family is one of the most distinguished of that republic" (31). As if anticipating this piece of domestic information, Walton has previously reminded his sister of the problems with their household and his education:

You may deem me romantic, my dear sister, but I bitterly feel the want of a friend.... How would such a friend repair the faults of your poor brother! ... [I]t is a still greater evil to me that I am self-educated: for the first fourteen years of my life I ran wild on a common, and read nothing but our uncle Thomas's book of voyages. At that age I became acquainted with the celebrated poets of our own country; but it was only when it had ceased to be in my power to derive its most important benefits from such a conviction, that I perceived the necessity of becoming acquainted with more languages than that of my native country. (19)

Subordinated by the shadow of the much more prepossessing Frankenstein, Walton laments his childhood, one that is based upon the tenets of romanticism Wordsworth could have easily espoused. Walton is educated not through the stultifying formal rules of an unimaginative curriculum (or at least one that arrests imaginative capacities) but the relative freedom of nature. Running "wild upon a common" and engaging an interest in learning other languages, far from being shameful, would have constituted the romantic educational ideal welcomed alike by Lake District poets and their latter-day expatriated descendants, the privileged circle of romantic ghost-story-tellers of which the Shelleys were a part. Bemoaning the liberating, revolutionary possibilities self-education offers, regretting a little the "gentle and feminine fosterage" his sister gives in their alternative domestic arrangement, Walton longs for "a friend who would have sense enough not to despise me as romantic, and affection enough for me to endeavour to regulate my mind" (19).

Frankenstein's family, on the other hand, is far more conventionally situated. His affiliation to Geneva is as strong as to his family. (The fact that Geneva would have been highly evocative of Rousseau suggests that Frankenstein's domesticity may be as vexed a site for Shelley as Rousseau was for Wollstonecraft.)[12] Alphonse Frankenstein's appropriative control, so very unlike Margaret Saville's sensitive refinement of Walton's sensibilities, manifests itself through his discovery of Caroline Beaufort, his "fair exotic," weeping over the coffin of her dead father. The commemoration of this moment in a painting hanging over the Frankenstein mantle—surely one of the stranger memorials in novel history—in effect stabilizes the delicacy of this fair exotic, rendering her far more enduring as an artifact than she is as a mother.[13] All in all, Alphonse Frankenstein presents a very solid picture of the benevolent paternal despot. His family history is unimpeachable, his dedication to the civic realm legendary. In fact, his son makes it very clear that most of his life is spent in public service and only the "decline" of his life witnesses the fruits of domesticity:

My ancestors had been for many years counsellors and syndics; and my father had filled several public situations with honour and reputation. He was respected by all who knew him, for his integrity and indefatigable attention to public businesses. He passed his younger days perpetually occupied by the affairs of his country. (31)

Nothing could be further from this case than Walton's family and Walton's sense of familial duty. Like Frankenstein, he disobeys patriarchal injunction and runs away to sea. Like Frankenstein, he also ignores the feminine entreaties of his sister who pleads her "evil forebodings" for his grandiose enterprise to discover "a passage near the pole to those countries to reach which at present so many months are requisite" (16). Crucially unlike Frankenstein, however, he manages to survive more or less intact, returning to England to piece together one of the most infamous cautionary tales of overweening ambition in the age of romanticism. To what does he owe his survival? Do conventional domestic alignments—not ones made or manufactured to order, like Frankenstein's—cast in the language of national identification, rescue him in spite of himself? How do the ideological configurations demonstrated by this novel affect the shape of romantic identity, especially by accommodating the troubled perimeters of feminine domesticity? In fact, it seems that the peregrinations made in this gothic novel, as well as in Wollstonecraft's *Mary* and *Maria* and in Brontë's *Villette* (unlike either Johnson or

De Quincey, Wollstonecraft, Shelley and Brontë are moving outside England) increasingly disrupt and complicate the masculine ideal of a stable home front.

The fact that Walton abandons his project and returns to England signals something very different from failure. His initial disappointment is moderated by the promise of returning to both his sister and England: "while I am wafted toward England, and towards you, I will not despond" (215). This return, even if it is bound up with the sense of disappointment, is far more complicated than personal failure (his desire for a seafaring, adventurous life)—or even imperial failure (the scope of his project to discover new trade routes)—would warrant. The personal imperfection Walton desires Frankenstein to "repair" provides a critical clue to reading the complications of Walton's untimely return to England. Clearly, Walton's use of "repair" in this context is in the sense of "ordering" or "strengthening." "Repair," however, also means "adorn, ornament, restore, furnish or provide with something," according to the *Oxford English Dictionary*, and these senses—of which Shelley would have been aware, especially given the obsessive copyediting to which she and her husband submitted the manuscript—change the ideological configurations of Walton's "failure." That is, if we read "repair" as adornment, Frankenstein's friendship, now commodified into an ordered set of letters and journals that constitute the narrative, serves primarily as a form of gilding, as the inconsequential (or at least inessential) ornamentation to the reliable frame of Walton's subjectivity. Frankenstein's friendship thus ceases to dominate and becomes, rather, the subordinate story to Walton's greater travel epic. Even more complicating is the notion of "furnishing" or "providing with something": as a native of England, Walton is incomplete—inviting foreign intrusion, knowing his need to learn other languages (and regretting past opportunities), embracing Frankenstein in order to supply himself with that central friendship he lacks. More abstractly, Walton's British romanticism extends a tempering invitation to Continental articulations of that discourse that are later materialized—turned into the educational book—and restored to their proper English place.[14] Such restoration performs the very crucial disembodiment of foreignness by reconstructing bodies of Frankenstein and his monster into other kinds of material objects. Such disembodiment also partially precludes the problems of accommodating space for physical otherness within the parameters of domestic culture. This form of restoration thus perpetuates the xenodochial-xenophobic economy upon which romantic writing rests.

Walton's xenophobic encounters are primarily relegated to the offhand remarks he makes about his crew, but his theatrical response to the monster exhibits the more typically British xenophobic behavior when confronted with an unthinkable other. So dramatic is this encounter that the novel ends quite abruptly shortly afterward. The monster's representation of difference—especially of racial difference—has been commented on by many scholars of postcolonial and cultural studies.[15] What I find interesting are the ways Walton's return—or restoration, reparation—to England precedes this encounter. Ostensibly thwarted because of inhospitable meteorological conditions, Walton's decision to comply with the demands of his mutinous crew does not yield to good sense but, rather, capitulates to ideology. It is not the physical sight of the monster (except a very distant and very brief glimpse early in the novel) that persuades Walton and his crew to return to England. Rather, the desire to return is far more effectively produced through Frankenstein's narrative (even if his final rallying invective against the putative cowardice of Walton's crew is enough to silence them, it does not turn them from their purpose). This narrative's implicit monstrosity, already made material by Walton's letters, notes, and journal, renders the corporeal presence of the creature himself excessive; his exorbitant physicality is too immoderate for domesticity even though it is just such a purchase that the monster has himself demonstrated—in some of the most moving language in the novel—so aptly deserving. But commodification has *already* occurred. Walton has already garnered his fair exotic—Frankenstein's narrative itself—and the presence of the true wonder of the tale, the monster, therefore gets relegated to the dark margins of the high seas, floating in no-man's land, citizen of nowhere.[16]

Walton is the self-deprecating brother and principal narrator sailing into uncharted territory with the intention of bringing more property—geographical and scientific knowledge—home to be domesticated and used in the service of an expanding British empire. Despite his attestations to his personal faults, Walton is the British representative and signifier for Shelley of a stable national identity. Interestingly, the strong representations of Genevese life only produce stories of disintegration, while the practically nonexistent, undetailed representations of British life clearly compose the moral vanguard of national affiliation that anchors the ideological situation of the novel.

Frankenstein's father's commitment to Genevese civic life may have initially established his paternal suitability, but it is also clear that his "decline"—by which Frankenstein means his age—is one that could also describe his domestic arrangements. Once the precedent has been established by Alphonse Frankenstein's benevolent appropriation of Caroline Beaufort, their family continues to reproduce itself in terms of the social mission. Caroline Frankenstein's status as "fair exotic" is duplicated in the daughter they procure "while making an excursion beyond the frontiers of Italy" (34). Here romanticism wars with feminized domesticity: the Frankensteins' "excursion," unlike Wordsworth's *Excursion,* does not refine the poetic imagination; their expedition rather ends in the acquisition of Elizabeth, the daughter who eventually kills the mother.[17] Elizabeth Lavenza, placed to nurse among Italian peasantry, blooms "fairer than a garden rose among dark-leaved brambles" (35). Frankenstein's mother is instantly and mimetically attracted, and she sets about securing the latest example of otherworldly loveliness to grace her household:

She appeared of a different stock. The four others were dark-eyed, hardy little vagrants; this child was thin, and very fair. Her hair was the brightest living gold, and, despite the poverty of her clothing, seemed to set a crown of distinction on her head. Her brow was clear and ample, her blue eyes cloudless, and her lips and the moulding of her face so expressive of sensibility and sweetness, that none could behold her without looking on her as of a distinct species, a being heaven-sent, and having a celestial stamp in all her features. (33–34)

Importing another "fair exotic" into the family, Caroline Beaufort—the mother, not the father—realigns the family along "natural" lines of class and race. In this way, familial structures are recast as national and cultural constructs but more importantly as structures that depend on feminine manipulation in order to maintain their ideological integrity. Like that of De Quincey's servant girl Barbara Lewthwaite, Elizabeth's difference from the other children demonstrates the peculiar relationship between physical fairness and moral rectitude; she is "fairer than a garden rose among dark-leaved brambles," an embodiment of Rousseauian sensibility. Her face is an allegory of romanticism, reflecting the sublime Alpine landscape. Yet despite Elizabeth's clear moral superiority she remains nonhuman: her features are of a "distinct species," an "apparition," language Frankenstein uses later to describe his monster. She is adopted by the Frankenstein family, yet she retains another surname.

The Frankensteins learn from the Italian peasant woman that Elizabeth's mother, a German, is dead and her father "was one of those Italians nursed in the memory of the antique glory of Italy,—one of the *shiavi ognor frementi,* who exerted himself to obtain the liberty of his country. He became the victim of its weakness" (35). Elizabeth's pedigree suggests that the "natural" family (blood ties) follows a pattern of social inheritance.[18] That is, even if she lives with her foster parents and "bloom[s] in their rude abode," "Providence" in the guise of the superior Frankenstein name "afford[s] her such powerful protection" (35). This name signifies a similarly nonhuman (or greater-than-human) authority (e.g., Nature) that assigns and aligns familial relations.[19]

The overriding significance of national identities in relation to familial ones is prominent in Elizabeth's background. Her father, the decayed Milanese nobleman, takes in as physical sustenance a national identity: "nursed in the memory of the antique glory of Italy," he "exert[s] himself to obtain the liberty of his country." He is, however, among the "*schiavi ognor frementi*"—the "slaves always fretting"—thus suggesting that this particular national identity is based on racial weakness. As if to confirm the xenophobic representation of Italy, he becomes a "victim of its weakness." His property is confiscated, his child becomes "an orphan and a beggar," and his own whereabouts are unknown. Shelley's allusions to the faults of the peasantry and noblemen alike (their "weakness") suggest a xenophobic hierarchy that serves the hegemonic purposes of anglicized cultures. Despite Elizabeth's father's pretensions to nobility, he is still cast as a slave to the insidious weakness of a contaminated nationality. Presumably, Elizabeth's Teutonic connection prevents her from immediately falling like her father into the same abyss of national weakness, and yet Elizabeth's place in the Frankenstein household is suspect, perhaps because she belongs to a "different species."

For all her exquisite external fairness, then, Elizabeth is similarly infected; she is farmed out to a wet-nurse and ingests an alien identity along with an alien milk. She is the blood-relation-turned-social-hybrid by Shelley's revisionary hand, nourished by mixed class (peasant, aristocracy) and nationality (Italian, German). Her propensity to infect is displayed most dramatically by her fatal transmission of scarlet fever to Caroline Beaufort. Similarly, her efforts to save Justine from execution fail and in fact seem only to hasten Justine's death. Domesticated by outward form and sensibility, these fair exotics—Caroline Beaufort and Elizabeth Lavenza—perform crucial cultural work to retain the integrity and coherence of the patriarchal name, especially in the context of its association with nationality (Geneva).

It would seem, then, that despite the faultless genealogy of the Frankenstein family there is something corrupt about the parameters of their domesticity—or the perimeters of their familial space—perhaps because they continue to seek reproduction elsewhere. Caroline Beaufort, Elizabeth Lavenza, Safie—even Justine Moritz—all represent versions of the fair exotic, dangerous for their seductive appearances, monstrously resistant to domestication. In particular, the perilous Elizabeth manages to "kill" thrice before she is killed herself: Caroline Beaufort, Justine Moritz, and William Frankenstein all meet their demise through her (indirect) agency.

Why Elizabeth? In one of her letters to Frankenstein, she articulates the delights of domesticity, perhaps as a foil to Frankenstein's self-created womb-workshop, imploring him to return to his former familial space of his father's making:

Get well—and return to us. You will find a happy, cheerful home, and friends who love you dearly. Your father's health is vigorous, and he asks but to see you. . . . How pleased you would be to remark the improvement of our Ernest! . . . Little alteration, except the growth of our dear children, has taken place since you left us. The blue lake, and snow-clad mountains, they never change;—and I think our placid home, and our contented hearts are regulated by the same immutable laws. (64)

Here a feminine Nature and domestic ideology—supported and regulated by women—together conspire to keep newly formed traditions of romanticism intact and "immutable." Elizabeth is primary arbiter not only of familial desire but of romantic law: not only does she govern the ways in which the family develops but she also fixes for posterity an enduring romantic formula for domesticity. Elizabeth thus functions as the hub of familial activity. Frankenstein, on the other hand, is moving outside the family home and therefore outside the scope of romanticism by indulging (some might argue transgressing) other realms of representation, particularly of science and natural history. Frankenstein's desires articulated in this field of representation may be inevitably doomed because of his refusal to attend to the conventions of domesticity.

However, Elizabeth is not alone in this role: other households demonstrate the ways in which the supporting ideological structures that hold the family in place, under the purported aegis of paternal rule, are governed by laws devised and upheld by the feminine. Walton's sister Safie's role in the De Lacey family and even that of the female monster are examples of this representation.[20] Not only do these characters share a similar position in relation to their families, their points of "origin" are similar. They are not "natural" to the patriarchal family, indeed, as no woman is, but are imported from other, less financially fortunate or foreign families—foreign, that is, to the national familial structures determined by English/Genevese dictation. Even if the women in *Frankenstein* assume a transparency that assures male reproductivity (not unlike the importance of virginity in Western culture), and even if they share a certain motility and expendability, their "unnecessariness" may be more difficult to document than feminist readings of the maternal in this novel would have us believe.[21]

For example, the notion that Shelley obviates or circumvents the place for the maternal is a popular feminist reading of this novel.[22] Certainly there seems to be an excess of dead women, particularly mothers, littering the pages of the novel, blocking an unproblematically romantic (as in inward subjectivity) trajectory for the narrative. But feminine and maternal characters also negotiate very interesting ideological lines that keep English domesticity safely intact and free from the Continental fissures Frankenstein introduces to his own household. Far from destroying or evading the place of the mother, these negotiations establish another space that, if abjected, is nevertheless crucial to the production of romantic ideology. These negotiations may keep the forms of romanticism that were dear to Shelley's husband's heart—generator of "the most melodious verse that adorns our language" (7)—discrete from excessive Continental corruption.

The most compelling example of such arbitration is the infamous scene of the near-creation of the female monster. After much agonized self-reflection, Frankenstein agrees to comply with the monster's desires to procure his own domesticity by creating for him a matching mate. In order to do so, however, it is necessary for Frankenstein to make a journey to England to learn the "knowledge and discoveries" of its "philosophers" (152). Once there, a letter from a friend in Scotland inviting Frankenstein and his companion, Henry Clerval, to come for a visit affords Frankenstein the excuse for finding a remote part of the Orkney Islands to institute his new laboratory. This laboratory witnesses one of the more gruesome scenes of mutilation when Frankenstein deliberately dismembers the half-finished body of the female monster that he destroys after reflecting "she might be ten thousand times more malignant than her mate" (165).

The ideological structuring of this enterprise is one that bears untangling. Strikingly, the keystone to monster-making lies in the heart of England, at the hub of intellectual activity: London. Frankenstein ventures there to have intercourse with these "philosophers" (152). Although these figures are natural philosophers engaged in speculative science, their disembodied presence in the narrative recalls the more recent meaning of "philosopher."

Frankenstein focuses as much on the bodies of his teachers at Ingolstadt as he does on their pedagogy; his relation to their skills is as informed by his immediate reaction to their physical presence:

> M. Krempe was a little, squat man, with a gruff voice and a repulsive countenance; the teacher, therefore, did not prepossess me in a favour of his pursuits. . . . M. Waldman . . . was very unlike his colleague. He appeared about fifty years of age, but with an aspect expressive of the greatest benevolence; a few grey hairs covered his temples, but those at the back of his head were nearly black. His person was short, but remarkably erect; and his voice the sweetest I had ever heard. . . . As he went on, I felt as if my soul were grappling with a palpable enemy. . . . So much has been done . . . more, far more, will I achieve: treading in the steps already marked, I will pioneer a new way, explore unknown powers, and unfold to the world the deepest mysteries of creation. (51)

His professors, the natural philosophers Krempe and Waldman, function as the material "steps already marked" that lead him to the more disembodied presence of English philosophers. Unlike his studies in Ingolstadt, the material he is examining now is less insistently scientific or historical (as in natural history) but more in the realm of an epistemological "philosophy." This suggests that the central philosophical standpoints espoused by romanticism (for example, Kantian forms of the sublime) are ones that rest in England after having been appropriated from elsewhere. These standpoints have, therefore, already taken into account ideas of foreign monstrosity. In effect, for the same reason that Walton doesn't press Frankenstein to relinquish his formula to make life out of death and doesn't bring the monster back as a natural curiosity, so Frankenstein is incapable of fully materializing his female monster. That is, in the context of the romantic ideal, the material reality of formulae and monsters is excessive and less valuable than their disembodied, narrative representation.

Interestingly, Frankenstein chooses the same outpost for monstrous fashioning as Shelley does: she mentions in her Introduction that the "blank and dreary northern shores of the Tay" are the only free (that is, away from others' eyes) place for her "waking dreams." Frankenstein's reasoning is similarly invested with the desire for liberty from prying eyes. The boundaries of British identity—here Scotland, or even more removed, the Orkney Islands—are the predictable sites for staging experimental shifts of epistemological morphology. Yet it is at the hub of Englishness—London—where the paradigms for such shifts are concocted. Thus, while the dramatization of epistemological shifts may usefully take shape as an unrecognizable other—an otherness that the monsters demonstrate altogether too clearly—the less visible, more insidious ideological framework structuring such fashioning is already in place within the parameters of British national identity. It is no accident that this monster is female: as an upholder of the new domesticity that Frankenstein speculates about, her body is as excessive in its material presence as that of her monstrous counterpart.

Contrary to the cultural logic of western imperialism that typically situates the feminine in uncontestable relationships with the body, *Frankenstein*'s representation of sexuality and maternity is most strikingly characterized by its disembodiment. If the female monster's grisly remains provide physical evidence of her material presence, she is also never put together with the same attention to coherence as the monster. Upon opening the door to his laboratory the morning after, Frankenstein "almost felt as if [he] had mangled the living flesh of a human being. [He] paused to collect himself, and then entered the chamber" (170). Such language demonstrates not only a momentary thaw of Frankenstein's moral high-handedness but his more crucial understanding of the female monster as a sentient being: an agency he never grants the monster despite plenty of evidence of this monster's Cartesian sensibilities. The female monster preexists her material formation. She is, a priori, an intuitively conceived being, internally produced: her phenomenological status in Scotland is a direct result of her epistemological production in London. She is, therefore, capable of the disembodied thinking with which Frankenstein endows her: "she, who in all probability was to become a thinking and reasoning animal, might refuse to comply with a compact made before her creation. . . . She also might turn with disgust from him to the superior beauty of man; she might quit him, and he be again alone" (165). Rather than the embodiment of female marginalization, the female monster may be read more complexly as "the imperialist project cathected as civil-society-through-social-mission."[23] That is, the monstrosity of the ideological structures informing her (re)production is reinvested as a disembodied philosophical concept enriching the epistemological trajectory of romanticism.

The notion of a biologically "natural" family is held up for questioning; the family in this novel is rewritten not as a product of sexual reproduction but as a self-consciously created social mission. Familial structures in the novel represent the stability of social relations in a bourgeois culture. That is, through the structure of the nuclear family Frankenstein's social interactions remain intact. Familial structures are also a way in which to announce national and political allegiance; such allegiances prove to be crucial to the production of romantic thinking. The romantic political (and scientific) resistance figured by Shelley in this novel is thus written as xenophobic representation. Her romantic narrative's primary concerns with national identity and culturally discrete reproduction (sexual and textual) are articulated through the language of imperialism that writes the myth of "origins"—the Miltonic complaint—as a myth of nationalism.[24]

More troubling, in fact, than the female monster's story is the story of Safie, whose eventual banishment from the scene of domesticity makes clear how nationalism orders and is ordered by familial ties. Embedded and ventriloquized by the monster's tale, Safie's story occupies the center of the series of concentric histories.[25] Because of the vivid attempts the monster makes to rescue Safie from her foreignness and prevent her from being completely cast out of the Eurocentric picture, her history is particularly notorious even if it only narrates the dangers of inappropriate exchange. Safie's father, a Turkish merchant ("Turk" and "Arab" are used interchangeably—discrete identities do not exist for the "Oriental"), unfairly tried and condemned for an unnameable crime, is yet able to excite a seemingly politically sensitive response from "Parisians": "The injustice of his sentence was very flagrant; all Paris was indignant; and it was judged that his religion and wealth, rather than the crime alleged against him, had been the cause of his condemnation" (122).

The issues of discrimination in terms of race and class are overtly articulated in his case; however, his native "orientalism" makes such efforts at European incorporation staged by Felix, the De Laceys, and even the monster finally fruitless.[26] Felix attempts to rescue that "unfortunate Mahometan" (who is not given a name beyond "Safie's father" or "Turk," "Arab," "Mahometan") and the "Turk, amazed and delighted, endeavoured to kindle the zeal of his deliverer by promises of reward and wealth" (123). National and racial characteristics betray themselves in spite of European domestication. The "Turk"'s greed only makes the morally and racially superior Felix respond with virtuous indignation: he rejects the Turk's offer of wealth with "contempt." If, however, Felix shuns promises of monetary gain, he displays no compunction about accepting the gift of another material good, a "treasure which would fully reward his toil and hazard," the daughter Safie herself (123).

Safie is a more apt and tractable figure for European domestication than her father. A "Christian Arab," born of a mother who teaches her to "aspire to higher powers of intellect, and an independence of spirit, forbidden to the female followers of Mahomet," Safie functions as a token of negotiation not only between her father and Felix but between the monster and the De Lacey family. Safie is the object of domestic desire. She is what the monster tries but fails to be because in the hierarchy of race, class, and gender, only the feminine is so completely and seamlessly commodified. That is, while masculine representations of the foreign—Safie's father, the monster—are cast out of European identification, they retain a certain integrity, a discrete identity as something coherently other. The women in the novel, however, does not hold such stable positions and are, therefore, able to function in several registers at once.

For example, while Safie and the monster both occupy positions on the margins of a dominant culture, the former's status as an "other," brought into the fold, is harder to detect: she is a "treasure" similar to the one Elizabeth dramatizes for her adopted family. Like Elizabeth, however, she has a propensity to ineffective nursing (mothering).[27] Safie "arrived in safety at a town about twenty leagues from the cottage of De Lacey, when her attendant fell dangerously ill. Safie nursed her with the most devoted attention; but the poor girl died" (127). But unlike Elizabeth, her "fairness" uncovers the radical difference race makes to properly aligned European families.

Safie is placed within the same scene of canonical instruction as the monster, but unlike the monster whose education only further alienates him from domestication, Safie's instruction in the master language signifies not only her putative incorporation within Eurocentric culture but the point at which she is "required to turn away from herself to embrace her new identity, not as a self, but as the image of someone else."[28] Such an embrace, however, is deeply vexed by her national and racial standpoint. Although she "appeared to have a language of her own, she was neither understood by, nor herself understand, the cottagers" (117). She is nominally included within a newly reconfigured national identity but this inclusion only makes more apparent her racial difference. This difference resurfaces in the final moment of trial and brands her as unmistakably non-European, at least in terms of British loyalty: she is "unable to attend to her friend" and leaves the scene of European domestication. Safie is commodified as a foreign object and this commodification both insures her appropriation into colonialist culture and confirms her racial otherness. Unlike Elizabeth's Teutonic rectitude or the female monster's Englishness, Safie's subjectivity has already been molded outside the margins of European domesticity. She may be a "treasure" gilded by Felix's lessons of European culture, but she is not the same sublime creature that Elizabeth promises her adopted family. She is therefore constitutionally incapable of sustaining the mainstays of domesticated romanticism in her household, and eventually flees from the scene entirely.

Thus it is that the feminine may operate as the "namer" of the sublime object of romanticism. The fair exotics peopling *Frankenstein* do more than embellish romantic discourse: they are crucial to its production and therefore critical to the reproduction of dominant ideologies of imperialism and colonialism that rely on metaphors of reproduction. Such ideologies, as I've argued, are framed by xenophobic language and deploy gender not only to clarify reproductive capacities of the feminine but also to disarticulate the space of the domestic in order to rearticulate that space as the scene of national identity. This formulation may disrupt desires—even feminist desires—to recontain women within a tightly theorized politics. This formulation may also cause us to speculate upon how those internal spaces (e.g., "domestic") may be less "safe" for identity politics than we may have thought.[29] To be complicit in reproducing an imperialist text is, to some extent, to claim an authority; Shelley's ambivalent acknowledgment to her "former production," to which her "account will only appear as an appendage," complicates the relation between women-as-other and the colonial subject by suggesting that one endorses the subordination of the other. Women, as the examples in Wollstonecraft and Shelley demonstrate, come from elsewhere to complete the national household and sustain its discourse.

Domesticity and Its Discontents

"The monster in the text is not woman, or the woman writer; rather it is this repressed vacillation of gender or the instability of identity—the ambiguity of subjectivity itself which returns to wreak havoc on consciousness, on hierarchy, and on unitary schemes designed to repress the otherness of femininity."[30] Mary Jacobus's point here locates the issue of monstrosity firmly within the province of an itinerant female subjectivity; even while overtly shifting the focus away from the material body of the woman, the instability of identity is unmistakably a problem of "femininity." Such an identification is not new; feminist recovery of women's texts has conventionally situated the complexities of their representation with the problems of being a woman. Habitations of femininity, however, have become increasingly complex, as materialist feminists have demonstrated. My reading of *Villette* is not primarily concerned with the issues of female authorship that have engaged many critics' attentions. Nor am I focusing on the medical aspect of Lucy's hysteria, especially in relation to the production of writing, although the body of work addressing issues of authorship and hysteria informs and makes possible my own reading of this novel.[31] Rather, as part of a xenophobic cultural contiguity, I will focus on how this novel actively represents cultural fantasies about the internal domestic coherence of the mother country. Even in the case of an unfixed feminine subject position, articulations of a feminist canon—which are embedded in the deeply complicated place women's writing occupies in this novel—are sustained by the same fantasy of internal domestic cohesion and external national integrity. The ways in which these fantasies are upheld attest to a powerfully implanted xenophobia that, as we have seen, depends on the deterritorialization invited by xenodochy.

It is impossible to discuss issues of constructed female subjectivity and domesticity without attending to Nancy Armstrong's revolutionary reading of the relationship between politics and domesticating culture. Rewriting domestic circumstances in order to accommodate the emerging middle classes effectively dismantled gendered registers of culture that in turn reshaped modern institutional history. My particular reading of domesticity extends this form of dismantling to address the shaping of imperial history: the way deterritorialization of domestic property reconfigures national integrity. The "language" is used in this instance to both dismantle and reassemble national property is xenophobic.[32]

Villette is a novel that self-consciously leaves the question of home territory in abeyance: while Lucy Snowe's allegiances plainly lie toward England, it's also clear that she deliberately chooses not to foreclose the question of a permanent exile. Unlike Wollstonecraft's Mary, whose repatriation to England is inevitable, both Shelley and Brontë entertain the idea of foreign habitation. Yet while they entertain the idea of expatriation, the domesticity their characters choose to inhabit is determined by the cultural laws of Englishness.

After experiencing a series of dramatic domestic pitfalls, Lucy Snowe decides to leave England and entertains hopes of household integrity elsewhere on the Continent. Unlike Walton's voyages, which are tempered with the hope of triumphant return, Lucy's travels are dogged by a melancholia that forecasts her metaphysical and material impoverishment: there is nothing she could possibly bring back to her mother country. Unlike Frankenstein, for whom London represents a seat of learning, a temple to epistemology, a place of amplified clarity, Lucy finds London is a foreign country: "the strange speech of the cabmen and others waiting round, seemed to me odd as a foreign tongue. I had never before heard the English language chopped up in that way."[33] Lucy's confusion over language here establishes her own problems with negotiating conditions outside the confines of domesticity; but her inability to make sense of urban speech may also signify problems with internal incoherence and domestic disorder for those without property or agency.

As such a disenfranchised citizen, Lucy has learned that household harmony within England is something from which she is barred. Her first experiences with the Bretton family make clear her odd status: neither an intrinsic nor an unproblematically extrinsic member of the family, Lucy is cast out of familial unanimity and has to find refuge with Miss Marchmont's diseased domicile:

> two hot, close rooms . . . became my world; and a crippled old woman my mistress, my friend, my all. . . . I forgot there were fields, woods, rivers, seas, an everchanging sky outside the steam-dimmed lattice of this sick-chamber. . . . All within me became narrowed to my lot. . . . I demanded no walks in fresh air; my appetite needed no more than the tiny messes served for the invalid. (97)

Miss Marchmont hardly offers a promising and lasting place for Lucy. Her sick-room—whose "tiny messes" supply Lucy with her only sustenance—affords a good deal of metaphysical pleasure to Lucy but can hardly supply even the daily wants of a healthy life.[34] If Miss Marchmont's stories and quick wit furnish Lucy with a "growing sense of attachment," the material conditions of such an existence are enervating (96–97). Ideologically, such a domicile represents for Lucy the problems with a model of identity (Miss Marchmont) too closely aligned to the disembodied notions of nation: material needs are held at bay and turned into diseased versions of themselves. As an affected political body, Lucy thus must venture elsewhere on a journey to find real sustenance for a frame deformed by the continual ingestion of invalid meals.

London does not afford such a respite to Lucy, as her descriptions of linguistic exchange suggest. This port city, however, does at least present to her possibilities for other scenes of consumption. After wandering about the city, she returns to the inn, "faint, at last, and hungry (it was years since I had felt such healthy hunger)," to dine on "two dishes—a plain joint, and vegetables; both seemed excellent (how much better than the small, dainty messes Miss Marchmont's cook used to send up . . . to the discussion of which we could not bring half an appetite between us)" (109). London's spectral, half-foreign, somewhat terrifying initial countenance ("I lie," thinks Lucy, "in the shadow of St. Paul's") cannot continue to provide for Lucy's welfare because Lucy herself cannot supply London with an adequately material citizenry (107). Although Lucy sees London the next day with clearer eyes—"I like the spirit of this great London which I feel around me," she tells herself in the morning (108)—London still resembles the abstract, the transcendental, a city with "not *too* dense a cloud of haze" (109, italics mine). Lucy's reasons for not remaining in London are vague at best, perhaps because the ideological grounds on which this decision has been made are not in her control, despite her narrative authority. Cast adrift from English soil because of gender and impoverished class conditions, Lucy nevertheless makes an admirable colonial missionary. Her inability to digest completely the food given her at her most recent home (Marchmont's) signifies, in part, the inadequacy of sustenance provided by her mother country: she needs to find a necessary supplement to such meager fare.35

What she is fed at Madame Beck's establishment in Villette is almost immediately restorative. The detail of Lucy's description—in some ways outweighing the scarcity of specific features of her London meal—furnishes us with an idea of the relish with which she begins her foreign life. Even if the "nature" of the meat is unknown, its "sauce" is pleasant, indicating the ways in which foreign matter is made palatable to imperial consumption in spite of the dangers it may mask:

A cook in a jacket, a short petticoat and sabots, brought my supper: to wit,—some meat, nature unknown, served in an odd and acid, but pleasant sauce; some chopped potatoes, made savoury with, I know not what: vinegar and sugar, I think; a tartine, or slice of bread and butter, and a baked pear. Being hungry, I ate and was grateful. (130)

Still, the "nature" of her meat is "unknown," masked by a sauce she can only guess at. The point of reading Lucy's meals as an index to her acculturation is to understand the idea of ingestion in relation to domesticity and nationality. Eating or not eating, actively ingesting or rejecting, are actions that become the surest sign of a self-identification, an independent stand at subject-formation. Such choices are ones determined by a Kristevan sense of abjection: "'I' want none of that element, sign of their desire.... But since the food is not an 'other' for 'me,' I abject *myself* within the same motion through which I claim to establish *myself*."36 In the case of Lucy Snowe, her rejection of Miss Marchmont's messes and consumption of Madame Beck's repast suggest an inscription of subjectivity entirely contingent on the nationalization of domesticity.

138   Chapter 4

Food marks another crucial cultural index in this novel; it is the trope that figures *Villette* as an early Victorian text that has introjected romantic desire. Lucy claims to have "something of the artist's faculty of making the most of present pleasure," and in this way allows her "fancy" or imagination to recreate the foreign landscape. The Belgian landscape, however, bears little resemblance to Shelley's sublime landscapes. This example of Continental terrain is

somewhat bare, flat, and treeless . . . slimy canals crept like half-torpid green snakes, beside the road; and formal pollard willows edged level fields, tilled like kitchen-garden beds . . . yet amidst all these deadening influences, my fancy budded fresh. . . . These feelings, however, were kept well in check by the secret but ceaseless consciousness of anxiety lying in wait on enjoyment, like a tiger crouched in a jungle. (122)

Lucy's first glimpse of foreign potential is a demystified landscape: fields are leveled and subdued into "kitchen-gardens," their boundaries neatly marshaled and formalized by willow trees. Far from the wild heaths of Walton's youth or the immutable Alpine vistas of Frankenstein's birthplace, Lucy Snowe's encounter with the natural is one mediated by the domestic. Perhaps as a result of her decision to closet herself away from open-air recreation at her Marchmont post, Lucy's understanding of landscape is accountable only through the language of interiors with which she has become familiar.

What Lucy imagines stretched out before her is a radically different scenario. Her "fancy," invested with romantic desire, implants "snakes" and "tigers" in the conventional Belgian fields. These monsters are not, however, of foreign origin. They are produced from within the recesses of English domesticated landscapes, interior and exterior. Lucy brings with her a history of understanding the foreign as monstrous, and yet those figures of monstrosity are fabricated from materials produced within the very bosom of the English household. Not unlike the crocodiles and tigers inhabiting De Quincey's household and produced by De Quincey's imagination, Lucy's anxiety about foreign pleasures takes shape as a self-produced "tiger" in order to provide her with visible boundaries of national and cultural affiliation.

Arguably, what the Imaginary of the novel conceives as the seductive though potentially dangerous pleasures of the forbidden foreign, Lucy's consciousness of cultural difference represses and rewrites as ambiguous anxiety, as the exotic tiger in the jungle.[37] In fact she later becomes the hunted prey as "two moustachioed men" figuring oppositely to the "true young English gentleman"—(whose virtuous intentions are also confounded by foreign deviousness)—follow her through the streets of Villette until finally her "dreaded hunters were turned from their pursuit" (125). Such an anxiety seems sexually based, yet it may also mark the romantic chiasmus of fear and desire for the contaminating touch: the xenophobic response propagated by xenodochial obsession. The monsters signifying alterity—tigers, snakes, mustachioed men—originate from within the strongholds of English domesticity. Such origins have manifold implications, but, perhaps most dramatically, they suggest that the imperial campaign to align cultural with racial difference may also originate on the home front. That is, while it is crucial to the integrity of British identity to invent visible markers of difference (such as race) to distinguish the other, it is of tantamount importance to present a unified British identity to those others. Lucy's national affiliation may protect her from the snakes and tigers (two animals, I might add, that are not typically associated with Belgium) of foreign ground, but her desire for and consumption of foreign food may leave her open to other more insidious contaminants. Lucy is protected from the full consequences of her desires because she stages, consciously or not, different sites of consumption.

The deep pleasure Lucy takes in eating Continental delicacies occurs in private. Her first meal is eaten in a small room buried in the recesses of Madame Beck's kitchen: "I was led through a long, narrow passage into a foreign kitchen, very clean, but very strange. . . . I was led forward to a small inner room termed a 'cabinet'" (130). Later, her desires for a paté à la crème take shape and are fulfilled in secluded spaces. They foment in an attic to which she is sequestered (to learn her lines for the fête): "A *paté*, or a square of cake, it seemed to me would come very *apropos*; and as my relish for these dainties increased, it began to appear somewhat hard that I should pass my holiday, fasting and in prison" (205). Released by her putative turnkey, Monsieur Paul, she is led "down—down—down to the very kitchen. I thought I should have gone to the cellar" in order to eat these cakes with "great joy" and "considerable willingness" (206).[38]

Lucy's public consumption in Villette is very differently staged. For example, she writes of both the typical breakfast routine at school and occasional forays into the Belgian countryside:

This allowance [of pistolets] being more than I needed, I gave half to Ginevra; never varying in my preference, though many others used to covet the superfluity; and she in return would sometimes give me a portion of her coffee. . . . I don't know why I chose to give my bread rather to Ginevra than to another; nor why, if two had to share the convenience of one drinking-vessel, as sometimes happened—for instance when we took a long walk into the country, and halted for refreshment at a farm—I always contrived that she should be my convive, and rather like to let her take the lion's share, whether of white beer, the sweet wine, or the new milk: so it was, however, and she knew it; and, therefore, while we wrangled daily, we were never alienated. (312–13)

The "superfluity" coveted by the other schoolgirls is tellingly vague; though meant to refer to the excess of food given Ginevra, it could equally allude to Lucy's excessive favoritism—something marked as desire by the largely foreign audience of onlookers. Lucy's display may, therefore, signify her need to demonstrate national affiliation to Ginevra Fanshawe who, like a British lion, willingly participates in such an exchange.[39] Even as a foreigner in a foreign land, Lucy is "never alienated" because she is provided with physical material for daily repatriation.

Repatriation here works according to the propriety of alignments: for all her moral flaws, Ginevra Fanshawe is a figure suitable to be Lucy's "convive" because of her class and, more importantly, because she is not simply British but English. Lucy's public display of national alignment reflects a more profoundly British anxiety about exhibiting their proper racial alignments for the benefit of the foreign. The most dramatic example of this is the "English" governess, Mrs. Sweeny, whom Lucy replaces. Lucy describes this personage as follows:

I need hardly explain to the reader that this lady was in effect a native of Ireland; her station I do not pretend: she boldly declared that she "had the bringing-up of the son and daughter of a marquis." I think, myself, she might possibly have been hanger-on, nurse, fosterer, or washer-woman, in some Irish family: she spoke with a smothered brogue, curiously overlaid with mincing cockney inflections. . . . This brisk little affair of the dismissal was all settled before breakfast: order to march given, policeman called, mutineer expelled, "chambre d'enfants" fumigated and cleansed, windows thrown open, and every trace of the accomplished Mrs. Sweeny—even to the fine essence and spiritual fragrance which gave token so subtle and so fatal of the head and front of the offending—was annihilated from the Rue Fossette. (132–33)

Lucy's appeal to her readers articulates with devastating accuracy the understanding of English cultural imperialism that would have resonated with Brontë's 1850s audience.[40] Her need to both explain and not explain "native" Irish propensities to drink enunciates British anxiety over what counts as "English." For Lucy, it is critical to make Madame Beck understand that this technically British subject is masquerading as an English governess, and that her ostensible mastery of the language—a "smothered brogue" gilded with "mincing cockney"—renders her highly unsuitable as a cultural instructor. If the Irish were the first manifestation of "race" in English usage, then Lucy's replacement of Mrs. Sweeny manifests a British anxiety of aligning nationalism with race. The thoroughness with which she is removed from the Rue Fossette—a removal that entails not only the command of Lucy's cultural authority on English matters and Madame Beck's institutional authority on matters pertaining to her school but the anonymous legal authority of the "agent of the police"—implies the various laws employed to insure that British national identity retains its proper representation abroad.

Mrs. Sweeny is not only the English teacher but a governess as well, a nursemaid to the young children of Madame Beck. Lucy first sees Mrs. Sweeny ensconced within the deep recesses of the nursery and, to "complete the picture, and leave no doubt as to the state of matters, a bottle and an empty glass stood at the sleeping beauty's elbow" (131). Infecting the sanctity of the "chambre d'enfants" is an adulterated version of Englishness: the monster of alterity takes shape most convincingly as a manifestation of outcast British identity and not as the foreign other. The notion of Britishness as a vexed identity in need of stabilizing ideological structures, particularly of race, constitutes much of the xenophobic rendering of Belgium in *Villette*. Mrs. Sweeny's capacities to nurse Madame Beck's children duplicate the ways in which monstrosity inhabits the most intimate places; in the case of *Villette*, ingestion (food or intoxicants) is an overdetermined activity closely linked to the production of identity.[41] (One needs only to think back to Wollstonecraft's—and Rousseau's—injunction for women to nurse patriotic duty as an another form of breastfeeding.) Sweeny functions, therefore, as Lucy's figure of the abject. Sweeny's infected body, despite its showy dress, solicits a panoply of authorities—legal, moral, national, linguistic—in order to fix her in the abjected position; her abjection therefore keeps intact Lucy's place as the native cultural informant. It is critical to British cultural integrity for Lucy Snowe to fill Mrs. Sweeny's shoes; yet her own predilections for consumption may render her equally vulnerable to the same contamination with which Sweeny infects the nursery.

There are two significant scenes in which Lucy's fall into the foreign (contamination) is performed. Putatively protected by the armor of her English (and Protestant) name, Lucy may have already been marked by the consumption of illicit substances, rendering her as diseased as Mrs. Sweeny were it not for other monsters defining the parameters of the domestic and the foreign. Left with "the dust of a town-summer departed," Lucy's "prop of employment" is withdrawn. The removal of this vital and integral part of her identity thus turns the familial institution into a profoundly unfamiliar scene. Lucy must fabricate a literal monster in order to insure herself of her place inhabiting that scene. Lacking the title "Engleesh school mees" that rallies her identity into a semblance of coherence, Lucy fashions the "*crétin*," a creature with a "poor mind [that] like her body, was warped" by a "propensity to evil" (229). Thus the school becomes a prison in which Lucy's cellmate is "some strange tameless animal," deprived of language and expressing herself by "moping and mowing and distorting her features with indescribable grimaces" (229). This moment is more than simply an illustration of the familiar Freudian topos in which the slide from *heimlich* to *unheimlich* becomes a metonym for the gothic text.[42] The *crétin* represents another self-created monster that demonstrates Lucy's turn from the enthusiastic consumption of Continental substances and return to more British habits of ingestion.

Lucy loses her appetite. Attending to the needs of the *crétin* deprives her "often of the power and inclination to swallow a meal," and also sends her "faint to fresh air, and the well or fountain in the court." In effect, the *crétin*'s presence, inert though it may be, quells Lucy's hunger for foreign delicacies and forces her to seek the relief of "fresh" air, not the spent foreign atmosphere of an enclosed former nunnery.[43] Furthermore, the *crétin* (by leaving the Rue Fossette) allows Lucy to venture forth outside the confines of the school, something she has not yet desired to do. What she eventually finds is a thoroughly British sanctuary in the Bretton household to which she becomes reunited. Thus the *crétin* is a boundary creature that returns Lucy from the lures of foreign desire to her English origins. How Lucy gets there, however, is another story.

Overcome by the "extremity of want," Lucy seeks comfort from the Catholic church and from a priest, who is fortunately "not a native priest," because "of that class, the cast of physiognomy is, almost invariably, groveling." Yet even if this priest responds to her confession with compassion, still she suspects he "would have tried to kindle, blow and stir up in me the zeal of good works" which would reduce her to "counting [her] beads in the cell of a certain Carmelite convent." No, sooner should she "[think] of walking into Babylonish furnace" than be affected by his "sentimental French kindness, to whose softness [she] knew [her]self not wholly impervious" (235). Lucy's wanderings in the heart of the city after her encounter with the priest evoke Freud's example of the uncanny in which he wanders through the heart of an unfamiliar Italian city, returning repeatedly to the red light district. Lucy writes:

> But I had become involved in a part of the city with which I was not familiar; it was the old part, and full of narrow streets of picturesque and mouldering houses. I was much too weak to be very collected, and I was still too careless of my own welfare and safety to be cautious: I grew embarrassed: I got inmeshed in a network of turns unknown. I was lost, and had no resolution to ask guidance of any passenger. (235–36)

Just as Freud locates the uncanny in the foreign (the Italian city), in prostitutes (the painted women), and in his own labyrinthine repetition as a streetwalker, Lucy journeys through the unfamiliar part of a foreign city, confused by "turns unknown," at the heart of which she finds the "painted and meretricious face [of the Church]" (516). Far from discovering any relief from her mental anguish, Lucy's repetitive wandering only locates the painted face of the foreign and feminine. For Lucy (and arguably for Freud), such a discovery freezes exoticism as a definitive entity that their desire may romanticize but never quite realize. Freud is rescued from his fall into the foreign by his consciousness of national and sexual difference: he abandons his experimental walk and hastens back to places of more familiarity. Lucy faints before she falls. Her swoon in the face of the uncanny foreign—embodied most visibly by the Catholicism—represents her unconscious protection from a sexual fall by a nationally discrete identity masquerading as a religious one, wheeled in as a defense at this crisis in her narrative. She reawakens within the domestically intact and magically relocated Bretton household: "Am I in England? Am I at Bretton? [she] muttered" (242). Thus the integrity of her English identity—an integrity achieved only after constructing an apotropaic monster—shields her unconscious desire for other forms of consumption.[44]

If Lucy is protected from her xenodochial desire for forbidden sweets, if she domesticates her outlandish appetites for the exotic by disciplining them to the structure of the conventional gothic romance, they return to baffle her and eventually ward off any neat closure to incipient love relationships. Once again, it is the maid in the household who is the agent for such blockage and betrayal. The cook, Goton, for whom Lucy is an especial pet ("chou-chou"), nevertheless participates in opiating Lucy, the result of which is to utterly confuse the plot and complicate the trajectory of imperial representation.

Lucy violates foreign integrity by falling in love with Madame Beck's cousin, Monsieur Paul; her interest in entering and disrupting this household is cause for alarm. Because she can find no permanent place in English homes—Miss Marchmont dies and her interest in entering the Bretton household as the conventional romance heroine is frustrated—she strives for foreign conquest in typically imperial style.[45] But her unconscious desires for foreign delectation are dangerous; her champion, Goton, bears the drug that will reconfigure her plot:

I went up-stairs. Presently I was in my bed—my miserable bed—haunted with quick scorpions. I had not laid down five minutes, when . . . Goton came, bringing me something to drink. I was consumed with thirst—I drank eagerly; the beverage was sweet, but I tasted a drug. . . . In fact, they had given me a strong opiate. (546)

Like any addict, Lucy already imagines monsters (scorpions) that infest her bed; her awareness of the sweetness of her poison underscores her unconscious desire for such contaminants. Interestingly, in the dream that follows her ingestion of opium Brontë connects fantasy, imagination, and Orientalism. Lucy's imagination has been roused before, especially in the episodes that feature the figure of the nun, but those moments are written by the discourse of an articulated, if unrequited, English romance. In this chapter, her inadequately repressed feeling for Monsieur Paul (the French teacher) emerges as a desire for an even more hideous object: Madame Walravens.

Lucy ventures out into the city in a state of hallucinatory vividness, recalling another voyage into the strange on the ship the *Vivid* on which Lucy sailed to Belgium in the first place: "The drug wrought. . . . Imagination was roused from her rest" (547). This chapter makes abundantly clear that, as an oriental product, opium's effects are connected to the production of both fantasy and Western-created notions of the "Orient" itself. Lucy's imagination "[brings] upon [her] a strange vision of Villette" (547). This vision is dominated by Egyptian artifacts:

a land of enchantment . . . a forest with sparkles of purple and ruby and golden fire gleaming the foliage; a region . . . of strangest architectural wealth—of altar and of pyramid, obelisk, and sphinx; incredible to say, the wonders and the symbols of Egypt teemed throughout the park of Villette. . . . While looking up at the image of a white ibis . . . I lost sight of the party which . . . I had followed. (550–51)

Fantasy, Egyptian artifact, and writing, figured here by the ibis who signifies Toth, the Egyptian god of Letters, come together in this opiated vision of Oriental wealth, improbably created—like any heart of darkness—in the center of Villette. The fact that Lucy loses "sight" of the party which she is following, distracted by an even more foreign representation of writing suggests that she may have already been foreclosed from the domestic delights of the foreign household and must look to other models to inscribe a place for herself. Lucy's gaze is somewhat appropriative, not to say touristic; she remains outside the arena of actions, hidden from view while her friends perform, positioning herself among the outermost circle of observers.

Lucy therefore changes her interpretation of her relationship to Monsieur Paul. The Oriental façade provides an appropriate backdrop for Lucy's moment of error in (wrongly) identifying Monsieur Paul's niece, Justine Marie, as his fiancée. Lucy thus self-consciously sets up a false identity for Monsieur Paul that connects sexual relationships with national ones. Even if this portion of the narrative is ostensibly produced by Lucy's drugged hallucinations, it is curious that those visions recapitulate British cultural fantasies about something further east. In effect, it is because Lucy has relinquished the idea of her own monstrosity by creating other parameters of domesticity (that the *crétin* has so usefully embodied) that she can indulge in British clichés about the foreign. The defamiliarization of the domestic mother country has been effectively reterritorialized by the language of xenophobia. The most clearly drawn example of how the mechanism of xenophobia operates to protect Lucy from the disgrace of foreign incorporation is the language with which describes Madame Walravens.

At the center of the concentric circles of observers, and at the center of the Oriental dream stands the grotesque figure of Madame Walravens, "hideous as a Hindoo idol" and covered with a "pile of merchandize." The strange and almost incidental appearance of Madame Walravens in the preceding chapter, "Malevola," would make her seem a gratuitous figure in the novel. However, not unlike the *crétin*, whose hastily constructed appearance functions as a way in which Lucy's identity is kept intact, the equally monstrous (but more powerful) Madame Walravens functions as a necessary monster demonstrating Lucy's coherent national identity.

Lucy loses herself in the old part of Villette and finds, at its heart, the scarlet harlot, the painted face of the Catholic Church. In the same manner, Madame Walravens is found "deep into the old and grim Basse-Ville." Lucy's first glimpse of her in the bowels of old Villette is resplendent:

This being wore a gown of brocade . . . covered with satin foliage . . . over the gown a costly shawl, gorgeously bordered. . . . But her chief points were her jewels; she had long, clear ear-rings, blazing with a lustre which could not be borrowed or false; she had rings on her skeleton hands, with thick gold hoops, and stones—purple, green, and blood-red. (481)

In the Egyptian scene Madame Walravens appears quite differently from Lucy's opiated perspective:

a strange mass it was—bearing no shape, yet magnificent. You saw, indeed, the outline of a face and features, but these were so cadaverous and so strangely placed, you could almost have fancied a head severed from its trunk, and flung at random on a pile of rich merchandize . . . neither the chasteness of moonlight, nor the distance of torches, could quite subdue the gorgeous dyes of the drapery. (558)

Ingesting opium has only duplicated for Lucy the (British) xenophobic understanding of orientalized figures. This "being," previously accorded the status of a knowing subject, is now at once a "mass" that has no "shape," a thing with the "outline" of a face and features, a cadaver, a head, and a trunk. This line-up of contradictory descriptions suggests the history of Lucy's repatriation. That is, Madame Walravens' steady disintegration from a putatively freestanding subjectivity to the monstrously shapeless mass charts Lucy's progressive integration as a citizened subject. Madame Walravens is the sign of successful English imperialism; her display of foreign finery only spells Belgian greed, while Lucy's altruistic desire to set up a school in Villette embodies British imperialism as a social mission. Because Madame Walravens has actively frustrated Lucy's relationship to Monsieur Paul, she is figured as monstrous and her monstrosity enables Lucy to free herself from the confines of the romance plot and redirect her ambitions toward an Anglicized version of domestic colonialism.[46]

The novel ends by placing at the center what seems on the surface so marginal—the foreign and the imperial—and making it an oriental mise-en-scène for Lucy's confrontation with her false identification with the foreign household. Madame Walravens's colonial exploitation of Monsieur Paul, despite her helpless and otherwise impoverished state, represents imperialist greed as hopelessly foreign. However blameless Monsieur Paul may be, he also supports this system and in doing so puts at risk his desire to establish a permanent English or anglicizable domestic space with Lucy. Thus competing imperialist ideologies are set up as a contest between domestic and imperialist goals. Monsieur Paul's Catholicism (what distinguishes him as most foreign), however, takes the form of a certain domestic piety that is expressed in his care of Justine Marie, Lucy, and even Madame Walravens. In this sense, his Catholicism may be read (and certainly is by Lucy) as a source of integrity, and his "otherness" turns into a model of Englishness, defined by his ability to sustain a household: English domesticity has been successfully exported.

Lucy's school is set up as a specifically English and Protestant rival to Madame Beck's Catholic discipline. Monsieur Paul himself implores Lucy to "remain a Protestant. My little English Puritan, I love Protestantism in you . . . it is the sole creed for 'Lucy'" (594–95). He conflates "creed" with "nationality" and collapses both ideologies into the single identity of "Lucy." Lucy's domesticity remains untouched by foreign experience, a product of Lucy's English hands: "My school flourishes, my house is ready" (595). Lucy successfully introjects the foreign through the agency of monstrosity: Monsieur Paul, the domesticated representation of the foreign, has at one time been of "low stature, wiry make, . . . angles . . . darkness . . . manner," but is now "more my own" (592,595). So much "her own" indeed that his bodily presence ceases to be requisite: Lucy has successfully ingested his supplemental necessity. He is cast out to sea amid the wrecks of the Atlantic, and is replaced by Lucy's (and the reader's) romantic "fancy," who exhorts us to "leave sunny imaginations hope . . . let them picture union and a happy succeeding life," and place Monsieur Paul in the exotic sphere, forever "reckoned amongst the jewels" (596, 595).

Thus *Villette* marks the ways imperialism depends on a system of deterritorializing the domestic in order to reterritorialize other registers of expanded empire. Lucy's situation in Villette repeats Miss Marchmont's story. Like Miss Marchmont, Lucy renounces the romance plot and sends her lover to oblivion; but crucially unlike Miss Marchmont, she has learned the lesson of the supplement. Monsieur Paul's foreignness supplies the imperial agent (Lucy) with what it lacks, buttressing Victorian fantasies of cultural coherence and simultaneously displaying its pathology whose symptom is xenophobia.

Afterword

The *Oxford English Dictionary* identifies the first use of the word "fair" (in England) to refer specifically to lightness of complexion as occurring in 1551 (in T. Wilson's *Logike*). The first appearance of Africans in London is generally dated around 1555, "when five Africans arrived to learn English and thereby facilitate trade, as the beginning of a continual black presence in Britain." There is not a transparent historical connection between these two events. Their proximity, however, does raise other questions: what was the necessity for this addition to the use of "fair's" earlier meaning of "pleasing form" and what kinds of cultural anxieties about identity did this necessity reflect? Gretchen Gerzina suggests that the more difficult task is "to decipher and reconstruct the attitude of earlier white Britons toward these 'newcomers'" and further proposes that the "English only began to see themselves as 'white' when they discovered 'black' people." The relatively sudden need to use "fair" to mean "light," then, in the face of the material presence of Africans (who, interestingly, were there first to engage in trade, not as labor) seems consistent with this logic.[1]

Forms of exoticism inhabit the domestic stronghold, although their origins are elsewhere. In a larger sense, the structure of alien identity is one that takes shape through xenodochial desire that in turn produces xenophobic representation. The romantic focus on the solitary, inward authorial voice—a phenomenon I am situating earlier than traditional historical accounts of the romantic literary period—suggests that romanticism as a psychological mode bears a resemblance to the dynamics of incorporation.

The "fair exotics" of *Frankenstein* and *Villette* address the ways in which the embodiments of liminality—for example, the Christian/Arab character of Safie—depend on white, Anglican British models for their meaning just as paradigms of whiteness are contingent on blackness. Even if Caroline Beaufort—to whom the phrase refers—is technically a Genevese and reflects the model of citizenry provided by Rousseau, the "fair exotic" is sanctioned by British writers Wollstonecraft and Shelley (who was much more invested in conservative and typically English forms of domesticity than her mother). Her fairness marks her exoticism, a phenomenon that resonates in her French surname. Caroline Beaufort's nominally French, socially Genevese, and metonytonymically British civic identity first invokes the French in order to later warrant the (re)production of more hideous forms of exoticism: the monster. But Frankenstein's mother's exoticism is not limited to her "fairness"; rather, that very conflation of fair/exotic engenders a series of dangerous supplements—her son, her daughter, and finally her "grandson" the monster. Troubling the integrity of the Genevese/British civic family is this fair exotic, nourished from within the most intimate domestic space.

Likewise, Lucy Snowe functions as a fair, although less transparent exotic. She is self-consciously English and articulates the hallmarks of British prejudice at every question of national or cultural identity. Her desire, however, remains elsewhere, projected onto a French erotic possibility (M. Paul) and a Belgian domestic reality (the school he enables her to run). The fairness promised by her surname and darkened by her xenodochial appetite marks her as a character; her fairness renders her into an exoticized figure. Lucy Snowe's association with French cultural identity produces a monstrously ambiguous narrative. This novel's closure operates as foreclosure: it defers both the return of French eroticism (her marriage to M. Paul) and the return to the British motherland (she remains in her English school) in order to sustain the fantasy that imperial Britishness can simultaneously inhabit the places of self/other/othered.

I have attempted to identify the psychological drives that structure such contradictory impulses. While it is probably true that the African presence in sixteenth-century white British culture might have stimulated a number of needs to differentiate Britons from Africans, equally compelling are the ways in which such drives became institutionalized and systematized, especially given the disparity of the white population versus the African one. How could Queen Elizabeth I issue an edict in 1596 to demand the repatriation of Africans because there were "so many black people in England" if it were not for some anxiety about the integrity of her constituency?[2]

Her formal edicts between the years 1596 and 1601 to remove their presence were apparently ineffectual. Queen Elizabeth's declaration that these people were "infidels having no understanding of Christ or his Gospel" reflects less her concerns for the ideological welfare of her subjects than her anxieties that black people would leach jobs and goods from English citizenry. Hence the black people who were, according to Gretchen Gerzina, already "ensconced in Britain's houses, streets and ports, and portrayed on its stages" were represented as "blackamoors" or "infidels."[3] It appears as if racial difference, invited as it were in 1555 by someone willing to teach these five Africans the language of trade, turned out to be a material means by which ideological configurations of hierarchy were established.

Such configurations, then, make possible Crusoe's negotiations with skins: his fine gradations of color, his self-conscious entertainment of the prospects of being othered himself, his secure knowledge that his whiteness predominates any exterior marking. The difference Defoe's novel foregrounds is the psychic internalization of external difference, distinguishing *Robinson Crusoe* as a precursor to the romantic internalization of otherness. Johnson's work addresses this internalization by acknowledging epistemology as the critical source of the superior capacities of European trade compared to "Asiatics" and "Africans," and invoking the "unsearchable will of the Supreme Being" as a final reason for this hierarchy.[4] His description of language clearly draws upon this logic. Yet Johnson's representations of European epistemology is not simply a black and white affair. The dialectical relation between xenophobia and xenodochy is mediated by both the French and that part of the British found wayward and wanting (represented in both *London* and the *Life of Savage*). Thus Johnson defines English epistemological production as originating from "pure sources" and is able to excoriate the language of British subjects working as "Indian traffickers" and "loose" translators who pose such threats to "genuine diction."[5]

De Quincey's *Confessions of an English Opium Eater* makes explicit the connection between exotic monstrosity and native domesticity: mediating between these terms (which are often entirely conflated) is not only the "spurious and defective sensibility of the French" but the thoroughly frightening and disarming presence of the Malay and his consorts. More terrifying, however, to De Quincey are the "fair exotics"—the servant girl, his children—who populate his household. Such beings threaten the intellectual integrity of his opiated dreams, obtruding their material presence upon his hallucinatory fantasies about scholarship (particularly his ambivalent desires for inclusion in Wordsworth's familial circle) and "Asiatic" scenarios alike.

My focus on Mary Wollstonecraft, Mary Shelley, and Charlotte Brontë in the second half of this study—three key figures in the history of feminist criticism—in the context of the other major figures of eighteenth- and nineteenth-century British authorship I examine raises questions about women's writing, which is often left in a category of its own, apparently untouched by ideological hierarchies about "othering." These chapters thus address not only the texts themselves but the assumptions and methods of feminist literary criticism. The focus on the domestic brings together the relationship between the maternal and the national that simultaneously—and paradoxically—make women eccentric to the domestic spheres they represent.

The fair exotic is at once engaging and eccentric. This figure negotiates encounters with foreign bodies and incorporates them within the province of a dominant (national) self. Displaying an alluring and seductive facade, its idiosyncracies nevertheless emerge as freakish and have the power to invoke a horror, a xenophobic drive that continues to excoriate even while it invites.

Notes

Introduction

1. Daniel Defoe, *Robinson Crusoe* (1719; New York: Bantam, 1981), 58. Subsequent material from *Robinson Crusoe* is from this text unless otherwise indicated, and will be noted in parentheses.

2. For example, Ella Shohat and Robert Stam claim that their exhaustive study, *Unthinking Eurocentrism: Multiculturalism and the Media* (New York: Routledge, 1994), is "written in the passionate belief that an awareness of the intellectually debilitating effects of the Eurocentric legacy is indispensable for comprehending . . . contemporary subjectivities" (1). Their argument reflects one of the earliest analyses of British imperialism, Gayatri Spivak's "Three Women's Texts and a Critique of Imperialism" (in *"Race," Writing, and Difference*, ed. Henry Louis Gates, Jr. [Chicago: University of Chicago Press, 1985]), in which she apprises readers of the impossibility of reading nineteenth-century literature without remembering the profound effects imperialism had on social representation. Both these articulations of postcolonial inquiry quite rightly point to material histories of dominance and subordination; less visible in these arguments is what defines the structure of hegemony, how the parameters of imperial identity might also be subjected to a materialist analysis.

3. Freud suggests that the mechanism of joking or recontaining a preconscious idea as comic represents an anxiety about the full articulation of that idea: "Evidence, finally, of the increase in activity which becomes necessary when these primary modes of functioning are inhibited is to be found in the fact that we produce a *comic* effect, that is, a surplus of energy which has to be discharged in *laughter, if we allow these modes of thinking to force their way through into consciousness.*" *The Interpretation of Dreams* (New York: Avon, 1965), 644.

In the case of Crusoe, his initial flight from England against the wishes of his family, his enslavement by the Moors (where he calls himself an English slave), and his later shipwreck on the island all attest to xenodochial desire. Crusoe's joke about riding through Yorkshire equipped as the foreign body can only be fully articulated *as* a joke, an ejaculation of surplus unconscious anxiety about expressing his desire not to embody British subjectivity.

4. Lest readers think that I'm using the terms "British" and "English" indiscriminately, let me point out that I engage these terms in the ways Linda Colley and Gerald Newman do. The politics of identity embedded in the uses of these terms are quite critical to imperial representations. For the most part I am associating notions of "Englishness" with a domestic colonialism (privileging the English territory over its

annexed portions of Scotland and Wales), while the term "British" identifies a coherent national identity, welded by various Acts of Union and wielded as an impregnable shield of imperial superiority to the rest of the world. I would also like to point out that Crusoe's anxiety about his British subjectivity, articulated from the onset of his narrative by a discourse on the incorporation of the original Teutonic "Kreutznaer" from Bremen into an anglicized "Crusoe," verifies the authority of English as a master discourse. See Linda Colley, *Britons: Forging the Nation, 1707–1837* (New Haven, Conn.: Yale University Press, 1991) and Gerald Newman, *The Rise of English Nationalism: A Cultural History 1740–1830* (New York: St. Martin's Press, 1987).

5. The terms "self-consolidating other" and "absolute other" are Gayatri Spivak's. See "The Rani of Sirmur" in Francis Barker et al., *Europe and Its Others*, vol. 1 (Colchester: University of Essex Press, 1986).

6. I invoke the terms "romantic" and "romanticism" throughout this study. I want to clarify exactly what I mean when I use them. In general, my use of these terms assumes the literary preoccupation with subjectivity, inwardness, and authorship that defines modernity. But I am also interested in the xenodochial features of romantic authorship (articulated, for example, by De Quincey's desire for the horrifying other). Although I really don't talk much about the sublime in relation to romanticism, I am interested (especially in this Introduction), in the ways in which the material conditions of literary representation are purified or refined into intellectual abstractions.

7. I refer to Crusoe's island as a "supplement," and I mean to use this term in its conventional sense—something that makes up a lack—but also in its Derridean sense, that is, as the site that simultaneously signifies the fantasy of the subject's absolute coherence and as its equally absolute incapacity for such agency.

8. I use "self" and "other" in a deliberately binary form in this section primarily to emphasize the ideological dimensions of the construction of *visible* difference. John Barrell has argued that the foreign is often invoked as a form of maintenance. The difference I bring to his discussion is the degree to which this invitation is a welcome one; I would argue that the extremities of British xenophobia can only make sense when matched by an equally keen interest and solicitation of the foreign.

9. Sigmund Freud, *Sexuality and the Psychology of Love*, trans. Philip Rieff (New York: Macmillan, 1963), 217.

10. Immanuel Kant, *Critique of Pure Reason*, trans. J. M. D. Meiklejohn (Amherst, Mass.: Prometheus Books, 1990): 21.

11. Some influential words on the romantic sublime come from Thomas Weiskel's account, who ventriloquizes the ways in which romanticism came to be understood in the academy prior to its problematization by forms of ideological critique. Weiskel claims that "not as theme or image, ideology or ethic" does the romantic sublime speak" to us. The sublime moment, Weiskel argues, "tends to have a typical or fictional status. The dialectic of continuity and originality can only be resolved in a fiction of some kind, and it may be that the origin, like a screen memory, is a compromise between what we cannot fail to know and what we need to believe—the latter usually a mystery to ourselves." Weiskel, *The Romantic Sublime: Studies in the Structure and Psychology of Transcendence* (Baltimore: Johns Hopkins University Press, 1986), 12; also see 136–64. Weiskel himself is troubled by the ideological structures on

which such transcendental notions as the sublime are dependent, and, though he addresses this problem using Lacanian paradigms of identity and the unconscious, he still privileges the existence of the sublime as an extant phenomenon, a thing in itself. My critique, beginning with Kant's material circumstances for producing the idea of transcendental aesthetics, suggests that all such structures are dependent on xenophobic drives among other things.

12. Kant, *Critique of Pure Reason*, 29–30.

13. One of the most striking examples of the ways xenophobia has structured our unconscious—according to psychoanalytic discourse—is Freud's definition of "phantasy," in which he declares, finally, that

On the one hand, they [phantasies] are highly organised, free from self-contradiction, have made use of every acquisition of the system Cs. and would hardly be distinguished in our judgment from the formations of that system. On the other hand they are unconscious and incapable of becoming conscious. Thus *qualitatively* they belong to the system Pcs., but *factually* to the Ucs. Their origin is what decides their fate. We may compare them with individuals of mixed race who, taken all round, resemble white men, but who betray their coloured descent by some striking feature or other, and on that account are excluded from society and enjoy none of the privileges of white people. (Phantasy [or Fantasy]," quoted in J. Laplanche and J.-B. Pontalis, *The Language of Psycho-Analysis* [New York: Norton, 1973], 317)

14. In order to distinguish my usage from the more conventionally Jungian uses of the collective unconscious, I would like to make clear that this is not the direction in which I am heading. Rather, I am considering the ways ideologies work as a "collective" effort in producing notions of individual agency.

15. M. H. Abrams, *Natural Supernaturalism: Tradition and Revolution in Romantic Literature* (New York: Norton, 1971), 170–71.

16. Benedict Anderson's argument for "imagined communities" is especially influential here, in which the cultural artifacts of national development relied on crossovers of discrete historical forces, but the consequent solidification of nations resulted in an unmoveable modularity. Anderson, *Imagined Communities: Reflections on the Origin and Spread of Nationalism* (New York: Verso, 1983), 14.

17. Even though Swift's novel was published a few years after Crusoe's (1726), Swift is not making the same "romantic" claims as Crusoe. Swift's *Gulliver's Travels*, I would argue, remains far more entrenched within Enlightenment discourse.

18. Wordsworth, *The Prelude* (1805), Book Nine: l.36–37, 122–25 (italics mine).

19. The work of Ernest Tuveson, *The Imagination as a Means of Grace: Locke and the Aesthetics of Romanticism* (Berkeley: University of California Press, 1960), and Hans Aarslef, *From Locke to Saussure: Essays on the Study of Language and Intellectual History* (Minneapolis: University of Minnesota Press, 1982), establish continuities between the eighteenth-century Enlightenment and romanticism, as do more recent books by Jules Law, Cathy Caruth, Jerome Christensen, Steven Knapp, and Adela Pinch. See Caruth, *Empirical Truths and Critical Fictions: Locke, Wordsworth, Kant, Freud* (Baltimore: Johns Hopkins University Press, 1991); Christensen, *Romanticism at the End of History* (Baltimore: Johns Hopkins University Press, 2000); Knapp, *Literary Interest:*

The Limits of Anti-Formalism (Cambridge, Mass.: Harvard University Press, 1993); Adela Pinch, *Strange Fits of Passion: Epistemologies of Emotion, Hume to Austen* (Stanford, Calif.: Stanford University Press, 1996).

20. Tim Fulford and Peter J. Kitson, *Romanticism and Colonialism: Writing and the Empire, 1780–1830* (Cambridge: Cambridge University Press, 1998), 1.

21. See John Barrell, *The Infection of Thomas De Quincey: A Psychopathology of Imperialism*, (New Haven, Conn.: Yale University Press, 1991); Marilyn Butler, *Romantics, Rebels, and Reactionaries: English Literature and Its Background, 1760–1830* (New York: Oxford University Press, 1981); Nigel Leask, *British Romantic Writers and the East: Anxieties of Empire* (Cambridge: Cambridge University Press, 1992) and "Colonialism and the Exotic," in *Romantic Writings*, ed. Stephen Bygrave (London: Routledge, 1996), 227–49; Jerome McGann, "The Failures of Romanticism," in *Romanticism, History, and the Possibilities of Genre: Re-Forming Literature, 1789–1837*, ed. Tilottama Rajan and Julia M. Wright (Cambridge: Cambridge University Press, 1998), 270–87 and "Rethinking Romanticism," in *The Challenge of Periodization: Old Paradigms, New Perspectives* Lawrence Besserman (New York: Garland, 1996), 161–78. In addition to these last two collections, also see Sonia Hofkosh and Alan Richardson, eds., *Romanticism, Race, and Imperial Culture, 1780–1834* (Bloomington: Indiana University Press, 1996), and John Beer, ed., *Questioning Romanticism* (Baltimore: Johns Hopkins University Press, 1995).

22. Saree Makdisi, *Romantic Imperialism: Universal Empire and the Culture of Modernity* (Cambridge: Cambridge University Press, 1998), 8–10.

23. I understand that all three of these examples fall under the rubric of "discursive"; yet, even in areas of cultural activity that are not primarily dependent on the dissemination of language, notions of containment are operative.

24. Gauri Viswanathan, *Masks of Conquest: Literary Study and British Rule in India* (New York: Columbia University Press, 1989) and Vinay Dharwadker, "Print Culture and Literary Markets in Colonial India," in *Language Machines: Technologies of Literary and Cultural Production*, ed. Jeffrey Masten, Peter Stallybrass, and Nancy J. Vickers (New York: Routledge, 1997), 108–33.

25. Here I am referring to what Deleuze and Guattari identify as the "intermezzo": a place where one can "be-between, to pass between" the dualisms set up by the machinery of ideology that enunciates social fields. I also must point out that, although my use of the term "domestic" here is primarily in the service of "native," I will make an argument for the relationship between domesticity and gender and sex. See Gilles Deleuze and Felix Guattari, *A Thousand Plateaus: Capitalism and Schizophrenia* (Minneapolis: University of Minnesota Press, 1987), 277.

26. Nigel Leask, *British Romantic Writers and the East*, 7.

27. Slavo Žižek, *The Plague of Fantasies* (London: Verso, 1997), 7.

28. One cannot deny the enormous influence of the German school of romanticism. For the purposes of this argument, however, I am focusing on British manifestations. And by codification I am not referring to the older historical sources romanticism is informed by; rather, my argument concerns the contemporary formation of this ideology.

29. Michel Foucault, "Nietzsche, Genealogy, History" in *Language, Counter-*

Memory, Practice, trans. Donald Bouchard and Sherry Simon (Ithaca, N.Y.: Cornell University Press,1977), 139.

30. It is safe to assume that Johnson's stature via his *Dictionary* was great enough for him to have been widely read and used by romantic writers.

Chapter 1. Institutionalizing Xenophobia

1. This connection is enhanced by the fact that French writers' use of the Oriental tale was primarily as a political tool: the East was infamous (according to European historiographers) for its despotism, and pre-republic critics of France's absolute monarchy could draw upon this parallel with relative ease. English readers of such tales, complacent in the knowledge that their particular monarchy was constitutional, could consume these pointed critiques with a kind of horrified pleasure and confirm their suspicion that it was but a short leap from France to the murky realms of the Other.

2. Johnson translated the French version of Father Lobo's travels when he was unsuccessful in finding a teaching position, after he had been convinced by a former school friend, Edmund Hector, to publish the book. Twenty-six years later, Johnson wrote *Rasselas* to defray the expenses of his mother's funeral but also, perhaps, to avoid the scene of her death.

3. Samuel Johnson, *Selected Poetry and Prose,* ed. Frank Brady and W. K. Wimsatt (Berkeley: University of California Press, 1977), 122. All subsequent quotations and page references to Johnson's *Rasselas, Preface to the Dictionary, London,* and *Life of Savage,* unless otherwise indicated, are from this edition and will be cited parenthetically.

4. Robert DeMaria, Jr., *Johnson's Dictionary and the Language of Learning* (Chapel Hill: University of North Carolina Press, 1986), 6–7.

5. See, for example, David Palumbo-Liu's *The Ethnic Canon: Histories, Institutions, and Interventions* (Minneapolis: University of Minnesota Press, 1995); Hans Ulrich Gumbrecht's and Palumbo-Liu's edited collection, *Streams of Cultural Capital: Transnational Cultural Spaces (Mestizo Spaces)* (Stanford, Calif.: Stanford University Press, 1998), Joel Reed's work on the institutionalization of learning in the eighteenth century; Pierre Bourdieu's, Jean-Claude Passeron's, and Monique de Saint-Martin's *Academic Discourse: Linguistic Misunderstanding and Professional Power,* Pierre Bourdieu's *Homo Academicus* (Stanford, Calif.: Stanford University Press, 1994); and Michael Berube's and Cary Nelson's *Higher Education Under Fire* (New York: Routledge, 1995).

6. Johnson's celebrated exchange with Lord Chesterfield to whom he had earlier applied for support in 1747, provokes, for Brady and Wimsatt, "a trumpet call in the progressive emancipation of the English man of letters from the auspices of the aristocracy" (9). Oddly, the academy seems removed from its association with the aristocracy in this comment, even though Johnson castigates both institutions, and even more oddly, was happy to take a stipend from George III in later years.

7. For example, in his biography of Johnson, Walter Jackson Bate describes the

creation of such a dictionary as Johnson's attempt to "try to do for England, as an individual and in a fraction of the time, what the Academies had done for Italy, France, and most recently, Spain" (Walter Jackson Bate, *Samuel Johnson* [New York: Harcourt, Brace, Jovanovich, 1977], 241–42). Bate claims that such a attempt was a "tempting challenge for Johnson, who for fifteen years had found one door after another barred to him for lack of a degree. If [he] succeeded, it would permanently establish his reputation and change the course of his life." Implicit in this observation is Johnson's scorn of academies and yet his dependence on them for a necessary authority.

8. Given this theoretical position, one would expect a radical restructuring of historical analysis in Cohen's study, and indeed Cohen engages recent reevaluations of the ways in which theorists like Kuhn and Foucault have problematized the notions of "paradigm" and "episteme" in the interests of developing methodologies of discursive practices. His reexamination of modes of analysis does not account for the radical differences made by the ideological concerns of gender or race.

9. Murray Cohen, *Sensible Words: Linguistic Practice in England 1640–1785* (Baltimore: Johns Hopkins University Press, 1977), xi–xiii.

10. Donna K. Haraway, *Simians, Cyborgs, and Women: The Reinvention of Nature* (New York: Routledge, 1991), 127–29.

11. DeMaria, *Johnson's Dictionary*, 7.

12. Raymond Williams, *Marxism and Literature* (Oxford: Oxford University Press, 1977), 80.

13. To discuss "selfhood" in an ideological context invariably invites psychoanalytic inquiry. What sorts of mystifications are implied in the production of subjectivity? For most critics, the notion of individual relies on mystification and reification; that is, one may accurately conceive the coherence of a self in terms of the fantasy of its coherence. Johnson's "self," articulated through public academic discourses (lexicography) and the private conditions of his life, is one that is invented and mystified in order to negotiate between these spheres.

14. See Linda Colley, *Britons: Forging the Nation, 1707–1837* (New Haven, Conn.: Yale University Press, 1992), 12–14, 373.

15. *Johnson's Dictionary: A Modern Selection*, ed. E. L. McAdam and George Milne (New York: Random House, 1963), 285.

16. Johnson's troubled association with the aristocracy is more pointedly defined in the *Life of Savage*, where he represents upper class indulgence in the same carnivalesque excess conventionally represented by the lower class. In the *Life of Savage*, the conjunction of aristocratic corruption and sexual corruption, embodied by the reviled and yet powerful position of the Countess of Macclesfield, is sharply drawn.

17. This may be related to the problematic status of British identity that Johnson writes in his poem *London* (1738), in which the "purity" of British nationalism is always in question because of the questionable status of Scotland and Wales. "Englishness" is a product of a constant vigilance and patrolling of the borders of language, as Johnson's lexicographical labor exemplifies.

18. Jacques Derrida, *Limited Inc* (Evanston, Ill.: Northwestern University Press, 1988), 5.

19. Raymond Williams, *Marxism and Literature* (Oxford: Oxford University Press, 1977), 44.

20. Homi K. Bhabha, "Signs Taken for Wonders: Questions of Ambivalence and Authority Under a Tree Outside Delhi, May 1817," in *"Race," Writing and Difference*, ed. Henry Louis Gates, Jr. (Chicago: University of Chicago Press, 1986), 163–84.

21. It is also interesting that Johnson specifies terms of "domestic" use that come from French. In *London* the figures that are most vilified are the foppish and francophilic young men who make a place for themselves in the home and heart of the unsuspecting Briton, and then stab him, suggesting that the domestic space is ironically the space most vulnerable and open to foreign appropriation.

22. The different uses of "fetishism," Marxist and Lacanian, may be articulated in this context. In marxist terms, fetishism is a material presence—the reification of social relations and products of labor—whereas in its lacanian use, the subject functions as a mask for the impossibility of its existence—fetishism is therefore about lack. Johnson's fetishism of a literary past can be read in both uses: he reifies a past literary and historical period as an idyllic moment of "real" linguistic coherence. According to Johnson himself, however,

> The language most likely to continue long without alteration would be that of a nation raised a little ... above barbarity, secluded from strangers ... either without books or, like some of the Mahometan countries, with very few. ... But no such constancy can be expected in a people polished by arts and classed by subordination, where one part of the community is sustained and accommodated by the labor of the other. Those who have much leisure to think will always be enlarging the stock of ideas, and every increase of knowledge, whether real or fancied, will produce new words or combinations of words. (294–95)

Here the accruement of language is represented as a continual process in which no specific moment characterizes its epitome. "Knowledge" operates (as Johnson points out) as both fact and fiction, as, in effect, both a reification and a lack. What's interesting here is how both uses of fetishism function in relation to nationalism and cultural imperialism. Johnson's fetishization of Englishness, manifested by the Elizabethan writers who represent, albeit problematically, "the wells of English undefiled," masks a fear of British nationalism (although almost perfunctorily posed against indiscriminate "Mahometan countries") as a necessary loosening of boundaries that have then to be continually regulated and policed.

23. In his "Signature Event Context," appearing in both *Limited Inc* and *Dissemination* (Chicago: University of Chicago Press, 1981), Derrida differentiates between the oral and the written as (traditionally) the difference between exhausting the presence of the subject that has emitted the (oral) communication and the written sign's capacity for extending beyond the presence of its inscription to a possible endless chain of iterability.

24. Defoe's earlier *Journal of the Plague Year* (1722) articulates similar anxieties when commercial ports function as places where wealth (in the form of imperial spoils) and disease (since the plague seems to be transported by mercantile ships) have equal accessibility to an English public.

25. Spivak's terminology here counteracts a fall into binarisms that most discussions of "othering" seem to produce because of the overdetermined relation of all three positions. The "self-consolidating" other, continually defined in relation to a

reification of a "fixed" self, consequently disrupts any stability that an "absolute" other may have. John Barrell's reformulation of Spivak's terms "dramatise[s] how what at first seems 'other' can be made over to the side of the self—to a subordinate position on that side—only so long as a new, and a newly absolute 'other' is constituted to fill the discursive space that has thus been evacuated." John Barrell, *The Infection of Thomas De Quincey: A Psychopathology of Imperialism* (New Haven, Conn.: Yale University Press, 1991), 10.

26. Bate, *Samuel Johnson*, 241–42.

27. Edward Said, *Orientalism* (New York: Random House, 1979), 20. Said argues for a Gramscian notion of cultural hegemony in the industrial West. I would agree that a place for Johnson's *Preface to the Dictionary* would be as a representation of those dominant ideas, institutions, and works achieved through cultural consent, but I also would argue that *any* reading of these texts is crucially connected to issues of gender in the process of interpreting cultural "meaning."

28. See Laura Brown's discussion of Belinda's dressing-table in *The Rape of the Lock* in *Alexander Pope* (London: Blackwell, 1985), 1–45.

29. Brown, 8. Also see John Barrell, *The Idea of Landscape and the Sense of Place, 1730–1840* (Cambridge: Cambridge University Press, 1972).

30. Another way of reading this is not simply as a native resistance to colonialist/imperial appropriation, which would, in some ways, presuppose the formulation of an intact, coherent "native" constructed out of Western fantasies about "other" cultures, but, more problematically and less easily recontained, as an instance of Homi K. Bhabha's subversive mimicry, with the danger that one *can't* readily identify the "native idiom."

31. DeMaria, *Johnson's Dictionary*, ix.

32. See Boswell, *Life of Johnson* (London: Oxford University Press, 1985); Walter Jackson Bate, *The Achievement of Samuel Johnson* (New York: Oxford University Press, 1961) and *Samuel Johnson*; DeMaria, "The Politics of Johnson's Dictionary," *PMLA* 104, 1 (January 1989): 64–74; Howard Weinbrot, *Britannia's Issue: The Rise of British Literature from Dryden to Ossian* (Cambridge: Cambridge University Press, 1995).

33. See Terry Eagleton, *The Function of Criticism: From the Spectator to Post-Structuralism* (London: Verso, 1984), Jürgen Habermas, *The Structural Transformation of the Public Sphere: An Inquiry into a Category of Bourgeois Society*, trans. Thomas Burger (Cambridge, Mass.: MIT Press, 1989); Michael Ketcham, *Transparent Design: Reading, Performance, and Form in the Spectator Papers* (Athens: University of Georgia Press, 1985); Jon Klancher, *The Making of English Reading Audiences, 1790–1832* (Madison: University of Wisconsin Press, 1987); and Neil Saccamano's review of Habermas's book, "The Consolations of Ambivalence," *MLN* 106, 3 (1991): 685–98, in which Saccamano argues that Habermas is engaged in the same sort of activity in creating a (reading) public sphere through the process of addressing it. These works specifically address the historical development of the bourgeoisie and its project for creating and refining a public discursive space allotted to the airing of middle class interests.

34. *London* is also complicated by the peculiar status of Juvenal's Third Satire in English neoclassical poetry. It is a poem already central to the canon of English poetry, one that every schoolboy would "translate" as a school exercise. The "imitation" (a loose and paraphrastic form of translation advocated by Denham and Cowley) is legit-

imized by eighteenth-century neoclassical practice. Denham writes, "If Virgil must needs speak English, it were fit he should speak not only as a Man of this Nation, but as a Man of this Age" (from the preface to *Destruction of Troy*, 1656). This is the tradition Johnson inherited, and in his *Life of Pope* he cites the imitation as a form of political satire. After Pope's enlistment of Horace as a classical moralist in order to articulate the Tory attack against Sir Robert Walpole, Johnson uses Juvenal's Third Satire as a way of ventriloquizing his scorn of the art of currying favor and his bitterness at unrecognized merit that again was part of the Tory position, although it differed from Pope's in the sense that Johnson was also personally invested. See John Butt and Geoffrey Carnall, *The Mid-Eighteenth Century*, Oxford History of English Literature (Oxford: Clarendon Press, 1979), 8–13.

35. If we understand the word "primer" to mean the kind of book children use to learn how to spell and read, as instructions on the "first principles of any subject," then the *Dictionary* announces, generally, the law of the father. It is a material body whose authority is announced only by "name."

36. With regard to "imported" politics, a phrase I lift from *London*, it seems important to underscore the crucial place antagonism occupies in the use of this term, which is invented in order to determine the position of the domestic. In Laclau and Mouffe's account of antagonism, its hegemonic capacities are deconstructed to show its force:

First of all, it is clear that an antagonism cannot be a *real* opposition. There is nothing antagonistic in a crash between two vehicles: it is a material fact obeying physical laws . . . .Real opposition is an *objective* relation—that is, determinable, definable—among things; contradiction is an equally definable relation among concepts; antagonism constitutes the limits of every objectivity, which is revealed as partial and precarious *objectification*. If language is a system of differences, antagonism is the failure of difference: in that sense, it situates itself within the limits of language and can only exist as the disruption of it—that is, a metaphor. . . . Antagonism escapes the possibility of being apprehended through language, since language only exists as an attempt to fix that which antagonism subverts. (Ernesto Laclau and Chantal Mouffe, *Hegemony and Socialist Strategy: Towards a Radical Democratic Politics*, trans. Winston Mome and Paul Commack [London: Verso, 1985], 123–25.)

Part of the anxiety of Johnson and his various speakers is precisely the impossibility to distinguish "disruption" as a real experience: hence, the insistent invention of such poetic discourse that figures, metaphorically, the problems of antagonism.

37. Henry Louis Gates, Jr., "Talkin' That Talk," in *"Race," Writing, and Difference*, 402. Said's *Orientalism* is also useful. He suggests that the "Orient" is a self-identical creation of European culture in order to establish and confirm ethnic and cultural difference (1–28). My own distinctions of "otherings" are more in line with Gayatri Spivak's terms of "self-consolidating other" and "absolute other," for the process of identity-making seems to involve a consolidation of the self, although the term "self-consolidating other" is even more slippery by its propensity to consolidate than what I will suggest to be the intermediary term (Gayatri Chakravorty Spivak, "Overdeterminations of Imperialism: David Ochterlong and the Ranee of Sirmoor," *Europe and Its Others*, vol. 1 [Colchester: University of Essex, 1985]). Also see Benedict Anderson,

Imagined Communities: Reflections on the Origin and Spread of Nationalism (London: Verso, 1983), 14–16.

38. Laclau and Mouffe, *Hegemony and Socialist Strategy*, 111.

39. Putative, of course, because the pastoral can only function when emptied of meaning; the idyllic is a place where, in the words of David Byrne, "nothing ever happens."

40. See Bate, *Samuel Johnson*, 172, and his note to that reference, and Boswell's *Life of Johnson*, 91. Bate appears puzzled by Johnson's invocation of the pastoral in this context, noting that "no writer has more effectively poured scorn on the whole concept of the 'pastoral' than has Johnson." My reading accounts for this apparent contradiction in which the pastoral functions not simply as a place for poetic contemplation but as another way in which "England" can establish and maintain a discrete identity through difference.

41. Terry Castle, *Masquerade and Civilization: The Carnivalesque in Eighteenth Century English Culture and Fiction* (Stanford, Calif.: Stanford University Press, 1986), 113. Castle also suggests in a footnote that Johnson's disapproval of the masquerade was not as much for moral reasons as for social ones, a distinction I find confusing because of the ways "morality" is fashioned in opposition to "social."

42. The regulation of the grotesque body by the bourgeoisie in order to clean and keep clean the public arena is an argument that Peter Stallybrass and Allon White propose in *The Politics and Poetics of Transgression* (Ithaca, N.Y.: Cornell University Press, 1986).

43. Stallybrass and White suggest that these contradictory impulses of representation create a strange relationship in which the *political* (bourgeois) imperative to get rid of the loathsome qualities of the "low" conflict "powerfully and unpredictably with a desire for this other" (5). In the context of *London*, Johnson's regulation of such conflicting desires is contained within an acceptable discursive space—that is, his "imitation"—and yet, as always with Johnson, the threat of breaking through this veil of illusion undermines his efforts at control.

44. It is impossible to escape the multifarious meanings that "shore" may have here. It is meant as a sewer, and yet the pun with shore as coast raises many interesting possibilities of territorial anxiety.

45. See Sigmund Freud, "Medusa's Head," in *Sexuality and the Psychology of Love* (New York: Macmillan, 1963), 212–13, for a discussion of apotropaia.

46. I am using, in part, the model of homosocial desire that Eve Kosofsky Sedgwick suggests as a way of triangulating the third figure of other, and as a "strategy for making generalizations about, and marking historical differences in, the structure of men's relations with other men" (*Between Men: English Literature and Male Homosocial Desire* [New York: Columbia University Press, 1985], 2).

47. Bate, *Achievement of Samuel Johnson*, 14.

48. Bate, *Achievement of Samuel Johnson*, 14. Clearly Bate doesn't feel the same need to apologize for Johnson's "propagation of falsehood" as Brady and Wimsatt do.

49. Toni O'Shaughnessy reads identity-making in terms of the relationship between Johnson and Savage in her illuminating essay "Fiction as Truth: Personal Identity in Johnson's *Life of Savage*," *Studies in English Literature* 30, 3 (Summer 1990): 487–501. She argues that Johnson's acceptance of Savage's claims to identity is a "con-

sciously partisan commitment, the informed nature of which is complicated but not belied by its apparently unproblematic presentation.... What Johnson must deal with is not merely that Richard Savage's identity is contested; the more fundamental problem is that in Savage's case, personal identity is shown to be radically and permanently contestable" (488). My reading of the relationship between Johnson and Savage focuses on Johnson's sense of identification *with* Savage—and consequent rewriting of his *own* identity—not his acceptance of a preconstructed identity. Also see Toni O'Shaughnessy Bowers, "Critical Complicities: Savage Mothers, Johnson's Mother, and the Containment of Maternal Difference," *AJ* 5 (1992): 115–46.

50. I must hasten to add that such a destiny may be manifest in numerous ways; that is, unlike pre-Enlightenment models of class, Johnson is particularly sensitive to the notion of middle-class virtue as a sustaining affect, one that presumably overrides the excesses practiced by either extreme.

51. As Stallybrass and White argue:

The primary site of contradiction, the site of conflicting desires and mutually incompatible representation, is undoubtedly the "low." Again and again we find a striking ambivalence to the representation of lower strata (of the body, of literature, of society, of place) in which they are both reviled and desired. Repugnance and fascination are the twin poles of the process in which a political imperative to reject and eliminate the debasing "low" conflicts powerfully and unpredictably with a desire for this other. (Stallybrass and White, *The Politics and Poetics of Transgression*, 4–5)

52. I refer to Lacan's formulations of the ways the articulation of the name of the father constitutes crucial ways of organizing (however fantastically) one's domestic and cultural space. It is this place, confused by the intervention of a differently gendered subjectivity, that Johnson the lexicographer seeks to proscribe and correct with his authorial account of the "true" origins of Richard Savage.

53. I want to mention here the sexual implications of such a "coupling." Savage's monomaniacal desire for his mother, projected, as it were, onto a more socialized need to be recognized as a son, obviously lends itself to other obsessional desires.

54. This text may represent, like Bates's biography, another attempt to locate subjectivity according to its time-honored parameters.

55. Clarence Tracy, *The Artificial Bastard* (Cambridge, Mass.: Harvard University Press, 1953), 17.

56. In a later chapter, I will discuss the ways in which motherhood is a "shield" completely penetrable by other ideological issues.

57. Johnson's relation to Francis Barber is interestingly argued by Gretchen Gerzina. Acknowledging the complexities of their long relationship, Gerzina suggests, a propos of Barber's stint on board a ship,

Yet, while Johnson freely admitted his "tenderness" and concern for Barber, he also indicated a kind of ownership. Barber was "given him" rather than hired by him, although it seems probable that Barber received some kind of financial remuneration. At the same time, his tone is exactly that of a father who wants the prodigal to return home. The prodigal may have returned, and he certainly served faithfully for the next twenty-five years, but years later Barber told Boswell that he did so "without any wish of his own." He was free for a time to choose his own employment and the path of his life, but the world acknowledged Johnson's de facto ownership over him. (Gretchen Holcomb Gerzina, *Black London: Life Before Emancipation* [New Brunswick, N.J.: Rutgers University Press, 1995], 46–47.)

58. The fact that "female" monstrosity—an atheist that talks you "dead"—gets transposed onto the effeminate bodies of men in *London* attests to the ways in which the monstrous feminine may well be too protean for comfort.

59. Stallybrass and White, *Politics and Poetics of Transgression*, 56.

60. See Homi K. Bhabha, *The Location of Culture* (New York: Routledge, 1994), 102–22.

61. Laclau and Mouffe, *Hegemony and Socialist Strategy*, 111.

62. On abjection see Julia Kristeva, *Powers of Horror: An Essay on Abjection* (New York: Columbia University Press, 1982); Kristeva, "Freud and Love: Treatment and Its Discontents" in *The Kristeva Reader*, ed. Toril Moi (New York: Columbia University Press, 1986), 240–71; and Neil Hertz's chapter "The End of the Line" in *The End of the Line: Essays on Psychoanalysis and the Sublime* (New York: Columbia University Press, 1985).

63. Julia Kristeva, "Freud and Love: Treatment and Its Discontents," in *The Kristeva Reader*, 240.

64. It is curious that Johnson was also with a wet-nurse from whom he allegedly contracted scrofula, the "king's evil," and on whom was blamed series of things, including his bodily deformity that was ostensibly responsible for his literary obscurity. See Bate, *Samuel Johnson*, 6–7, 14–17. The ingestion of maternal milk and what that ingestion signifies is a thematic concern not only for De Quincey, but for Wollstonecraft and Mary Shelley as well. This putatively pure maternal impulse becomes deeply anxious for the formation of national identity; in later chapters I will explore how this impulse is articulated.

65. Stallybrass and White, *Politics and Poetics of Transgression*, 159. See their chapter on "The Maid and the Family Romance" for a detailed discussion of nurse as social hybrid.

66. Thomas De Quincey, *Confessions of an English Opium Eater, 1856 Revision*, ed. Alethea Hayter (London: Penguin, 1971), 188.

Chapter 2. DeQuincey and the Topography of Romantic Desire

1. Bate's descriptions of Johnson's relations to his mother, Hannah Grey, Hester Thrale, and the other female occupants of his extensive social circle suggest that they attempted to regulate his domestic life. Bate describes their interest in Johnson's daily life as a form of meddling. Perhaps, however, it might make sense to read his often vexed relations with women as reflections of his psychic problems with depression (among other things) and sexuality that may have been exacerbated—if not instigated—by an infecting maternal body. See Bate, *The Achievement of Samuel Johnson* (New York: Oxford University Press, 1961) and his biography *Samuel Johnson* (New York: Harcourt Brace, 1977). Also see Boswell's treatment of Johnson's melancholia in

The Life of Samuel Johnson (1791; London: Oxford University Press, 1965).

2. Bate describes quite poignantly the stultifying depression from which Johnson suffered. The ways Johnson coped with such a disease may exemplify his ultimate belief in an eighteenth-century disciplinary system that, for him, was the only way to maintain or forbear the disintegrating possibilities of psychic pain.

3. This phrase remains constant in both the 1805 text and the 1850 revision.

4. The most compelling account of De Quincey's fraught relations with the first circle of Lake District poets, especially Coleridge, is Nigel Leask's chapter on De Quincey in his study on Romantic writers. Leask, *British Romantic Writers and the East: Anxieties of Empire* (Cambridge: Cambridge University Press, 1992), 170–228.

5. Barrell and Leask have certainly had their influence on the proliferation of critical work on De Quincey's previously neglected corpus.

6. Thomas De Quincey, *Confessions of an English Opium Eater*, ed. Alethea Hayter (New York: Penguin, 1971), 108–9. All subsequent quotations from the 1822 *Confessions* will be made from this edition unless otherwise indicated, and will be noted in parentheses.

7. Donna J. Haraway, *Primate Visions: Gender, Race, and Nature in the World of Modern Science* (New York: Routledge, 1989), 115.

8. Interestingly, Crusoe's architectural household may also be read as a cultural hybrid: he fabricates a space that resembles an English domestic stronghold almost entirely out of indigenous materials. The cats' miscegenation, however, is something out of Crusoe's control and therefore dangerous.

9. Julian North records the mixed criticism De Quincey's *Confessions* received when it first was published. Hailed as a celebrated example of the "egotism [that] is the spirit of the age" and condemned for being "something excessively disgusting in being obliged to look into any man's private life," De Quincey's autobiographical project challenged concepts of serious writing. Because of the sheer range of his critical reception, he stands in sharp contrast to Wordsworth, whose writing was much more uniformly acclaimed; thus De Quincey's constant anxiety about his status as an intellectual and writer, and thus his importance to the discursive structures of romanticism. See North, *De Quincey Reviewed: Thomas De Quincey's Critical Reception, 1821–1994* (Columbia, S.C.: Camden House, 1997).

10. Michel Foucault, *The Order of Things: An Archaeology of the Human Sciences* (New York: Random House, 1973), 132.

11. One should also note that "framing" doesn't simply resituate the constitutive subject within specific boundaries of meaning but also works as an architectural metaphor. That is, a frame also signifies the structural apparatus onto which are hung or built various fabrics of meaning. Thus the discovery of dinosaur bones and the consequent motive to formulate skeletons (which are really the only convincing "material" evidence of the existence of such species) also articulate the impulse to derive histories of meaning (that are, grandiosely enough, figured as "prehistory") that may serve to situate, contextualize, and eventually mythologize the place of human history. I would argue that tigers have functioned in a similar way in late eighteenth- and early nineteenth-century England, in that they function as extra-British, extra-Christian, but nevertheless quite material cultural monsters whose most crucial act may be to situate,

contextualize, and mythologize the place of Christian history in the face of otherness. Hence, Blake's question: "Did He who made the lamb make thee?"

12. John Barrell, *The Infection of Thomas De Quincey: A Psychopathology of Imperialism* (New Haven, Conn.: Yale University Press, 1991), 50.

13. In fact, it is difficult not to be reminded of Johnson's ties with nursery-milk in this context. As I pointed out in the previous chapter, Bate champions the rumor that Johnson's wet-nurse was to blame for his scrofula; this articulates the kind of vulnerability of the nursery and unreliability of the maternal body. Equally at issue may be the food to which infants graduate once they are weaned from their mothers' bodies: like maternal milk, nursery food can be dangerous because it doesn't resemble anything recognizable *as* food and could therefore harbor potentially dangerous and contaminating agents. Without continual regulation, debilitating disease disfigures the products of national subjectivity, and children themselves are prey to monstrosity.

14. *See Freud, Civilization and Its Discontents,* trans. James Strachey (New York: Norton, 1961).

15. See Barbara Johnson, "My Monster/My Self," *Diacritics* 12, no. 2 (Summer 1982): 2–10.

16. Barrell, The Infection of Thomas De Quincey, 50.

17. For a more detailed argument about the history of tigers in De Quincey's unconscious, see Barrell, 47–66. Barrell also argues that De Quincey would have almost certainly seen the 1808 exhibit of Tipu's tiger (based on a letter dated July 1, 1813).

18. Leask points out that "De Quincey admits that he 'paid a heavy price in distant years' for his midnight cruising and that his wife Margaret became 'infected with the spectacle of my dread contest with phantoms and shadowy enemies.' . . . [H]is pun on the 'antimercurial' quality of opium in *Confessions*, p. 72 suggests an allusion to its contemporary indication either as a counter to the iatrogenic illness caused by a regime of mercury pills, the principal cure for 'lues venera,' or as a cure for venereal disease itself." Leask, *British Romantic Writers,* 189.

19. Donna J. Haraway, Simians, Cyborgs, and Women: The Reinvention of Nature (New York: Routledge, 1991), 2.

20. Although, as Leask has suggested, the putative subject of his original *Confessions* is opium, only in the later 1856 revisions does the narrative become more unmistakably autobiographical. Nevertheless, the 1823 text displays enough self-representation to be considered an autobiographical text.

21. As Laplanche and Pontalis define, "In psychoanalysis the bounds of the body provide the model of all separations between an inside and an outside. Incorporation involves this bodily frontier literally. Introjection has a broader meaning in that it is no longer a matter only of the interior of the body but also that of the psychical apparatus, of a psychical agency, etc." (J. Laplanche and J.-B. Pontalis, *The Language of Psycho-Analysis* [New York: W.W. Norton, 1973], 229–30). I would like to point out that the *fantasy* of introjection is what is crucial to its operation. That is, the romantic (and contemporary) belief in the existence of an internal kernel unshaped by external machinery is what sustains the production of the phenomenon of the unconscious. I argue that such a belief is utterly contingent on the ideological apparatus.

22. North, *De Quincey Reviewed*, 11–19.

23. Also see the really fine study of De Quincey's writing and the "genealogy of the modern self" (as she terms it) by Alina Clej, and the equally persuasive and provocative work by Josephine McDonagh for alternative readings of De Quincey's confessional writing. Alina Clej, *A Genealogy of the Modern Self: Thomas De Quincey and the Intoxication of Writing* (Stanford, Calif.: Stanford University Press, 1995); Josephine McDonagh, De Quincey's Disciplines (Oxford: Clarendon Press, 1994).

24. Slavoj Žižek, *The Sublime Object of Ideology* (London: Verso, 1989), 18.

25. Leask argues that De Quincey "*rewrites* the *Biographia* in a pathological rather than a normative moral/aesthetic register, showing Genius, Imagination, Will and Principle to be conditioned by the complex nervous organization of civilization and all its discontents, in particular, the conditioning of what I call the 'preternatural stimulants' of opium on the body" (*British Romantic Writers*, 186). His persuasive and illuminating chapter unfolds the various ways in which De Quincey's material consumption of opium reflect the politics of imperialism.

26. Charles J. Rzepka, *Sacramental Commodities: Gift, Text, and the Sublime in De Quincey* (Amherst: University of Massachusetts Press, 1995), 167. See the chapter "Home at Grasmere" for more on the status of De Quincey's relationship to the Wordsworths.

27. See Mary Jacobus's treatment of gender and the De Quincey/Wordsworth relationship in *Romanticism, Writing, and Sexual Difference: Essays on the Prelude* (Oxford: Clarendon Press, 1989).

28. Rzepka, *Sacramental Commodities*, 169.

29. In a twist to Harold Bloom's anxiety of influence, De Quincey functions as the less strong writer who adopts a father instead of seeking to displace him.

30. I would also point out that De Quincey's father's inadequacies are sexual; the long-dead body of the "real" father is replaced by the fantasy father whose sexual potency is materialized in his child, though even this potency has to be domesticated for De Quincey. Kate Wordsworth is, after all, dead and poses no threat to De Quincey's sibling rivalry.

31. For a detailed biographical account of De Quincey's intellectual relationship to Wordsworth, see John E. Jordan, *De Quincey to Wordsworth: A Biography of a Relationship* (Berkeley: University of California Press, 1962).

32. Later in the narrative, De Quincey's so-called mastery of Greek comes into question when the Malay visits him in his Lake District cottage. During this exchange, De Quincey can only quote lines from the *Iliad* to the bemused Malay. Not even adequate to harangue an Athenian mob, De Quincey's mastery of any kind of language remains illusory and fantastic, and yet also speaks volumes about the paternal impotence of his teachers.

33. De Quincey magnanimously excepts Coleridge from the unhappy list of pretenders to the title "philosopher" that "England can . . . show" (*Preliminary Confessions*, 33), but it is clear that he has issues of rivalry with Coleridge which he takes up in "Coleridge and Opium Eating," after having been accused by Coleridge that he continued his use of opium for its pleasure-giving effects.

34. The mother's language performs a Derridean supplementary function; in its accessorizing operation—the disposable item that also happens to be, in the rhetoric of

fashion, "indispensable"—his mother's tongue furnishes the stabilizing fantasy on which he can rest his talent for writing and scholarship.

35. Barrell reads the surprise appearance of the uncle—interrupting the anticipated pleasure of seeing his eldest sister Mary—as one that is at once "an intruder and a barrier . . . ambiguously, or equally, between Thomas and his sister, and between Thomas [the uncle] and his mother." Barrell then discusses the ways De Quincey projects his guilty, perhaps sexual, fantasies about his relation to Mary onto the supposed guilt of a sexual liaison between his uncle and mother (themselves brother and sister): "The narrative seems to work just as well if the tiger is the bringer of death or the bringer of love, dividing Thomas from his sister, or alienating the affections of his mother; it seems to condense the stories of the death of Elizabeth and the sexual pollution attached to that death, while still permitting them to be seen as different stories that may involve different female victims, the different sisters of different brothers" (*The Infection of Thomas De Quincey*, 57). While it seems certain that De Quincey's later explication of the circumstances in which he finds himself a peripatetic in Wales is overdetermined—informed by the various levels of guilty family liaisons—also crucially operative here is the way in which he constructs his domestic relations as already foreign, already othered, already open to strange infection.

36. Leask, *British Romantic Writers*, 172–73. On the reception of De Quincey's Confessions as an intervention into the debates surrounding the uses of opium, Leask writes: "From the beginning, however, there was uncertainty about the work's moral tendencies, perhaps understandable when one looks at the 'reader's response' to the *Confessions*, which make the tears shed over Richardson's *Clarissa* or Rousseau's *La Nouvelle Héloïse* seem rather tame by comparison" (173). The suspicion (medical, scientific, literary) that always accompanied even enthusiastic responses to De Quincey's oeuvre suggests that although "settled comfortably" within a sanctioned genre, De Quincey would, consciously or not, demonstrate the abysmal strangeness of that space.

37. De Quincey's bondage to confession, expressed here in the phrase "bound to confess," is resonant with a moment from Descartes, in which Descartes's theory of cogito seems equally overdetermined by issues of boundaries and bondage or of bondage to boundaries. Descartes writes: "At the same time we must at least confess that the things which are represented to us in sleep are like painted representations which can only have been formed as the counterparts to something real and true" (Descartes, selections from "Meditations on First Philosophy," in *From Modernism to Postmodernism*, ed. Lawrence Cahoone [New York: Blackwell, 1996], 31). Elsewhere (in the Introduction) I have problematized the issue of "at least"; here, I am more interested in the word "confess." Such a choice (in both French and the English translation) suggests that it is upon confession—that most notoriously unreliable and mendacious of accounts—that the entire Enlightenment notion of cogito ergo sum (the Cartesian subject) rests. Similarly, De Quincey employs this contestable venue to venture forth a scientific (and therefore "truthful") account of addiction.

38. Haraway, *Simians, Cyborgs, and Women*, 7.

39. Here one must remember that such an institution was only emerging in its

capacity to produce "objective" discourse. It seems that such discursive practices were much more overtly politically informed than their contemporary counterparts.

40. See Appendix A and B to the *Confessions*, 117–215.

41. Perhaps a different way of putting this would be to suggest that the biological effects of fathering are far inferior to the authorial ones. De Quincey performs the role of biological father, but this is less powerful than being acknowledged as an authorial father.

42. I would like to point out that De Quincey is capitalizing on a history of showcasing the feminine in order to establish a masculinized power. Here Kate Wordsworth, while lamented as a dearly loved child, may be singled out and displayed as the monstrous block to De Quincey's filial association to Wordsworth, not unlike the ways in which exotic monsters—dinosaurs, for example—are contained within museums in order to recontain their monstrosity and define the parameters of imperial power.

43. Jacques Lacan, "Subversion of the Subject and Dialectic of Desire," in *Écrits: A Selection*, trans. Alan Sheridan (New York: W.W. Norton, 1977), 292.

44. See Mark Bracher, "Lacan's Theory of the Four Discourses," *Prose Studies* 11, no. 3: 32–49, for an illuminating reading of these ideas from Lacan's 17th Seminar. In fact, one can extend this reading to think through the overdetermination of Wordsworth's and Coleridge's *Lyrical Ballads*. Published in 1798, it was—and perhaps more crucially still is—hailed as the revolutionary text that forever changed the course of poetics. This fantasy continues to be sustained in academic institutions precisely because we have invented Wordsworth as the master romanticist, and sustain such mastery through our own supplements to *Lyrical Ballads*' serious lacks.

45. Lacan, *Écrits*, 299.

46. Alethea Hayter in fact suggests in her Introduction to the edition that this scene is a poetic "working-out of this complex of feeling," viz. the insult De Quincey felt leveled at his wife by the Wordsworths. Margaret Simpson's image then "coalesced with those other betrayed and suffering girls who already haunted [De Quincey's] imagination" (13).

47. See Bracher, "Lacan's Theory," 43–45.

48. The Wordsworth reference is to *The Power of Music*. It seems that Wordsworth's "obligation" in the context of De Quincey's *Confessions* is to provide the empty signifier of romantic discourse. As a master, Wordsworth cannot know what counts as "true" poetics; it is left to the not-masters to sustain the apparatus of romanticism by a process of negation. Romanticism is, then, utterly formulated through xenophobia, a fear of what is not romantic: addiction.

49. De Quincey's apostrophe is resonant with Johnson's representation in the *Life of Savage* of Lady Macclesfield, who according to his account feeds upon the abjected body of Richard Savage in order to sustain her title and her place. The stability of Oxford-street, both as a topographical site and as a romantic one may, according to De Quincey, depend on just such cannibalistic consumption.

50. Ann stands as the most fully described prostitute in a pantheon of streetwalkers with whom De Quincey visited.

51. Leask links this loss with De Quincey's failure to obtain credit, which in turn is metonymically linked to his own "fears of being submerged in an ocean of undifferentiated humanity" (*British Romantic Writers*, 195). I wonder, however, whether the overdetermined circumstances of these failures and loss are also deliberately invoked in order to justify De Quincey's inevitable link to the maternal body: without monetary agency, without a transcendental authorial status, unable even to lay claim to Ann because she belongs to another patronymic.

52. Robert Markley argues compellingly about the anxieties over reforestation in seventeenth- and eighteenth-century England. He writes a propos of Arthur Standish's *The Commons Complaint*:

Standish clearly understands the economic consequences of ecological stress. The scarcity of timber sets of a chain reaction of consequences, hindering building and repair work and forcing the use of other resources—dung for fuel, for example—which depresses agricultural productivity. His formulation, "no wood, no Kingdome,"—is not a simplistic lament for vanishing forests, but an acute analysis—borne out by rising prices—of timber shortages that, he argues, can be remedied only by encouraging landowners to undertake an aggressive program of reforestation. ("'Gulfes, Deserts, Precipices, Stone': Marvell's 'Upon Appleton House' and the Contradiction of 'Nature,'" in *The Country and the City Revisited: England and the Politics of Culture, 1550–1850*, ed. Gerald Maclean, Donna Landry, and Joseph P. Ward [Cambridge: Cambridge University Press, 1999], 91)

53. For example, Alexander Pope's 1713 celebration of the Treaty of Utrecht, *Windsor-Forest*, specifically championed oak as the sign of British naval power might that was associated with national peace and prosperity. Pope writes:

Thou too, great Father of the British Floods!
With joyful Pride survey'st our lofty Woods,
Where tow'ring Oaks their growing Honours rear,
And future Navies on thy Shores appear.   (*Windsor-Forest*, ll. 219–22)

54. I realize that the appellation "romanticism" is one that has been awarded posthumously, and I don't mean to suggest that Wordsworth, his sister, and Coleridge actively conspired to keep their circle exclusive—although there may well be convincing evidence to support this idea. Rather, the idea that their poetic projects—particularly for Wordsworth—seemed destined to make a mark implies a certain self-consciousness of a radical poetic destiny.

55. Rzepka accounts for De Quincey's ambivalence toward the Lake District circle as a reenactment of his early adolescent attempts to enter the adult world. See *Sacramental Commodities*, 107–8.

Chapter 3. Mothered Identities

1. Anne McClintock, Jenny Sharpe, and Sara Suleri in particular have complicated later nineteenth-century models of othering and the discipline of postcolonial stud-

ies itself. Suleri reminds us that "a simple correlation of gender with colonizer and colonized can lead only to interpretive intransigence of a different order, through which an attempt to recognize marginality leads to an opposite replication of the uncrossable distance between margin and center" (Suleri, *The Rhetoric of English India* [Chicago: University of Chicago Press, 1992], 15). My departure from their arguments is only in the service of addressing romanticism specifically, especially in relation to the production of a xenophobic discourse of national identity. Interestingly, contemporary studies in romanticism may have been guilty of too careless an impulse to collect marginalized subjectivities under the monolithic rubric of "other." See McClintock, *Imperial Leather: Race, Gender, and Sexuality in the Colonial Contest* (New York: Routledge, 1995); Sharpe, *Allegories of Empire: The Figure of the Woman in the Colonial Text* (Minneapolis: University of Minnesota Press, 1993).

2. See Cora Kaplan's chapter, "Pandora's Box" in *Sea Changes: Culture and Feminism* (London: Verso, 1986), 147–76 for a detailed account of Wollstonecraft's relation to Rousseau and for a provocative critique of *A Vindication of the Rights of Woman*. For a fascinating reading on Wollstonecraft's relationship to conventional eighteenth-century Republican ideology, see Virginia Sapiro, *A Vindication of Political Virtue: The Political Theory of Mary Wollstonecraft* (Chicago: University of Chicago Press, 1992).

3. Jacques Derrida, *Of Grammatology*, trans. Gayatri Spivak (Baltimore: Johns Hopkins University Press, 1974): 144–45.

4. Margaret Homans, *Bearing the Word: Language and Female Experience in Nineteenth-Century Women's Writing* (Chicago: University of Chicago Press, 1989), 153.

5. Linda Colley, *Britons: Forging the Nation, 1707–1837* (New Haven, Conn.: Yale University Press, 1992), 238–50.

6. Landry notes Richard Polwhele's poem *The Unsex'd Females* as a crucial example of the ways Wollstonecraft's status as a pro-revolutionary, feminist, democratic writer is in part an invention of various men threatened by the possible enfranchisement of British women. Landry writes: "Wollstonecraft looms as a sinister spectre of radicalism within the text, a woman whose writing serves as a rallying cry for impressionable females shamed by her raillery into imitating her dangerous militancy. Polwhele hyperbolically turns Wollstonecraft's plea for women's rights into female tyranny, a sexual world turned upside down." Landry, *The Muses of Resistance: Laboring-Class Women's Poetry in Britain, 1739–1796* (Cambridge: Cambridge University Press, 1990), 254.

7. Landry, *Muses of Resistance*, 254.

8. Judith Butler, *Gender Trouble: Feminism and the Subversion of Identity* (New York: Routledge, 1990), 142.

9. Benedict Anderson argues that the concept "nation" implies several things. First, it is *imagined* because each member of a nation "lives [in] the image of their communion" (nationalism invents nation), the imagined nation has clearly defined borders ("no nation imagines itself coterminous with mankind"), the nation is imagined as "sovereign" because "the concept was born in an age when Enlightenment and Revolution were destroying the legitimacy of divinely-ordained, hierarchical dynastic realm," and finally the nation is perceived as a *community* because "regardless of the actual inequality and exploitation that may prevail in each, the nation is always conceived as a deep, horizontal comradeship" (15–16). Benedict Anderson, *Imagined Com-*

munities: *Reflections on the Origin and Spread of Nationalism* (London: Verso, 1983), 15–16.

10. Butler, *Gender Trouble*, 142.

11. Gayatri Spivak, "Three Women's Texts and a Critique of Imperialism," in *"Race," Writing and Difference*, ed. Henry Louis Gates, Jr. (Chicago: University of Chicago Press, 1986), 262.

12. See Marilyn Butler, *Romantics, Rebels, and Reactionaries: English Literature and Its Background, 1760–1830* (New York: Oxford University Press, 1981); Moira Ferguson, *Colonialism and Gender Relations from Mary Wollstonecraft to Jamaica Kincaid* (New York: Columbia University Press, 1994) and "Mary Wollstonecraft and the Problematic of Slavery," in *Mary Wollstonecraft and 200 Years of Feminism*, ed. Eileen Jones Yeo (London: Rivers Oram, 1997), 89–103; Mary Jacobus, "The Difference of View," in *Women Writing and Writing About Women* (New York: Barnes and Noble, 1979), 10–21 and *Reading Woman: Essays in Feminist Criticism* (New York: Columbia University Press, 1986); Landry, *Muses of Resistance*; Mary Poovey, *The Proper Lady and the Woman Writer: Ideology as Style in the Works of Mary Wollstonecraft, Mary Shelley, and Jane Austen* (Chicago: University of Chicago Press, 1985).

13. Even if the French Revolution dramatized for women on both sides of the Channel the potential for other radical departures from established roles, Landry has pointed out that the very notion of "revolutionary women" in Britain is a contradiction in terms.

14. Colley, *Britons*, 240.

15. Colley, *Britons*, 241.

16. Colley, *Britons*, 240.

17. Gretchen Holcomb Gerzina, *Black London: Life Before Emancipation* (New Brunswick, N.J.: Rutgers University Press, 1995), 4–7.

18. Mary Wollstonecraft, *A Vindication of the Rights of Woman* (1792; New York: Norton, 1988), 8–29. Subsequent material quoted from this text will be made from this edition and will be noted in parentheses. Landry discusses the "Turkish prejudice" in Wollstonecraft, Hannah More, and Ann Yearsley as a "traditional figure of otherness within British culture." Using Gayatri Spivak's formulations of different forms of otherness, she persuasively argues that in the case of Hannah More references to Eastern alterity performed the necessary task of consolidating "her audience's sense of cultural identity" precisely because it capitalized upon a collective cultural imaginary about the "Orient." I am arguing, however, that Wollstonecraft's undifferentiated use of orientalist imagery, like More's, capitalizes on conventional figures of otherness in order to invoke a xenophobic exercise that would retain a dominant notion of national identity.

19. From unpublished manuscript (Charlotte Sussman) in author's possession.

20. See Poovey, *Proper Lady*, 48–81.

21. See Mary Jacobus, *Romanticism, Writing, and Difference: Essays on* The Prelude (New York: Oxford University Press, 1989), for a fuller account of Wollstonecraft's relation to Rousseau.

22. Colley, *Britons*, 274.

23. Julia Kristeva, "Revolution in Poetic Language," in *The Kristeva Reader*, ed. Toril Moi (New York: Columbia University Press, 1986), 101.

24. Anna Wilson, "Mary Wollstonecraft and the Search for the Radical Woman," *Genders* 6 (1989): 91.

25. See Janet Todd's "Introduction" to her collection of Mary Wollstonecraft's *Mary, Maria, or the Wrongs of Woman*, and Mary Shelley's *Matilda, Maria/Mary Wollstonecraft; Matilda/Mary Shelley* (London: Penguin, 1992), x–xiii. All references to *Mary* and *Maria* will be made from this text and will be noted in parentheses.

26. Colley, *Britons*, 240.

27. Colley, *Britons*, 31–33. Colley argues that "one of the most powerful transmitters of the idea of Britain as Israel" can be located in Handel's oratorios. She points out that Handel deliberately inserted comparisons between moments of British history and the exploits of the prophets and heroes in the Old Testament in order to establish the moral that Israel's violent and uncertain past could be recovered by the Protestant Hanoverian dynasty:

It was because he celebrated Britain in this glowing fashion that Handel became such a national institution. As the eighteenth century progressed, his oratorios were performed at Westminster Abbey, at cathedral concerts like the annual Three Choirs Festival at Worcester, Gloucester and Hereford, in northern dissenting chapels, in Welsh assembly rooms and in Scottish cities and towns eager to advertise their fashionability . . . the men and women . . . listening so intently were indeed engaged in an act of faith. Only what many of them were worshipping was Great Britain, and indirectly themselves. (33)

28. One needs to keep in mind the ways middle-class feminine identity was problematized by the convention of wet-nursing, especially vis-à-vis the new political identification of a vocation of motherhood for women. Nevertheless, I would still maintain that ideologies of class and race were often called up as justifications for such anxious solicitude.

29. Here the various dramas representing Tipu and his demise popular during the 1790s would certainly be informing Wollstonecraft's use of the popular metaphor of ferocity.

30. Kaplan, *Sea Changes*, 159.

31. Homi K. Bhabha, "Signs Taken for Wonders: Questions of Ambivalence and Authority Under a Tree Outside New Delhi, May 1817," in *"Race," Writing, and Difference*, ed. Gates, 173.

Chapter 4. Fair Exotics

1. Mary Wollstonecraft, *A Vindication of the Rights of Woman*, ed. Carol H. Poston (New York: Norton, 1988), 7.

2. Mary Shelley, *Frankenstein*, ed. M. K. Joseph (New York: Oxford University Press, 1983), 33. All material quoted from *Frankenstein* and the author's introduction,

unless otherwise indicated, will be made from this edition and will be noted in parentheses. My reasons for using the 1831 edition are to examine the Introduction Shelley writes vis-à-vis the novel. I am also interested in some of the editorial changes Shelley makes from the 1818 to the 1831 edition concerning Rousseau and the status of natural philosophy.

3. For an in-depth discussion of the Shelleys' writing habits, see Anne K. Mellor, *Mary Shelley: Her Life, Her Fiction, Her Monsters* (New York: Routledge, 1988). Also see James B. Carson, "Bringing the Author Forward: *Frankenstein* Through Mary Shelley's Letters," *Criticism* 30, 4 (Fall 1988): 431–53, Percy Bysshe Shelley, "On Frankenstein," in *The Works of Percy Bysshe Shelley in Verse and Prose*, 8 vols., ed. Harry Buxton Forman (London: Reeves and Turner, 1880), 7: 11–14. On feminist appropriations of *Frankenstein* see Ellen Cronan Rose, "Custody Battles: Reproducing Knowledge About *Frankenstein*," *New Literary History* 26, 4 (Autumn 1995): 809–32.

4. See Barbara Johnson, "My Monster/My Self," *Diacritics* 12, 2 (Summer 1982): 2–10, and Marc A. Rubenstein, "'My Accursed Origin': The Search for the Mother in *Frankenstein*," *Studies in Romanticism* 15 (Spring 1976): 165–94. Also see David Collings, "The Monster and the Imaginary Mother: A Lacanian Reading of *Frankenstein*" in *Case Studies in Contemporary Criticism: Frankenstein*, ed. Johanna M. Smith (Boston: Bedford, 1992), 245–58; Elissa Marder, "The Mother Tongue in *Phèdre* and *Frankenstein*," *YFS* 76 (1989): 59–77; Veronica Hollinger, "Putting on the Feminine: Gender and Negativity in *Frankenstein* and *The Handmaid's Tale*," in *Negation, Critical Theory, and Postmodern Textuality*, ed. Daniel Fischlin (Dordrecht: Kluwer, 1994), 203–24; and Bette London, "Mary Shelley, *Frankenstein*, and the Spectacle of Masculinity," *PMLA* 108, 2 (March 1993): 253–67.

5. Johnson, "My Monster/My Self." Johnson is referring primarily to autobiographical works by women—in this article she examines Nancy Friday's *My Mother/Myself* and Dorothy Dinnerstein's *The Mermaid and the Minotaur*—but in fact her remarks on the autobiographical genre extend to self-representations by men. Particularly in the case of De Quincey's *Confessions*, in which he codifies the mother only as the bringer of language and describes his stepchild relation to Oxford-street's opiated ministrations, Johnson's argument opens up another crucial place for gender.

6. Gayatri Spivak, "Three Women's Texts and a Critique of Imperialism," in *"Race," Writing, and Difference*, ed. Henry Louis Gates, Jr. (Chicago: University of Chicago Press, 1986), 244. Spivak's article is one of the first to address the ways feminist narratives (or narratives recovered solely in the service of an undifferentiated feminist inquiry) are embedded with other dominant ideological discourses—in this case imperialism. My departure from this argument is not to quarrel with the imperialist axioms she so persuasively uncovers but, rather, to disclose xenophobia as the language bearing such axioms. Also see Jeffrey Cass, "The Contestatory Gothic in Mary Shelley's *Frankenstein* and J. W. Polidori's *Ernestus Berchtold*: The Spectre of a Colonialist Paradigm," *JAISA* 1, 2 (Spring 1996): 33–41; Joseph W. Lew, "The Deceptive Other: Mary Shelley's Critique of Orientalism in *Frankenstein*," *Studies in Romanticism* 30, 2 (Summer 1991): 255–83; H. L. Malchow, *Gothic Images of Race in Nineteenth-Century Britain* (Stanford, Calif.: Stanford University Press, 1996).

7. See Johnson, "My Monster/My Self." I am also thinking of Margaret Homans's

framing of the horror of maternity. She suggests that the monster's creation "depends on and then perpetuates the death of the mother and motherhood" and that the monster's murder of Elizabeth is "only the logical extension of its existence as the reification of Frankenstein's desire to escape the mother." Homans, *Bearing the Word: Language and Female Experience in Nineteenth-Century Female Writing* (Chicago: University of Chicago, 1986), 103. In the same vein, Adam's rebellion parallels the rebellion of Satan that Percy Shelley canonizes in *Prometheus Unbound* and Mary Shelley allegorizes in *Frankenstein*.

8. Gayatri Spivak notes that, along with the monster's perusal of *Paradise Lost*, he reads Plutarch's *Lives*, a text he compares with "the patriarchal lives of [his] protectors" (*Frankenstein*, 123–24), and that his "*education* comes through Volney's *Ruins of the Empire* . . . an attempt at an enlightened universal secular, rather than a Eurocentric Christian, history, written from the perspective of a narrator 'from below,' somewhat like the attempts of Eric Wolf or Peter Wolseley in our own time."

9. Sandra Gilbert and Susan Gubar, *The Madwoman in the Attic: The Woman Writer and the Nineteenth Century Literary Imagination* (New Haven, Conn.: Yale University Press, 1979), 223.

10. Although the inscription appears in the 1831 edition and may arguably have had a limited audience in terms of the acknowledgment of paternal influence, for posterity (to which Shelley would have been sensitive, given her discourse on posterity in her Introduction to the 1831 edition) it has had a larger public and political function. On matters related to Mary Wollstonecraft's and William Godwin's work specifically in relation to Mary Shelley, see Marilyn May, "Publish and Perish: William Godwin, Mary Shelley, and the Public Appetite for Scandal," *Papers on Language and Literature* 26, 4 (Fall 1990): 489–512.

11. I don't mean to limit this reading of Shelley's novel to an autobiographical rendition. Such readings refuse women writers the agency automatically granted writers from within privileged literary circles, and continue to propagate the notion that women can only write about their own lives. However, for Wollstonecraft and Shelley as for De Quincey, their deliberate invocation of autobiographical data makes it impossible not to account for it in a critical analysis.

12. The allusion to Geneva was in fact written by Percy Bysshe Shelley, not Mary Shelley. The description of a public-spirited Geneva may be read as Percy Shelley's understanding of Rousseau philosophical standpoints. Shelley herself, however, later demonstrates her problems with Rousseau's constructions of subjectivity. The status of Geneva is at the very least a vexed site for her immediate relation to romanticism through her husband and less directly with Rousseau. For fuller treatments of Shelley's relation to Rousseau, see James O'Rourke, "Nothing More Unnatural: Mary Shelley's Revision of Rousseau," *English Literary History* 56, 3 (Fall 1989): 543–69; Alan Richardson, "From *Émile* to *Frankenstein*: The Education of Monsters," *European Romanticism Review* 1, 2 (Winter 1991): 147–62; and Johanna M. Smith, *Mary Shelley* (New York: Twayne, 1996).

13. The mantel that frames the fireplace is a common metaphor of domesticity and an especially apt location for this painting, since it simultaneously demonstrates the ways its centrality to the household is also most vulnerable to outside intrusion.

That is, it at once forms the center of the household while offering an aperture to the outside world. In this context, then, women, imported from elsewhere to act as domestic staffs constitute both the center and margins of domestic space.

14. I have argued earlier that imperialism and imperialism as England's social mission occupies what Jacques Lacan identifies as the "discourse of the master" and as such does not know "lack" because as the master it cannot know to want. In the case of Shelley's *Frankenstein*, however, the master signifier—Walton's Britishness—resembles more the "discourse of the hysteric": the position more likely to know "lack" and to supply the master with what it perceives the master as lacking. Part of what complicates Shelley's representation of the seamlessness of British mastery is, I believe, the complications of gender. If Shelley, as a subordinated writer, is extolling the necessities of hegemony, she is also extolling them from the subject position of the hysteric. Hence her contradictory representation of Walton.

15. See Anca Vlasopolos, "*Frankenstein's* Hidden Skeleton: The Psycho-Politics of Oppressions," *Science Fiction Studies* 10, 2 (July 1983): 125–36. Also Cass, "The Contestatory Gothic"; Lew, "The Deceptive Other"; Malchow, *Gothic Images of Race*.

16. Bringing travelers' tales back to England is also the theme of Percy Shelley's 1818 poem, *Ozymandias*, in which the poetic voice articulates a tale of imperial failure and poetic (epistemological) continuity, even triumph. The idea of epistemological endurance, especially in poetics, prevailed in the Shelley household during the writing of *Frankenstein*.

17. It would be impossible to imagine the full significance of this excursion without thinking of Wordsworth's *The Excursion*, the only completed part of his grand project, *The Recluse*. Although I'm not necessarily drawing a one-to-one correspondence between *Frankenstein* and *The Excursion*, I am struck by the ways in which the only completed production of a philosophical conversation that takes place between the Poet, the Wanderer, the Solitary, and the Parson (a conversation that is the structure of *The Recluse*) is the part that roams. That is, in order to represent British romanticism at its reclusive best, excursions are necessary, even if they only occur within the parameters of the imaginary.

18. I realize that in the 1818 edition Elizabeth is Victor's first cousin; however, the fact that Shelley made this change for the 1831 edition suggests more than just a way of rendering their relationship less incestuous. Such a change may also have been made in order to demonstrate the argument I make about the social and cultural "origins" of familial relations. Curiously, at the time of the 1831 revision, Mary Shelley was a pro-Italian, pro-Greek republican. It seem, then, that her xenophobic response to this particular representation of a movement—the *schiavi ognor frementi*—to which she was apparently sympathetic is overdetermined. On the one hand, her commiseration with pro-Italian/pro-Greek republicanism reflects the revolutionary politics espoused by her husband; on the other, her representation of Elizabeth's father and her pointed decision to change the nature of Elizabeth's relationship to the Frankenstein family reflect a deep ambivalence to this political identification when it enters the domestic space.

19. The position of "nature" in this novel is a very vexed one, and a thorough discussion would require another chapter. For the purposes of brevity, I suggest that the feminized "natural" abode is one that repeats the same alignments of ideology that I'm arguing happen with cultural constructions of domesticity. For a more developed

argument on feminism, science, and nature, see Anne K. Mellor, "A Feminist Critique of Science," in *Frankenstein/Mary Shelley*, ed. Fred Botting (New York: St. Martin's Press, 1995), 107–39.

20. In the case of the female monster, her "hub" is defined by the monster's incessant desire for her imagined companionship and possibilities of domestic bliss, but I will argue more about this later.

21. Regarding domesticity and dominant ideology, see Johanna M. Smith, "Cooped Up": Feminine Domesticity in *Frankenstein*," in Smith, *Case Studies*, 270–85.

22. Margaret Homans, for example, is an especial champion of the notion of circumventing the maternal, as distinct from merely getting rid of the mother by killing her off. But others, including early feminist readings such as those of Johnson, Ellen Moer, Gilbert and Gubar, Mary Jacobus, and Mary Poovey, also suggest that the problems with a *feminine* domesticity are bound up with their transparency in the service of masculine social relations. Johanna Smith's provocative reading of *Frankenstein*'s domestic spheres, while persuasively outlining the contestations between domesticity and experience—how ideologies of patriarchy and domesticity are pitted against one another—also falls back onto this idea of feminine transparency. While I am not disagreeing with these critical standpoints—indeed, I am relying quite heavily on the critical pathways laid before me—I am suggesting that there may be ways of reading domesticity not only as an instrument of patriarchal ideology but as an expression of xenophobia that provides the representational field for national and cultural identity.

23. Spivak, "Three Women's Texts," 263.

24. Spivak accounts for these gratuitous moments of xenophobia as an abundance of "incidental imperialist sentiment." My argument suggests that while these moments may be both gratuitous and incidental, they are nevertheless articulating romantic ideology.

25. Most critics have noted that the monster's tale is the center of the novel, thus locating the "uncanny" or the foreign at the heart of Shelley's text. My claim complicates this figuration a little by placing the fair exotic at the novel's heart. The fact that her tale may be appropriated by the most obviously subaltern figure suggests the problems with a domesticity that relies too heavily on improperly imported women for their reproduction.

26. Safie's father's history is a case of the ideological nature of identity that allows racial difference to negate class difference.

27. Elizabeth's impotence as a nurse is more vividly demonstrated through the deaths of Justine and William, two figures she attempts to care for who die despite her attempts.

28. Homans, *Bearing the Word*, 105.

29. By "safe" I am referring back to my argument in the first chapter, where Murray Cohen discusses the ways Johnson has been made "safe" for our reading. In this context, the recontextualization of "women" within the scope of feminist theory may not always yield entirely promising results.

30. Jacobus, *Reading Woman: Essays in Feminist Criticism* (New York: Columbia University Press, 1986), 5.

31. On women's writing in *Villette*, see Ali Behdad, "Visibility, Secrecy, and the Novel: Narrative Power in Brontë and Zola," *Literature Interpretations and Theory* 1, 4 (May 1990): 253–64; Gilbert and Gubar, *Madwoman in the Attic*, 399–440; Jacobus,

Reading Woman, 41–61; Patricia S. Yaeger, *Honey-Mad Women: Emancipatory Struggles in Women's Writing* (New York: Columbia University Press, 1988). On medical discourse see Charles Burkhart, *Charlotte Brontë: A Psychosexual Study of Her Novels* (London: Trinity Press, 1973); Beverly Forsyth, "The Two Faces of Lucy Snowe: A Study in Deviant Behavior," *Studies in the Novel* 29, 1 (Spring 1997): 17–25; Sally Shuttleworth, "The Surveillance of a Sleepless Eye: The Constitution of Neurosis in *Villette*," in *One Culture: Essays in Science and Literature*, ed. George Levine and Alan Rausch (Madison: University of Wisconsin Press, 1987), 313–35; Athena Vrettos, "From Neurosis to Narrative: the Private Life of the Nerves in *Villette* and *Daniel Deronda*," *Victorian Studies* 33 (1990): 551–79. On religious discourse see Marit Fimland, "On the Margins of the Acceptable: Charlotte Brontë's *Villette*," *Literature and Theology: An International Journal of Theory, Criticism, and Culture* 10, 2 (June 1996): 148–59; Gayla McGlanery, "'The Unlicked Wolf-Cub: Anti-Catholicism in Charlotte Brontë's *Villette*," *CVE* 37 (April 1993): 55–71; Kate Sawson, "Reading Desire: *Villette* as 'Heretic Narrative'," *ESC* 17, 1 (March 1991): 53–71; Michael Schiefebein, "A Catholic Baptism for *Villette*'s Lucy Snowe," *C&L* 45, 3–4 (Spring–Summer 1996): 319–29.

32. Nancy Armstrong, *Desire and Domestic Fiction: A Political History of the Novel* (New York: Oxford University Press, 1987).

33. Charlotte Brontë, *Villette*, ed. Tony Tanner (New York: Penguin, 1979), 106. Subsequent references to the text unless otherwise indicated will be made to this edition and will be noted in parentheses.

34. Interestingly, the "lattice" defining the space of the "sick-room" is a powerful metaphor for incarceration and domesticity alike.

35. True, her London meals are more substantial, but London itself stands in relation to Lucy as a "foreign" country. It is a transitional place, negotiating between the rural domesticity in which she has been raised and the expatriated future to which she looks forward.

36. Julia Kristeva, *Powers of Horror: An Essay on Abjection* (New York: Columbia University Press, 1982), 3.

37. My use of the term "imaginary" in this context is Lacanian. I argue that the novel itself creates an imaginary space for endless possibilities of subject-formation. Like the young baby in the mirror-phase who draws upon the pre-symbolic field of representation to sustain the fantasy of freestanding subjectivity, so the ideological structures of this novel depend on a similar field that employs fantasies of national identity to maintain its construction of the foreign.

38. In order to prevent any confusion, I must add that, even while Lucy eats with a good deal of gusto in front of Monsieur Paul, his particular role in relation to Lucy's realigned domesticity is very different from her less intimate relations with Madame Beck and the students of Rue Fossette.

39. It also seems equally compelling to read this scenario as part of a homoerotic exchange. See Ann Weinstone, "The Queerness of Lucy Snowe," *Nineteenth-Century Contexts* 18, 4 (1995): 367–84.

40. I use this term in the sense Edward Said has identified, separating "culture" as an arena of representation putatively free from political or ideological engagement, a concept "that includes a refining and elevating element, each society's reservoir of

the best that has been known and thought, as Matthew Arnold put it in the 1860s. Arnold believed that culture palliates, if it does not altogether neutralize, the ravages of a modern, aggressive, mercantile, and brutalizing urban existence." Edward Said, *Culture and Imperialism* (New York: Vintage, 1993), xiii. In the case of *Villette*, Lucy Snowe's demystification of Mrs. Sweeny is automatic, schooled by her solid background in English education. Mrs. Sweeny's engagement with vulgar commercialism, a traffic identified by her ill-gotten silk gowns and most significantly a cashmere shawl (what Madame Beck calls "un véritable Cachmire"), not only uncovers her as a manifestation of brutal urbanism but also shows her to have deserved such a fate.

41. Though Mrs. Sweeny isn't technically a wet-nurse, she superintends the feeding of the children and is therefore metonymically connected to more maternal forms of nursing.

42. See Sigmund Freud, "The Uncanny," in *Studies in Parapsychology*, ed. Philip Rieff (New York: Macmillan, 1963), 19–60.

43. Another compelling discourse of otherness at work in this novel, of course, is the contestations between Protestantism and Catholicism. Although I make some allusion to the Catholic Church, this is not an angle that I emphasize. See note 31 for more references on this argument.

44. This "apotropaic monster" (by which I mean the *crétin*) performs similarly to the decapitated head of Medusa Freud identifies in "Medusa's Head." Freud, "Medusa's Head," in *Sexuality and the Psychology of Love*, ed. Philip Rieff (New York: Macmillan, 1961), 212–13.

45. I might add that Lucy's desires to enter these English households would violate the demands of class. Miss Marchmont's cousin inherits her riches—the sum she had promised Lucy is never formally recognized—and Paulina Home, whose family matches the Brettons in every respect, marries Graham Bretton. In characteristically imperial style, then, Lucy has to venture abroad in order to improve the material conditions of her life.

46. Part of Madame Walravens's monstrosity is her transgendered overturning of imperial hierarchies; she (not some patriarch) controls the colonial injunction placed upon Monsieur Paul.

Afterword

1. Gretchen Holbrook Gerzina, *Black London: Life Before Emancipation* (New Brunswick, N.J.: Rutgers University Press, 1995), 3–5.

2. Gerzina, *Black London*, 3.

3. Gerzina, *Black London*, 3–4.

4. Samuel Johnson, *Rasselas*, in *Samuel Johnson: Selected Poetry and Prose*, ed. Frank Brady and W. K. Wimsatt (Berkeley, Calif.: University of California Press, 1977), 91.

5. Johnson, *Rasselas*, 289.

Works Cited

Aarslef, Hans. *From Locke to Saussure: Essays on the Study of Language and Intellectual History*. Minneapolis: University of Minnesota Press, 1982.
Abrams, M. H. *Natural Supernaturalism: Tradition and Revolution in Romantic Literature*. New York: Norton, 1971.
Anderson, Benedict. *Imagined Communities: Reflections on the Origin and Spread of Nationalism*. New York: Verso, 1983.
Armstrong, Nancy. *Desire and Domestic Fiction: A Political History of the Novel*. New York: Oxford University Press, 1987.
Barrell, John. *The Idea of Landscape and the Sense of Place*. Cambridge: Cambridge University Press, 1972.
———. *The Infection of Thomas De Quincey: A Psychopathology of Imperialism*. New Haven, Conn.: Yale University Press, 1991.
Bate, Walter Jackson. *The Achievement of Samuel Johnson*. New York: Oxford University Press, 1961.
———. *Samuel Johnson*. New York: Harcourt Brace, 1977.
Beer, John, ed. *Questioning Romanticism*. Baltimore: Johns Hopkins University Press, 1995.
Behdad, Ali. "Visibility, Secrecy, and the Novel: Narrative Power in Brontë and Zola." *Literature Interpretations and Theory* 1, no. 4 (May 1990): 253–64.
Bérubé, Michael and Cary Nelson, eds. *Higher Education Under Fire: Politics, Economics, and the Crisis of the Humanities*. New York: Routledge, 1995.
Bhabha, Homi K. *The Location of Culture*. New York: Routledge, 1994.
———. "Signs Taken for Wonders: Questions of Ambivalence and Authority Under a Tree Outside Delhi, May 1817." In *"Race," Writing, and Difference*, ed. Henry Louis Gates, Jr. Chicago: University of Chicago Press, 1986. 163–84.
Boswell, James. *The Life of Samuel Johnson*. London, 1791. London: Oxford University Press, 1965.
Bourdieu, Pierre. *Homo Academicus*. Trans. Peter Collier. Stanford, Calif.: Stanford University Press, 1988.
Bourdieu, Pierre, Jean-Claude Passeron, and Monique de Saint Martin. *Academic Discourse: Linguistic Misunderstanding and Professional Power*. Stanford, Calif.: Stanford University Press, 1994.
Bracher, Mark. "Lacan's Theory of the Four Discourses." *Prose Studies* 11, no. 3 (December 1988): 32–49.
Brontë, Charlotte. *Villette*. Ed. Tony Tanner. New York: Penguin, 1979.
Brown, Laura. *Alexander Pope*. London: Blackwell, 1985.

Butler, Judith. *Gender Trouble: Feminism and the Subversion of Identity.* New York: Routledge, 1990.
Butler, Marilyn. *Romantics, Rebels, and Reactionaries: English Literature and Its Background, 1760–1830.* New York: Oxford University Press, 1981.
Cahoone, Lawrence, ed. *From Modernism to Postmodernism.* New York: Blackwell, 1996.
Carson, James B. "Bringing the Author Forward: *Frankenstein* Through Mary Shelley's Letters." *Criticism* 30, 4 (Fall 1988): 431–53.
Caruth, Cathy. *Empirical Truths and Critical Fictions: Locke, Wordsworth, Kant, Freud.* Baltimore: Johns Hopkins University Press, 1991.
Cass, Jeffrey. "The Contestatory Gothic in Mary Shelley's *Frankenstein* and J. W. Polidori's *Ernestus Berchtold*: The Spectre of a Colonialist Paradigm." *Journal of the Association for the Interdisciplinary Studies of the Arts* 1, no. 2 (Spring 1996): 33–41.
Castle, Terry. *Masquerade and Civilization: The Carnivalesque in Eighteenth-Century English Culture and Fiction.* Stanford, Calif.: Stanford University Press, 1986.
Christensen, Jerome. *Romanticism at the End of History.* Baltimore: Johns Hopkins University Press, 2000.
Clej, Alina. *A Genealogy of the Modern Self: Thomas De Quincey and the Intoxication of Writing.* Stanford, Calif.: Stanford University Press, 1995.
Cohen, Murray. *Sensible Words: Linguistic Practice in England, 1640–1785.* Baltimore: Johns Hopkins University Press, 1977.
Colley, Linda. *Britons: Forging the Nation, 1707–1837.* New Haven, Conn.: Yale University Press, 1992.
Collings, David. "The Monster and the Imaginary Mother: A Lacanian Reading of *Frankenstein*." In *Case Studies in Contemporary Criticism: Frankenstein*, ed. Johanna M. Smith. Boston: Bedford, 1992. 245–58.
Defoe, Daniel. *Robinson Crusoe.* 1719. New York: Bantam, 1981.
Deleuze, Gilles and Felix Guattari. *A Thousand Plateaus: Capitalism and Schizophrenia.* Minneapolis: University of Minnesota Press, 1987.
DeMaria, Robert, Jr. *Johnson's Dictionary and the Language of Learning.* Chapel Hill: University of North Carolina Press, 1986.
———. "The Politics of Johnson's Dictionary." *PMLA* 104, no. 1 (January 1989): 64–74.
De Quincey, Thomas. *Confessions of an English Opium-Eater.* 1821–24. New York: Penguin, 1971.
Derrida, Jacques. *Of Grammatology.* Trans. Gayatri Spivak. Baltimore: Johns Hopkins University Press, 1974.
———. *Dissemination.* Trans. Barbara Jordan. Chicago: University of Chicago Press, 1981.
———. *Limited, Inc.* Evanston, Ill.: Northwestern University Press, 1988.
Dharwadker, Vinay. "Print Culture and Literary Markets in Colonial India." In *Language Machines: Technologies of Literary and Cultural Production*, ed. Jeffrey Masten, Peter Stallybrass, and Nancy J. Vickers. New York: Routledge, 1997.
Eagleton, Terry. *The Function of Criticism: From the Spectator to Post-Structuralism.* London: Verso, 1984.

Ferguson, Moira. *Colonialism and Gender Relations from Mary Wollstonecraft to Jamaica Kincaid*. New York: Columbia University Press, 1994.

———. "Mary Wollstonecraft and the Problematic of Slavery." In *Mary Wollstonecraft: 200 Years of Feminism*, ed. Eileen Jones Yeo. London: Rivers Oram, 1997. 89–103.

Fimland, Marit. "On the Margins of the Acceptable: Charlotte Brontë's *Villette*." *Literature and Theology: An International Journal of Theory, Criticism, and Culture* 10, no. 2 (June 1996): 148–59.

Forsyth, Beverly. "The Two Faces of Lucy Snowe: A Study in Deviant Behavior." *Studies in the Novel* 29, no. 1 (Spring 1997): 17–25.

Foucault, Michel. *The History of Sexuality*. Vol. 1, *The Birth of the Prison*. Trans. Robert Hurley. New York: Random House, 1980.

———. *Language, Counter-Memory, Practice: Selected Essays*. Ed. Donald F. Bouchard, trans. Bouchard and Sherry Simon. Ithaca, N.Y.: Cornell University Press, 1977.

———. *The Order of Things: An Archaeology of the Human Sciences*. New York: Random House, 1970.

Freud, Sigmund. *Civilization and Its Discontents*. Trans. James Strachey. New York: Norton, 1961.

———. *The Interpretation of Dreams*. Trans. James Strachey. New York: Avon, 1965.

———. *Sexuality and the Psychology of Love*. Ed. Philip Rieff. Collected Papers, vol. 7. New York: Macmillan, 1961.

———. *Studies in Parapsychology*. Ed. Philip Rieff. Collected Papers, vol. 10. New York: Macmillan, 1963.

Fulford, Tim and Peter J. Kitson. *Romanticism and Colonialism: Writing and Empire, 1780–1830*. Cambridge: Cambridge University Press, 1998.

Gates, Henry Louis, Jr., ed. *"Race," Writing, and Difference*. Chicago: University of Chicago Press, 1985.

Gerzina, Gretchen Holcomb. *Black London: Life Before Emancipation*. New Brunswick, N.J.: Rutgers University Press, 1995.

Gilbert, Sandra M. and Susan Gubar. *The Madwoman in the Attic: The Woman Writer and the Nineteenth-Century Literary Imagination*. New Haven, Conn.: Yale University Press, 1979.

Gumbrecht, Hans Ulrich and David Palumbo-Liu. *Streams of Cultural Capital: Transnational Cultural Spaces*. Stanford, Calif.: Stanford University Press, 1998.

Habermas, Jürgen. *The Structural Transformation of the Public Sphere: An Inquiry into a Category of Bourgeois Society*. Trans. Thomas Burger. Cambridge, Mass.: MIT Press, 1989.

Haraway, Donna J. *Primate Visions: Gender, Race, and Nature in the World of Modern Science*. New York: Routledge, 1989.

———. *Simians, Cyborgs, and Women: The Reinvention of Nature*. New York: Routledge, 1991.

Harris, Nigel. *The End of the Third World: Newly Industrialized Countries and the Decline of an Ideology*. New York: Penguin, 1987.

Hertz, Neil. *The End of the Line: Essays on Psychoanalysis and the Sublime*. New York: Columbia University Press, 1985.

Hofkosh, Sonia and Alan Richardson. *Romanticism, Race, and Imperial Culture, 1780–1834*. Bloomington: Indiana University Press, 1996.
Hollinger, Veronica. "Putting on the Feminine: Gender and Negativity in *Frankenstein* and *The Handmaid's Tale*." In *Negation, Critical Theory, and Postmodern Textuality*, ed. Daniel Fischlin. Dordrecht: Kluwer Academic, 1994. 203–24.
Homans, Margaret. *Bearing the Word: Language and Female Experience in Nineteenth-Century Female Writing*. Chicago: University of Chicago Press, 1986.
Jacobus, Mary. *Reading Woman: Essays in Feminist Criticism*. New York: Columbia University Press, 1986.
———. "Reading Woman (Reading)." In *Feminisms: An Anthology of Literary Theory and Criticism*, ed. Diana Price Herndl and Robyn R. Warhol. New Brunswick, N.J.: Rutgers University Press, 1997.
———. *Romanticism, Writing, and Sexual Difference: Essays on* The Prelude. Oxford: Clarendon Press, 1989.
Jameson, Frederic. *Postmodernism, Or the Cultural Logic of Late Capitalism*. Durham, N.C.: Duke University Press, 1991.
Johnson, Barbara. "My Monster/ My Self." *Diacritics* 12, no. 2 (Summer 1982): 2–10.
Johnson, Samuel. *Johnson's Dictionary: A Modern Selection*. Ed. E. L. McAdam and George Milne. New York: Random House, 1963.
———. *Life of Savage*. 1744. In *Selected Poetry and Prose*, ed. Brady and Wimsatt.
———. *London*. 1738. In *Selected Poetry and Prose*, ed. Brady and Wimsatt.
———. *Preface to the Dictionary*. 1755. In *Selected Poetry and Prose*, ed. Brady and Wimsatt.
———. *Rasselas*. In *Selected Poetry and Prose*, ed. Brady and Wimsatt.
———. *Selected Poetry and Prose*. Ed. Frank Brady and W. K. Wimsatt. Berkeley: University of California Press, 1977.
Jordan, John E. *De Quincey to Wordsworth: A Biography of a Relationship*. Berkeley: University of California Press, 1962.
Kaplan, Cora. *Sea Changes: Culture and Feminism*. London: Verso, 1986.
Kant, Immanuel. *Critique of Pure Reason*. 1781. Trans. J. M. D. Meiklejohn. Amherst, Mass.: Prometheus Books, 1990.
Ketcham, Michael. *Transparent Design: Reading, Performance, and Form in the Spectator Papers*. Athens: University of Georgia Press, 1985.
Klancher, Jon. *The Making of English Reading Audiences, 1790–1832*. Madison: University of Wisconsin Press, 1987.
Klein, Richard. *Cigarettes Are Sublime*. Durham, N.C.: Duke University Press, 1995.
Knapp, Steven. *Literary Interest: The Limits of Anti-Formalism*. Cambridge, Mass.: Harvard University Press, 1993.
Kristeva, Julia. *The Kristeva Reader*. Ed. Toril Moi. New York: Columbia University Press, 1986.
———. *Powers of Horror: An Essay on Abjection*. New York: Columbia University Press, 1982.
Lacan, Jacques. *Écrits: A Selection*. Trans. Alan Sheridan. New York: Norton, 1977.
———. *Four Fundamental Concepts of Psycho-Analysis*. New York: Norton, 1981.
Laclau, Ernesto and Chantal Mouffe. *Hegemony and Socialist Strategy: Towards a Radi-*

cal Democratic Politics. Trans. Winstan Moore and Paul Cammack. London: Verso, 1985.
Landry, Donna. *The Muses of Resistance: Laboring-Class Women's Poetry in Britain, 1739–1796.* Cambridge: Cambridge University Press, 1990.
Landry, Donna and Gerald MacLean. *Materialist Feminisms.* Cambridge, Mass.: Blackwell, 1993.
LaPlanche, J. and J.-B. Pontalis. *The Language of Psycho-Analysis.* New York: Norton, 1973.
Law, Jules David. *The Rhetoric of Empiricism: Language and Perception from Locke to I. A. Richards.* Ithaca, N.Y.: Cornell University Press, 1993.
Leask, Nigel. *British Romantic Writers and the East: Anxieties of Empire.* Cambridge: Cambridge University Press, 1992.
———. "Colonialism and the Exotic." In *Romantic Writings*, ed. Stephen Bygrave. London: Routledge, 1996.
———. "Toward a Universal Aesthetic: De Quincey on Murder as Carnival and Tragedy." In *Questioning Romanticism*, ed. John Beer. Baltimore: Johns Hopkins University Press, 1995.
Lew, Joseph W. "The Deceptive Other: Mary Shelley's Critique of Orientalism in *Frankenstein*." *Studies in Romanticism* 30, no. 2 (Summer 1991): 255–83.
London, Bette. "Mary Shelley, *Frankenstein*, and the Spectre of Masculinity." *PMLA* 108, no. 2 (March 1993): 253–67.
Makdisi, Saree. *Romantic Imperialism: Universal Empire and the Culture of Modernity.* Cambridge: Cambridge University Press, 1998.
Malchow, H. L. *Gothic Images of Race in Nineteenth-Century Britain.* Stanford, Calif.: Stanford University Press, 1996.
Marder, Elissa. "The Mother Tongue in *Phèdre* and *Frankenstein*." *Yale French Studies* 76 (1989): 59–77.
Markley, Robert M. "'Gulfes, Deserts, Precipices, Stone': Marvell's 'Upon Appleton House' and the Contradiction of 'Nature'." In *The Country and the City Revisited: England and the Politics of Culture, 1550–1850*, ed. Gerald MacLean, Donna Landry, and Joseph P. Ward. Cambridge: Cambridge University Press, 1999. 89–105.
May, Marilyn. "Publish and Perish: William Godwin, Mary Shelley and the Public Appetite for Scandal." *Papers on Language and Literature* 26, no. 4 (Fall 1990): 489–512.
McClintock, Anne. *Imperial Leather: Race, Gender, and Sexuality in the Colonial Contest.* London: Routledge, 1995.
McDonagh, Josephine. *De Quincey's Disciplines.* Oxford: Clarendon Press, 1994.
McGann, Jerome. "The Failures of Romanticism." In *Romanticism, History, and the Possibilities of Genre: Re-Forming Literature, 1789–1837*, ed. Tilottama Rajan and Julie M. Wright. Cambridge: Cambridge University Press, 1998.
———. "Rethinking Romanticism." In *The Challenge of Periodization: Old Paradigms, New Perspectives*, ed. Lawrence Besserman. New York: Garland, 1996.
———. *The Romantic Ideology: A Critical Investigation.* Chicago: University of Chicago Press, 1983.

McGlanery, Gayla. "'The Unlicked Wolf-Cub': Anti-Catholicism in Charlotte Brontë's *Villette*." *Cahiers Victoriens et Edouardiens* 37 (April 1993): 55–71.

Mellor, Anne K. "A Feminist Critique of Science." In *Frankenstein/Mary Shelley*, ed. Fred Botting. New York: St. Martin's Press, 1995.

———. *Mary Shelley: Her Fiction, Her Monsters*. New York: Routledge, 1988.

Newman, Gerald. *The Rise of English Nationalism: A Cultural History, 1740–1830*. New York: St. Martin's Press, 1987.

O'Rourke, James. "Nothing More Unnatural: Mary Shelley's revision of Rousseau." *ELH* 56, no. 3 (Fall 1989): 543–69.

O'Shaughnessy, Toni. "Critical Complicities: Savage Mothers, Johnson's Mother, and the Containment of Maternal Difference." *AJ* (1992): 115–46.

———. "Fiction as Truth: Personal Identity in Johnson's *Life of Savage*." *Studies in English Literature* 30, no. 3 (Summer 1990): 487–501.

Palumbo-Liu, David. *The Ethnic Canon: Histories, Institutions, and Interventions*. Minneapolis: University of Minnesota Press, 1995.

Pinch, Adela. *Strange Fits of Passion: Epistemologies of Emotion, Hume to Austen*. Stanford, Calif.: Stanford University Press, 1996.

Pope, Alexander. *Windsor-Forest*. In *Poetry and Prose of Alexander Pope*. Ed. Aubrey Williams. Boston: Houghton Mifflin, 1969. 65–77.

Poovey, Mary. *The Proper Lady and the Woman Writer: Ideology as Style in the Works of Mary Wollstonecraft, Mary Shelley, and Jane Austen*. Chicago: University of Chicago Press, 1984.

Reed, Joel. "Academically Speaking: Language and Nationalism in Seventeenth- and Eighteenth-Century England." PhD dissertation, University of California at Irvine, 1991. *Dissertation Abstracts International* 52, no. 12 (1992): 4341A.

———. "Restoration and Repression: The Language Projects of the Royal Society." *Studies in Eighteenth-Century Culture* 19 (1989): 399–412.

Rzepka, Charles J. *Sacramental Commodities: Gift, Text, and the Sublime in De Quincey*. Amherst: University of Massachusetts Press, 1995.

Richardson, Alan. "From *Émile* to *Frankenstein*: The Education of Monsters." *European Romanticism Review* 1, no. 2 (Winter 1991): 147–62.

Rose, Ellen Cronan. "Custody Battles: Reproducing Knowledge About *Frankenstein*." *New Literary History* 26, 4 (Autumn 1995): 809–32.

Rubenstein, Marc A. "'My Accursed Origin': The Search for the Mother in *Frankenstein*." *Studies in Romanticism* 15 (Spring 1976): 165–94.

Saccamano, Neil. "The Consolations of Ambivalence." *MLN* 106, no. 3 (1991): 685–98.

Said, Edward. *Culture and Imperialism*. New York: Random House, 1993.

———. *Orientalism*. New York: Random House, 1979.

Sapiro, Virginia. *A Vindication of Political Virtue: The Political Theory of Mary Wollstonecraft*. Chicago: University of Chicago Press, 1992.

Sawson, Kate. "Reading Desire: *Villette* as 'Heretic Narrative'." *ESC* 17, no. 1 (March 1991): 53–71.

Schiefebein, Michael. "A Catholic Baptism for Lucy Snowe." *Christianity and Literature* 45, no. 3–4 (Spring–Summer 1996): 319–29.

Sedgwick, Eve Kosofsky. *Between Men: English Literature and Male Homosocial Desire*. New York: Columbia University Press, 1985.

Sharpe, Jenny. *Allegories of Empire: The Figure of the Woman in the Colonial Text.* Minneapolis: University of Minnesota Press, 1993.
Shelley, Mary. *Frankenstein.* 1831. Ed. M. K. Joseph. New York: Oxford University Press, 1983.
Shelley, Percy Bysshe. "On Frankenstein." In *The Works of Percy Bysshe Shelley in Verse and Prose.* Ed. Harry Buxton Forman. 8 vols. London: Reeves and Turner, 1880. 7: 11–14.
Shohat, Ella and Robert Stam. *Unthinking Eurocentrism: Multiculturalism and the Media.* New York: Routledge, 1994.
Shuttleworth, Sally. "'The Sleepless Eye': The Constitution of Neurosis in *Villette.*" In *One Culture: Essays in Science and Literature,* ed. George Levine and Alan Rausch. Madison: University of Wisconsin Press, 1987.
Smith, Johanna M. "Cooped Up: Feminine Domesticity in *Frankenstein.*" In *Case Studies in Contemporary Criticism: Frankenstein,* ed. Smith. Boston: Bedford, 1992. 270–85.
———. *Mary Shelley.* New York: Twayne, 1996.
Spivak, Gayatri. "Three Women's Texts and a Critique of Imperialism." In *"Race," Writing, and Difference,* ed. Henry Louis Gates, Jr. Chicago: University of Chicago Press, 1985.
———. "The Rani of Simur." In *Europe and Its Others: Proceedings of the Essex Conference on the Sociology of Literature,* vol. 1, ed. Francis Barker et al. Colchester: University of Essex Press, 1985.
Stallybrass, Peter and Allon White. *The Politics and Poetics of Transgression.* Ithaca, N.Y.: Cornell University Press, 1986.
Suleri, Sara. *The Rhetoric of English India.* Chicago: University of Chicago Press, 1992.
Todd, Janet, ed. *Maria/ Mary Wollstonecraft; Matilda/ Mary Shelley.* London: Penguin, 1992.
Tracy, Clarence. *The Artificial Bastard.* Cambridge, Mass.: Harvard University Press, 1953.
Tuveson, Ernest Lee. *The Imagination as a Means of Grace: Locke and the Aesthetics of Romanticism.* Berkeley: University of California Press, 1960.
Viswanathan, Gauri. *Masks of Conquest: Literary Study and British Rule in India.* New York: Columbia University Press, 1989.
Vlasopolos, Anca. "*Frankenstein*'s Hidden Skeleton: The Psycho-Politics of Oppressions." *Science Fiction Studies* 10, no. 2 (July 1983): 125–36.
Vrettos, Athena. "From Neurosis to Narrative: The Private Life of the Nerves in *Villette* and *Daniel Deronda.*" *Victorian Studies* 33 (1990): 551–79.
Waldron, Jan L. "None of My Business." *New York Times Magazine,* June 18, 1995: 22.
Weinbrot, Howard. *Britannia's Issue: The Rise of British Literature from Dryden to Ossian.* Cambridge: Cambridge University Press, 1995.
Weiskel, Thomas. *The Romantic Sublime: Studies in the Structure and Psychology of Transcendence.* Baltimore: Johns Hopkins University Press, 1986.
Weinstone, Ann. "The Queerness of Lucy Snowe." *Nineteenth-Century Context* 18, no. 4 (1995): 367–84.
Williams, Raymond. *Marxism and Literature.* Oxford: Oxford University Press, 1977.
Wilson, Anna. "Mary Wollstonecraft and the Search for the Radical Woman." *Genders* 6 (1989): 88–101.

Wollstonecraft, Mary. *A Vindication of the Rights of Woman*, 1792. New York: Norton, 1988.
Wordsworth, William. *The Excursion*. 1814. New York: Norton, 1979.
———. *The Prelude*. 1805. New Haven, Conn.: Yale University Press, 1988.
Yaeger, Patricia S. *Honey-Mad Women: Emancipatory Struggles in Women's Writing*. New York: Columbia University Press, 1988.
Žižek, Slavoj. *The Plague of Fantasies*. London: Verso, 1997.
———. *The Sublime Object of Ideology*. London: Verso, 1989.

Index

abjection: in Brontë's *Villette*, 141; food loathing as, 118; of maternal body, 60, 62; of Orientalism, 18; xenophobia constructs cultural identities through, 7–8

Abrams, M. H., 12

absolute other, 39, 154 n5, 159 n25, 161 n37, 172 n18

academic culture: importance of in eighteenth-century England, 28; Johnson's relation to, 28, 32, 40, 158 n7

The Achievement of Samuel Johnson (Bate), 51–53, 164 n1

addiction: autobiographies of, 77; as domesticating habit, 71; meanings of, 76, 77

Africans, in Britain, 104–5, 148, 149

Allegories of Empire: The Figure of the Woman in the Colonial Text (Sharpe), 170 n1

Anderson, Benedict: *Imagined Communities: Reflections on the Origin and Spread of Nationalism*, 100, 155 n16, 170 n9

antagonism, 161 n36

anti-slavery sentiment, 104

Armstrong, Nancy, 135

Arnold, Matthew, 178 n40

Asia, place in English cultural unconscious, 69

Augustine, St., 84

authorship: and Johnson's *Dictionary of the English Language*, 27, 45, 65–66; obstructed by domestic concerns in Johnson's *Life of Savage*, 27, 54, 56, 58–59, 66; romantic idea of produced through inward contemplation, 12–13; stunting of Mary Shelley's, 119–20; xenophobia connecting addiction to in DeQuincey's *Confessions*, 75–78; xenophobic belief in essential subjectivity of, 16

The Author To Be Let (Savage), 56

autobiography: of addiction, 77; and fantasy of self-birth, 71; as literary genre in 1820s, 70

Barrell, John: *The Infection of Thomas DeQuincey*: on absolute other, 159 n25; on DeQuincey's othered domestic relations, 168 n35; on DeQuincey's pathological relation to romantic scholarship, 19; on foreign as form of maintenance, 17, 77, 84, 154 n8; on importance of historical materialism to romanticism, 14; on ramifications of DeQuincey's addiction, 75; on representation of prostitute in *Confessions*, 91; on tiger in eighteenth-century British imagination, 65, 70, 71, 72

Barretier, Philip, 44

Bate, Walter Jackson: *The Achievement of Samuel Johnson*, 51–53, 164 n1; *Samuel Johnson*, 157 n7, 162 n40, 164 n1, 166 n13

Bearing the Word: Language and Female Experience in Nineteenth-Century Female Writing (Homans), 98, 121, 174 n7, 177 n22

Beer, John: *Questioning Romanticism*, 14

Bhabha, Homi, 43, 60, 115, 160 n30

Blake, Robert, 44

Blake, William: *The Tyger*, 65, 165 n11

Bloom, Harold, 167 n25

Boerhaave, Herman, 44

Boswell, James: *The Life of Samuel Johnson*, 29, 164 n1

boundary creatures, 73–74, 142

Brady, Frank, 44

Britain, eighteenth and early nineteenth century: association of "British" with coherent national identity, 153 n4; association of tigers with orient, 65, 70, 71, 72; black population in, 104–5, 148, 149; collection of exotic objects, 69; commodification of women's bodies to represent a healthy nation, 103–4; cultural differences fetishized as color difference, 8, 11, 17; increase of consumerism, 35; and India, popular dualism between, 16–17; internal anxieties about national identity, 14–15; social movements of 1780s and 1790s, 99; women's place in nation, problems of, 99–100

190 Index

Britons: Forging the Nation (Colley), 102–3, 104, 153 n4, 173 n27

Brontë, Charlotte: Villette: anxiety of aligning nationalism with race, 140–41; consumption, 137–41; fair exotics, 148–49, 151; fall into foreign, 141–43; gender and romantic identity, 116, 123–24; inadequacy of sustenance provided by mother country, 136–37; introjection of foreign through monstrosity, 147; monstrousness as manifestation of outcast British identity, 141; monstrousness fabricated from domestic landscapes, 138, 142; opium's connection to fantasy and notions of orient, 144–46; repatriation through public display of nationality, 140; xenophobic response to xenodochy, 138–39, 141, 144–46

Brown, Laura, 42

Buffon, Georges Louis Leclerc, Compte de: The Natural History of Animals, Vegetables, and Minerals, 65, 70

Butler, Judith, 99, 100

Butler, Marilyn, 14, 102

Byrne, David, 162 n39

Byron, George Gordon, 18, 19

cannibalism, 18

capitalism, versus bourgeois impulse to protect national borders, 38

Cartesian subjectivity, 11, 66, 168 n37

Castle, Terry: Masquerade and Civilization: The Carnivalesque in Eighteenth-Century English Culture and Fiction, 47, 162 n41

castration, 7–8, 107

Catholicism, 143, 145, 146–47

Clej, Alina, 14

Cohen, Murray: Sensible Words, 29, 158 n8

Coleridge, Samuel Taylor: DeQuincey and, 68, 79, 167 n33; Kubla Khan, 67; Lyrical Ballads, 169 n44; Preface to the Lyrical Ballads, 21

Colley, Linda: Britons: Forging the Nation, 102–3, 104, 153 n4, 173 n27

colonialism: and definitions, 16; domestic, association of Englishness with, 153 n4; effect on romantic literature, 14; mother and children as prototypes for, 21, 101, 102–4; use of gender to disarticulate domestic space, 134. See also imperialism

Comments on the Confessions (DeQuincey), 79

communities: ideologies of, 100; imagined, 155 n16, 171 n9

consumerism, increase of in 18th century, 35

consumption: in Brontë's Villette, 137–41; as mark of difference between skin and flesh in Crusoe, 3–4; of Oriental artifacts; of the other as maintenance, 17–18

containment: in Britain's relation to India, 16; in romantic literature, 16

The Critique of Pure Reason (Kant), 8–10

crocodiles, 70, 74, 85

crossover creatures, 70–77

cultural materialism, in Johnson's representation of language, 31

cultural purity, fantasy of, 25

cultural studies, 11, 22

Culture and Imperialism (Said), 178 n40

Descartes, René, 168 n37

definitions, and colonial relations, 16

Defoe, Daniel
—Journal of the Plague Year, 159 n24
—Robinson Crusoe: cats as threat to Crusoe's position and power, 4, 165 n8; celebration of commercialism, 6, 13, 165 n8; consumption as mark of difference between skin and flesh, 3–4; Crusoe's ability to monitor and regulate reproduction, 4–5; Crusoe's clothing as protection from fall into otherness, 2–3; Crusoe's incapacitating worries, 1–2, 18; Crusoe's journal as discursive authority, 5, 6; epistemological superiority of British national subjectivity, 15–16; fetishization of skin, 1, 2, 5, 150; identity dependent upon perception of visible other, 2, 5–6, 68; ideological incapacity of Englishman to be a savage, 2; joking as anxiety about British subjectivity, 153 n3, 153 n4; romantic issues, 6, 150; as transitional text, 6–7, 14, 23; xenophobia as defense against xenochial desire, 5, 6–7

Delacroix, Eugène, 72

Deleuze, Gilles, 156 n25

DeMaria, Robert, 30, 43

DeQuincey Reviewed: Thomas DeQuincey's Critical Reception, 1821–1994 (North), 165 n9

DeQuincey, Thomas: ambivalence about political economy, 84; Comments on the Confessions, 79; othered writing, 71–72; paternal attachment to Wordsworth, 80, 81; Preliminary Confessions, 87; reference to

family members in generic terms in works, 79; *Suspiria de Profundis*, 79; traffic in prostitutes and venereal disease, 73, 86, 166 n18
—*Confessions of an English Opium Eater*: ambivalence about Lake District circle, 68, 78–79, 81, 83, 88, 89, 94; assignments of color to race, 92; "authentic" British imperial authorship, 77–78; on authorial success, 63; biological fathering vs. authorial fathering, 169 n41; burlesque of Wordsworth's poetic language, 90; Coleridge in, 68, 79, 167 n33; compulsion to show mastery of Greek, 81, 92, 167 n32; confession, 77, 168 n37; critical reception of, 75, 165 n9, 168 n36; DeQuincey's position as hysteric, 87–89; family relations, 85–86; fantasy of self-birth, 71; feminine monstrosity used to establish masculine power, 169 n42; foreign infecting body of Malay, 92, 93–94; invocation of the French, 84–85; Kate Wordsworth, 87, 167 n30; maternal body, 81–83, 88–91, 170 n51; monsters and children, 85–86, 93–94; monstrous domestic origin, 82–83; monstrous interruption of narrative integrity, 85–87; monstrous other's incorporation into domestic, 20, 67–68, 70–71, 74, 75, 94, 101, 104, 105, 150; mother as bringer of language, 167 n34, 174 n5; Orientalism to represent coherent English national identity, 68–69, 74, 77; Oxford-street as monstrous stepmother, 90–91, 169 n49, 174 n5; paternal fantasies, 79–81, 89, 167 n29, 167 n30; politicized self-representation through scientific discourse, 83–84; romanticism, 19–20, 74–75, 76, 88–89, 169 n48; self-marginalization, 75; shift from romanticism and toward writing as cultural practice, 95; tiger as metaphor for effects of opium habit on scholarship, 70; unnatural knowledge, 86–87; writing as both disease and cure, 78

Derrida, Jacques: formulation of supplement, 97; "Signature Event Context," 33, 159 n23
Devonshire, Duchess of, 99
dialect, Johnson's linking of to moral depravity, 41
difference: color, cultural differences fetishized as, 8, 11, 17; identity in terms of, 38; introjection of as strategy of national self-identification, 6; racial, and establishment of hierarchy, 149–50; racial, negating class difference, 177 n26; threat to integrity of European mastery, 10; visible, 2, 5–6, 68, 154 n8. *See also* other

displaced identification, 55
domestic: deterritorialization of through gender, 98, 100–101, 107, 134, 135, 147; feminine as external to, 118–19; feminine upholding romantic formula of, 128–29, 134; incorporation of otherness into, 18, 70, 72–73, 75, 94, 115; obstruction to English authorship, 27, 54, 56, 58–59, 66; romantic conflation of exotic with, 66
domestic colonialism, association of Englishness with, 153 n4
domesticity: foreign, failure of, 109–10; notion of, 29
Drake, Francis, 44

Eco, Umberto, 43
The Education of Mothers of Families (Martin), 98
Elizabethan writers, Johnson on, 34, 35
Elizabeth I, 149
Emile (Rousseau), 98, 99, 107
encyclopedic project, ideological impetus of, 43
"English," association of with domestic colonialism, 153 n4
Enlightenment: origin of romanticism in, 13, 14, 18–19, 66, 68; reasoning, 9–10, 12
Eurocentrism, 1, 45
The Excursion (Wordsworth), 176 n17
expatriation, 135

fair exotics: in *Frankenstein*, 177 n25, 118, 123, 126–128, 134; in *Frankenstein* and *Villette*, 148–49, 151
"fair," use of in England, 148
fantasy: of cultural purity, 25; and desire, 18; Freud on, 61, 155 n13; opium's connection to, 144–46; and representation, 61; of self-birth, 63, 71
feminine body: association with corruption of language, 37–39, 40, 150; and the domestic, 118–19, 128–29, 134; essentialism, 96–97; as foreign body, 48–51, 96–97, 133–34, 164 n58; invasion of masculine integrity by, 48–51, 54, 61; monstrous, 59–60, 169 n42; and national identity, 96–97, 134; regulation of in 18th-century Britain, 103–4; as self-

consolidating other, 39. *See also* gender; maternal body
feminine transgression, 54, 55, 56–63
feminist epistemology, and Johnson's lexicography, 29–30
Ferguson, Moira, 102
fetishism: in relation to nationalism and cultural imperialism, 159 n22; xenophobia as,
"Fiction as Truth: Personal Identity in Johnson's *Life of Savage*" (O'Shaughnessy), 162 n49
figural inversion, 57
food loathing, as abjection, 118
foreign body: as absolute other, 39; in DeQuincey's *Confessions*, 92, 93–94; disembodiment of, 124; feminized, 48–51, 96–97, 133–34, 164 n58; as form of maintenance, 17, 77, 84, 154 n8; masculine representations of, 132–33; maternal as, 55, 56–58; monstrous, 115, 147; mother as in *Life of Savage*, 56–58; and national identity, 45–46, 73; supplemental necessity of to imperialism, 147
Foucault, Michel, 18, 70
The Four Fundamental Concepts of Psycho-Analysis (Lacan), 1
framing, as architectural metaphor, 165 n11
francophilia, 109
francophobia: in Johnson's works, 21, 40, 47, 48–51, 109, 159 n21; in Wollstonecraft's *Vindication*, 97
French Revolution, 9, 21, 172 n13
Freud, Sigmund: on the fetish, 7; on mechanism of joking, 153 n3; "Medusa's Head," 179 n44; nurse, 62; oceanic state, 71; on "phantasy," 61, 155 n13; on processes of incorporation and introjection, 11; on uncanny, 142–43; on the unconscious, 10
"Freud and Love: Treatment and Its Discontents" (Kristeva), 61
Fulford, Tim (and Peter J. Kitson): *Romanticism and Empire*, 14

Gates, Henry Louis, 45
gender: and competing drives of xenophobia and xenodochy, 97; confusion of authorship with inversions of, 58–59; and deterritorialization of domestic, 98, 100–101, 107, 134, 135, 147; effect on lexicography, 30, 37; and romantic identity, 20, 116, 123–24; as a supplement, 97–98. *See also* feminine body; maternal body
gender studies, 22
Gentleman's Magazine, 43, 44
Gerzina, Gretchen, 104–5, 148, 149, 163 n57
Gilbert, Sandra, 177 n22
Grey, Hannah, 164 n1
Guattari, Felix, 156 n25
Gubar, Susan, 177 n22
Gulliver's Travels (Swift), 13, 155 n17
gynophobia, 27, 46, 51

Handel, Georg Friedrich, 110, 173 n27
Haraway, Donna, 29–30, 34, 43, 69, 73–74, 84
Harris, Thomas, 5
Hayter, Alethea, 169 n46
Hegemony and Socialist Strategy: Towards a Radical Democratic Politics (Laclau and Mouffe), 161 n36
historical materialism, 14
historiography, 10
Hofkosh, Sonia (and Alan Richardson): *Romanticism, Race, and Imperial Culture*, 14
Homans, Margaret: *Bearing the Word: Language and Female Experience in Nineteenth-Century Female Writing*, 98, 121, 174 n7, 177 n22

identity: authorial, 45; class ambiguity in relation to, 53–54; as contradictory relations of high and low, 60–61, 62, 64; dependence upon perception of visible other, 2, 5–6, 68; effects of preconceived formation of on women, 100; familial, 56; romantic, 116, 123–24; shift from Enlightenment to romanticism, 66, 68; in terms of difference, 38. *See also* national identity
identity politics, 99, 153 n4
imagination, 11, 13
imagined communities, 155 n16, 171 n9
imitation, 27, 44, 160 n34
imperialism: and cultural representation, 14, 101, 140–41, 153 n2; and deterritorialization of domestic through gender, 98, 100–101, 107, 134, 135, 147; effect on romantic literature, 14; justified as the overcoming of material differences, 9–10; in late 18th- and early 19th-century Britain, 16; monsters as physical representation of understanding of colonies, 70–71; as a social mission, 146, 176 n14; supplemental necessity of foreign to,

147; women as prototypes for, 101, 103–4
Imperial Leather: Race, Gender, and Sexuality in the Colonial Contest (McClintock), 170 n1
incorporation: Freud on, 11; of otherness within domestic scene, 18, 72–73, 75, 94; of otherness within self, 19; in psychoanalysis, 166 n21
India, and England, popular dualism between, 16–17
industrialism, fetishizing of moralizing aspects, 8
intellectual histories, 29
introjection: of difference as strategy of national self-identification, 6; fantasy of, 166 n21; of foreign through monstrosity, 147; Freud on, 11; material effects of in DeQuincey's *Confessions*, 75–76
intuition, 8, 9

Jacobus, Mary, 102, 134, 177 n22
Johnson, Barbara: "My Monster/My Self," 71, 120, 174 n5, 177 n22
Johnson, Joseph, 96
Johnson, Samuel: conflicted relation to the academy, 28, 32, 40, 158 n7; connection of French to oriental exoticism, 24; on dangers of translation, 24, 39–40, 42; depression, 165 n2; dual position as lexicographer and intellectual authority, 42; friendship with Richard Savage, 51–52; *The History of Rasselas, Prince of Abyssinia*, 19, 24, 25–27, 157 n2; honorary degree from Oxford, 29; *The Life of Pope*, 160 n30; *Lives of the Poets*, 53, 54; as Oedipal figure, 19; practice and attitude toward historical writing, 44; predominantly eighteenth-century sensibility, 66–67; relations with mother and other women, 164 n1; relation to Francis Barber, 163 n57; representation of British imperialism, 45; representation of internal self, 31, 66–67, 158 n13; restoration of authorial space to its proper place, 65–66; romantic move toward incorporating otherness within the self, 19, 21; as subject and voyeur of other bodies, 63–64; ties with nursery milk, 164 n64, 166 n13; use of Oriental tale, 25–26; view of patronage, 28, 32, 157 n6; *A Voyage to Abyssinia*, by Father Jerome Lobo (trans.), 24, 25, 26, 157 n2
—*A Dictionary of the English Language*: cultural representation, 32, 35; definition of aristocratic patronage, 32; Johnson's authorial presence, 27, 45; as means of control of oral language, 36; as primer, 45, 161 n35; publication of, 29; strategies involved in standardization of language, 24
— *Life of Savage*: affirmation of masculine authority, 27, 57; association of low places with high discourse, 53; class ambiguity in relation to personal identity, 53–54; confusion of authorship with inversions of commerce, gender, and class, 58–59; conjunction of aristocratic and sexual corruption, 55, 158 n16; English authorship obstructed by domestic concerns, 27, 54, 56, 58–59, 66; familial identity as overdetermined, 56; fantasy of self-birth, 63; feminine transgression, 54, 55, 56–63; grotesque hybridity, 59–60, 61; identity as contradictory relations of high and low, 60–61, 62, 64; imperialism dependent on commodified bodies, 58; Johnsonian self-representation, 162 n49; legitimacy dependent on masculine honor, 58; maternal as foreign body, 55, 56–58; maternal as monstrous, 54, 55, 56–63, 169 n49; nurse, representation of, 61–62; Oedipal scenario, 63, 163 n53; other alternatively as class and gender opposite, 57; questions of cultural and personal identity, 19, 45; "true" origins of Richard Savage, 56, 163 n52
—*London*: female monstrosity transposed onto effeminate bodies of men, 164 n58; francophobia, 27, 47, 48–51, 109, 159 n21; invasion of masculine integrity by feminine and sexually unstable, 48–51, 54, 61; masquerade, 47, 48, 50, 162 n41; model of coherent internal self, 19, 66; pastoral values, 27, 46–47, 48, 50; problematic status of British identity, 40, 51, 65, 158 n7; questions of poetic voice and poetic authority, 44–45; repugnance toward and fascination with "low life," 55, 162 n43; romantic conflation of exotic with domestic, 66
—*Preface to A Dictionary of the English Language*, 24, 66; affirmation of masculine authority, 57; authorial identity, 45; conflicting representations of capitalism, 38; on corruption of language, 15, 28, 30, 32–33; corruption of language associated with

exotic other/feminine, 37–39, 40, 150; cultural imperialism in national representation, 35, 41; difference between English and foreign lexicographers, 41; difference between oral and written language, 36, 41; on Elizabethan writers, 34, 35; francophobia, 40; identity in terms of difference, 38; ideological positioning of language and lexicographers, 34; on impossibility of fixing linguistic meaning, 34–35, 159 n22; Johnson's placement of himself as final literary authority, 32; Johnson's position as slave of science, 30–31; language as cultural barometer, 24; language as material, 31; model of national language and identity, 19, 30–31, 32, 36, 40, 43, 158 n17; orienting of English toward the past, 39; "othering" strategy, 35–43; vulnerability of Englishness to the "other," 26; written language as marker of cultural identity, 41–42; xenophobic response to adoption of foreign words, 35
Journal of the Plague Year (Defoe), 159 n24
Juvenal's satires, 44, 48, 160 n34

Kant, Immanuel: *The Critique of Pure Reason*, 8–10; forms of sublime, 130; internal "other" in model of mind, 10; transcendental aesthetic, 11, 154 n11
Kaplan, Cora, 115
Kristeva, Julia: formulation of mother, 107; "Freud and Love: Treatment and Its Discontents," 61; *Powers of Horror: An Essay on Abjection*, 60, 118; *Revolution in Poetic Language*, 96
Kubla Khan (Coleridge), 67

Lacan, Jacques: on articulation of name of father, 163 n52; definition of symbolic, 77; "discourse of the master," 176 n14; formulation of language as symbolic order, 76; formulation of unconscious, 12; *The Four Fundamental Concepts of Psycho-Analysis*, 1; on problem of being a philosopher, 87, 88; "Subversion of the Subject and Dialectic of Desire," 88
Laclau, Ernesto, 45–46, 60, 161 n36
Lake District poets, 20, 67, 68, 75, 93, 122
Landry, Donna: *The Muses of Resistance: Laboring-Class Women's Poetry in Britain, 1739-1796*, 102, 170 n6

language: adoption of foreign words, 35; association of feminine with corruption of, 37–39, 40, 150; as embodiment of cultural unconscious, 11; and ideology, 34; impurity of as means of representation, 36; institutionalization of, 24; Johnson's material view of, 31; and maternal, 167 n34, 174 n5; oral vs. written, 36, 41–42; purity of, 32–34; as symbolic order, 76
The Language of Psycho-Analysis (Laplanche and Pontalis), 166 n21
Laplanche, J., 166 n21
Lawson, Charles, 80
Leask, Nigel: on autobiographical tone of later revisions of *Confessions*, 166 n20; on consumption of other as maintenance, 17–18, 77, 84; on DeQuincey's connection to maternal body, 170 n51; on DeQuincey's consumption of opium as politics of imperialism, 167 n25; on DeQuincey's pathological relation to romantic scholarship, 19; on DeQuincey's references to Coleridge, 79; on DeQuincey's relation to Asia, 69; on DeQuincey's traffic in prostitution, 166 n18; on importance of historical materialism in relation to romanticism, 14; on ramifications of DeQuincey's addiction, 75; on reception of *Confessions*, 168 n36
Le Brun, Charles, 91
lexicography: documentation of coherence of national culture, 30–31; effect of ideologies of imperialism, gender, and sexuality on, 30; 18th century, 29
The Life of Samuel Johnson (Boswell), 29, 164 n1
Lyrical Ballads (Coleridge and Wordsworth), 169 n44

Macclesfield, countess of, 54–59
Macclesfield, earl of, 55
Makdisi, Saree, 14–15, 15, 16, 75
Malthus, Thomas, 84
Markley, Robert, 170 n52
Martin, Louis Aime, *The Education of Mothers of Families*, 98
masculine: invasion of by feminine, 48–51, 54, 61; Johnson's affirmation of authority of, 27, 57; Johnson's association with permanence, 37; Shelley's representations of foreignness, 132–33

masquerade, 47, 48, 50, 162 n41
Masquerade and Civilization: The Carnivalesque in Eighteenth Century English Culture and Fiction (Castle), 47, 162 n41
maternal body: abjection of, 60, 62; and the concept of nation, 20, 98, 100–101; delicate state of in Shelley's *Frankenstein*, 118; as monstrous in DeQuincey's *Confessions*, 82–83, 89–91; as monstrous in Johnson's *Life of Savage*, 54, 55, 56–63, 169 n49; and national identity in Wollstonecraft's *Maria*, 108, 111–15; as prototype of imperial relation to colonies, 21, 101, 102–4; as site of contamination and disease, 89, 92, 104; unreliability of, 164 n64, 166 n13, 177 n27
maternal milk, 71, 164 n64, 166 n13
McClintock, Anne: *Imperial Leather: Race, Gender, and Sexuality in the Colonial Contest*, 170 n1
McDonagh, Josephine, 14
McGann, Jerome J., *The Romantic Identity*, 14
"Medusa's Head" (Freud), 179 n44
modernism, 15–16, 154 n6
Moer, Ellen, 177 n22
monstrosity: boundary creatures as, 73–74, 142; crossover creatures as, 70–77; cultural meanings of in eighteenth and nineteenth centuries, 68; of fair exotics in Shelley's *Frankenstein*, 127, 128, 133; of foreign bodies, 115, 147, 164 n58; function of stabilizing cultural positions, 73–74; incorporation into domestic scene in DeQuincey's *Confessions*, 67–68, 70, 74, 75, 94, 101, 104, 105, 150; and itinerant female subjectivity, 134; maternal, in DeQuincey's *Confessions*, 82–83, 89–91; maternal, in Johnson's *Life of Savage* and *London*, 54, 55, 56–63, 169 n49; as outcast British identity in Brontë's *Villette*, 141; vulnerability of nursery to, 86, 141, 164 n64, 166 n13
More, Hannah, 20, 22, 99, 104, 172 n18
Mouffe, Chantal, 45–46, 60, 161 n36

national identity: achieved by traffic in foreign others, 45–46, 73; association with oak, 93; and deterritorialization of domestic through gender, 98, 100–101, 107, 134, 135, 147; as a domesticating shield, 118; and the feminine, 96–97, 134; internal anxieties about, 14–15; introjection of difference as strategy of, 6; motherhood and, 98, 100–101, 114–15; and notions of universalized manhood, 98; Orientalism as, 68–69, 74, 77; problems of foundational assumptions about, 99–100; in relation to familial, 127, 131–32; xenophobia and, 7–8
nationalism, and imperialism, 14
The Natural History of Animals, Vegetables, and Minerals (Buffon), 65
Newman, Gerald: *The Rise of English Nationalism: A Cultural History, 1740–1830*, 153 n4
North, Julian: *DeQuincey Reviewed: Thomas DeQuincey's Critical Reception, 1821–1994*, 165 n9
nursery, vulnerability to monstrosity, 86, 141, 164 n64, 166 n13

oak, association with English national self-identity, 93, 170 n53
opium: connection to fantasy and notions of orient, 144–46; consumption of as politics of imperialism, 167 n25
oral language, 36, 41
Orientalism (Said), 40, 160 n27, 161 n37
Oriental tale, 24, 25, 26, 157 n1
Orient/Orientalism: abjection of, 18; association of tigers with, 65, 70, 71, 72; connection to opium in *Villette*, 144–46; effect on romantic literature, 14; and English national identity in *Confessions*, 68–69, 74, 77; imagery of in *A Vindication of the Rights of Woman*, 105, 172 n18; in late eighteenth- and early nineteenth-century Britain, 16; Said on, 161 n37
O'Shaughnessy, Toni: "Fiction as Truth: Personal Identity in Johnson's *Life of Savage*," 162 n49
other: absolute, 39, 154 n5, 159 n25, 161 n37, 172 n18; consumption of as maintenance, 17–18, 77, 84; in DeQuincey's *Confessions*, 67–68, 70, 72–74, 75, 94, 101, 104, 105, 115, 150; 18th-century strategies of coping with, 75; exotic, incorporation into British fold, 72–73; internal, in Kantian model, 10; and national identity, 45–46, 73; romantic strategies of coping with, 19, 26, 75; self-consolidating, 39, 84, 154 n5, 159 n25, 161 n37, 172 n18; visible, and identity, 2, 5–6, 68; versus self, 154 n8; vulnerability of Englishness to in John-

son's *Preface*, 26. *See also* feminine body; foreign body; monstrosity
overdetermination, 56, 60, 62
"Overdeterminations of Imperialism: David Ochherlong and the Ranee of Sirmoor" (Spivak), 154 n5, 161 n37
Ozymandias (Shelley), 176 n16

Paine, Thomas: *The Rights of Man*, 9
paleontology, 69
pastoral, 27, 162 n39, 162 n40
patronage, Johnson's view of, 28, 32, 157 n6
poetics, understanding of transcendental sublime through, 10
The Politics and Poetics of Transgression (Stallybrass and White), 162 n42, 162 n43, 163 n51
Pontalis, J.-B., 166 n21
Poovey, Mary, 102, 177 n22
Pope, Alexander, 160 n34, 170 n53
Porter, Robert Ker, 72
postcolonial studies, 1, 14, 22, 153 n2
postmodern studies, 14, 16
Powers of Horror: An Essay on Abjection (Kristeva), 60, 118
Preface to the Lyrical Ballads (Coleridge and Wordsworth), 21
Preliminary Confessions (DeQuincey), 87
Prelude (Wordsworth), 67, 91–92
Price, Richard, 21
primatology, 69
Prometheus Unbound (Shelley), 174 n7, 175 n12
psychoanalysis, 116, 166 n21
psychosubjectivity, 116
purity, of language, 32–34

Questioning Romanticism (Beer), 14

race: anxiety of aligning nationalism with in Brontë's *Villette*, 140–41; assignments of color to in DeQuincey's *Confessions*, 69, 92; otherness, in Shelley's *Frankenstein*, 132, 133–34
racial difference: and establishment of hierarchy, 149–50; negating class difference, 177 n26
Rambler, 25, 26
recovery narrative, 87
reference works: authoritativeness, 19, 27; ideologies informing production of knowledge in, 29, 43; models of standardization for, 30
Revolution in Poetic Language (Kristeva), 96

The Rhetoric of English India (Suleri), 170 n1
Ricardo, David, 84
The Rights of Man (Paine), 9
The Rise of English Nationalism: A Cultural History 1740-1830 (Newman), 153 n4
Robespierre, Maximilien, 91
romance (medieval), 12, 13
The Romantic Identity (McGann), 14
romanticism: as articulation of xenophobic/xenodochial drives, 6–7, 8, 15, 19, 20; conceptions of self, 13–14; containment in, 16; defined, 154 n6; in Defoe's *Robinson Crusoe*, 6, 150; DeQuincey and, 19–20, 74–75, 76, 88–89, 169 n48; educational ideal, 122; Enlightenment notions in, 13, 14, 18–19, 74; formula of domesticity in Shelley's *Frankenstein*, 128–29, 134; German, 156 n26; historical materialism in relation to, 14; idea of author produced through inward contemplation, 12–13; and imagination, 11; incorporation of exoticism, 14, 17, 18, 66; material reality of monsters less valuable than narrative representation, 130–31; and modernism, 15; as reaction against Enlightenment reasoning, 12; reliance on abject to sustain poetic identity, 68; self-definition through change, 66–67; strategies of coping with other, 19, 26, 75; subjectivity reproduced within a national frame, 96; Wollstonecraft's relation to, 20
Romanticism, Race, and Imperial Culture (Hofkosh and Richardson), 14
Romanticism and Empire (Fulford and Kitson), 14
The Romantic Sublime: Studies in the Structure and Psychology of Transcendence (Weiskel), 154 n11
Rousseau, Jean Jacques: DeQuincey and, 84; *Emile*, 98, 99, 107; link of patriotism with mothering, 55; model of citizenry, 148; Wollstonecraft and, 21, 99, 107–8
Rzepka, Charles, 14, 75, 80, 170 n55

Said, Edward: *Culture and Imperialism*, 178 n40; *Orientalism*, 40, 160 n27, 161 n37
Samuel Johnson (Bate), 157 n7, 162 n40, 164 n1, 166 n13
Savage, Richard: association with Thales in Johnson's *London*, 27, 45, 47, 51; *The Author To Be Let*, 56; *The Wanderer*, 56. *See also* Johnson, Samuel, *Life of Savage*
Savage, Richard, 4th Earl Rivers, 55, 56, 57

Sedgwick, Eve Kosofsky, 162 n46
Seged, 25
self: differences between eighteenth- and nineteenth-century versions, 68; Johnson's incorporation of otherness within, 19, 21; Johnson's representation of, 31, 66–67, 158 n13; vs. other, 154 n8. *See also* identity
self-birth, fantasy of, 63, 71
self-consolidating other, 39, 84, 154 n5, 159 n25, 161 n37, 172 n18
self-definition: romantic notion of through change, 66–67; shift in at end of 18th century, 8–9
Sensible Words (Cohen), 29, 158 n8
Sharpe, Jenny: *Allegories of Empire: The Figure of the Woman in the Colonial Text*, 170 n1
Shelley, Mary, *Frankenstein*: authorial stunting, 119–20; change in familial relations in 1831 edition, 176 n18; disembodied foreignness, 124–25; disembodied maternity and sexuality, 131; epigraph from Milton, 121, 122; exchange between xenophobia and xenodochy, 119; fair exotics, 118, 123, 126–28, 134; female monster as imperialist project, 131; feminine as external to domestic space, 118–19; feminine representations of foreignness, 133–34; feminine upholding of romantic formula of domesticity, 128–29, 134; Introduction to 1831 edition, 119–20; masculine representations of foreignness, 132–33; maternal body, 22, 118; monster-making, England as keystone to, 129–31; monstrous resistance of fair exotics to domesticity, 127, 128, 133; national identities in relation to familial, 127, 131–32; racial otherness, 132, 133–34; representation of Italy, 127; and Rousseau's constructions of subjectivity, 175 n12; Shelley's inscription to her father, 121–22, 175 n10; Shelley's position of hysteric, 176 n14; social hybridity, 127; Walton as signifier of stable national identity, 124–25, 176 n14; xenophobia, 22, 120, 124–25, 127
Shelley, Percy Bysshe: *Ozymandias*, 176 n16; *Prometheus Unbound*, 174 n7, 175 n12
Sheridan, Richard, 103, 106
Shohat, Ella, 153 n2
sign, impurity of, 33, 35–36
"Signature Event Context" (Derrida), 33, 159 n23
The Silence of the Lambs, 5
Simpson, Margaret, 73, 86, 88, 169 n46

Sinclair, James, 59
slavery, 22, 23, 104–5
Smith, Adam, 84
Smith, Johanna, 177 n22
social hybridity: in *Frankenstein*, 127; in Johnson's *Life of Savage*, 59–60, 61
Southey, Robert, 78
Spenser, Edward, 80
Spivak, Gayatri: on encyclopedia project, 43; on imperialism, 101, 177 n24; notion of self-consolidating and absolute others, 39, 159 n25, 161 n37, 172 n18; "Overdeterminations of Imperialism: David Ochherlong and the Ranee of Sirmoor," 154 n5, 161 n37; "Three Women's Texts and a Critique of Imperialism," 120, 121, 153 n2, 174 n6, 175 n8
split subject, 8
Stallybrass, Peter, 57, 59, 62, 162 n42, 162 n43, 163 n51
Stam, Robert, 153 n2
subjectivity: Cartesian, 11, 66, 168 n37; fabrication of through xenophobia, 13; reproduced within a national frame in romanticism, 96; eighteenth-century construction of, 13; xenophobic belief in essential authorial, 16
sublime, 130, 154 n11
"Subversion of the Subject and Dialectic of Desire" (Lacan), 88
subversive mimicry, 160 n30
Suleri, Sara: *The Rhetoric of English India*, 170 n1
supplement: logic of, 97, 147; notion of, 154 n7
Suspiria de Profundis (DeQuincey), 79
Sussman, Charlotte, 106
Swift, Jonathan: *Gulliver's Travels*, 13, 155 n17

Taunton march, 99
A Thousand Plateaus: Capitalism and Schizophrenia (Deleuze and Guattari), 156 n25
Thrale, Hester, 164 n1
"Three Women's Texts and a Critique of Imperialism" (Spivak), 120, 121, 153 n2, 174 n6, 175 n8
tigers: association with Orient, 65, 70, 71, 72; in DeQuincey's *Confessions*, 70, 74, 82; incorporation into domestic British fold, 72–73; in late eighteenth- and early nineteenth-century Britain, 165 n11
timber, cultural importance of in eighteenth and nineteenth centuries, 92–93
Tipu, Sultan of Mysore, 71, 72, 74, 173 n29
tourism, 25

Tracy, Clarence, *The Artificial Bastard*, 56
transcendental aesthetic, 8, 9, 11
transgression: feminine, 54, 55, 56–63; politics of, 57
translation, Johnson's view of, 24, 39–40, 42
The Tyger (Blake), 65, 165 n11

unconscious, 8, 19
Unthinking Eurocentrism: Multiculturalism and the Media (Shohat and Stam), 153 n2

vernacular, and rise of nation state, 13
visible difference, 2, 5–6, 68, 154 n8
Viswanathan, Gauri, 16
Voltaire, 24, 25, 67

The Wanderer (Savage), 56
Weiskel, Thomas: *The Romantic Sublime: Studies in the Structure and Psychology of Transcendence*, 154 n11
wet-nursing, 62, 173 n28
White, Allon, 57, 59, 62, 162 n42, 162 n43, 163 n51
Williams, Raymond, 30, 34
Wilson, Anna, 108
Wimsatt, W. K., 44
Wollstonecraft, Mary: relation to romanticism, 20, 21; status as feminist writer, 170 n6
—*An Historical and Moral View of the Origin and Progress of the French Revolution*, 21
—*Maria, or The Wrongs of Woman*: ambivalence toward Rousseauian ideal for women, 111, 113; foreign as monstrous invader of domestic, 115; language of incarceration, 111–12, 113; maternal image, 112–13; metaphors of enslavement, 113; mothering and national identity, 108, 114–15; narrative of breast-feeding, 114; reading and feeling, 112–13, 114
—*Mary*, 108–11, 116, 123, 135
—*A Vindication of the Rights of Woman*: call for feminine essentialism, 96–97; conflicted relationship to Rousseau, 97, 107–8; cultural impact of, 99; different concepts of reading, 106; on education for women, 97–98, 105–6; francophobia, 97; Introduction, 105–6; orientalist imagery, 105, 172 n18; rejection of sensibility, 96, 102, 118; use of "slave" to describe position of women, 104–5; xenophobic rhetoric, 21, 97, 98, 102

women: effects of preconceived formation of identity on, 100; problems of place in eighteenth- and early nineteenth-century Britain, 99–100; as prototypes for imperialism, 101, 103–4; threat of enfranchisement to British men, 99; writers, and xenophobic models of imperialism, 20–21, 22–23, 150–51. *See also* feminine body; gender
Wordsworth, Dorothy, 78, 88
Wordsworth, Kate, 87
Wordsworth, William: DeQuincey and, 78, 80, 81; *The Excursion*, 176 n17; interest in French Revolution, 13–14, 20; *Lyrical Ballads*, 169 n44; *Preface to the Lyrical Ballads*, 21; *Prelude*, 67, 91–92; relation to exotic forms, 18, 68

xenodochy: contamination of domestic identity, 8; definitions of, 6; shaping of foreign body, 148; and xenophobia, 6–7, 8, 15, 17, 19, 20, 38, 46; xenophobic response to in Brontë's *Villette*, 138–39, 144–46; xenophobic response to in Shelley's *Frankenstein*, 119
xenophobia: and abjection, 7–8; and belief in essential authorial subjectivity, 16; construction of other through, 7; in current postmodern and postcolonial studies, 14; as defense against xenodochy in Defoe's *Robinson Crusoe*, 5, 6–7; in DeQuincey's *Confessions*, 75–78; fabrication of subjectivities through, 13; as fetish, 7; in Johnson's *Preface*, 35; and national identity, 7–8; and notion of sublime, 154 n11; process by which other is constructed, 7; as response to xenodochy in Brontë's *Villette*, 138–39, 144–46; romanticism and, 8, 15, 20; in Shelley's *Frankenstein*, 22, 120, 127; and situation of objects in domestic discourse, 11, 17; structuring of unconscious, 10; Wollstonecraft's, 21, 97, 98, 102; of women writers in late eighteenth and early nineteenth century, 20–21, 22–23, 150–51; and xenodochy, 6–7, 8, 15, 17, 19, 20, 38, 46

Yearsley, Ann, 20, 22, 23, 99, 104, 172 n18
Young, Robert, 14

Žižek, Slavoj, 18, 20, 77

Acknowledgments

I have long fantasized about the time when I would finally be able to thank the many people who have contributed to the making of this book. Now that I am actually writing these acknowledgments, however, I find the moment more poignant than jubilant and somewhat daunting because I have incurred so much intellectual debt. My first debt is to Mary Jacobus, Laura Brown, and Cynthia Chase, who inspired and guided this project from the beginning and whose teaching has been invaluable throughout my career. Conversations with Lynn Enterline, Billy Flesch, Suvir Kaul, Blake Leland, Dorothea von Mucke, Tom Reinert, Charlotte Sussman, and Marty Wechselblatt helped me identify and think through some of the struggles I had with the earlier stages of this project.

My professional career has been somewhat peripatetic, and the colleagues from whom I have learned at various institutions have had an integral part in writing this book. At Bowdoin College, Ann Louise Kibbie was and has continued to be a source of inspiration and cherished friendship. Julia Alvarez, Cates Baldridge, Alison Byerly, Sarah Hardy, Diana Henderson, and Tom Hecimovich made life at Middlebury College both intellectually stimulating and a whole lot of fun. I will always be grateful to my graduate students and colleagues at the University of Texas at Arlington for the many ways in which they contributed to my growth as a scholar. In particular, Martin Danahay, Tim Morris, and Susan Hekman have been very important as critics and friends. Johanna Smith's detailed and sensitive reading of my chapter on *Frankenstein* made it much stronger than it would have otherwise been. For enlightening discussions about cultural studies, weathering the hazards of pre-tenure years, and an enduring and profound friendship, I thank Stacy Alaimo.

The intellectual community at Southern Methodist University has been extraordinarily supportive and congenial; Rick Bozorth, Dennis Foster, Bruce Levy, Martha Satz, Willard Spiegelman, and Trysh Travis have made this department a particularly wonderful place to be. To Beth Newman and Nina Schwartz I owe deep debts for their rigorous readings of this manuscript as well as for their strong support and free psychoanalysis.

I also would like to thank Adela Pinch and the anonymous reader of this manuscript for the University of Pennsylvania Press and my other anonymous external reviewers for tenure; their labor can never be fully repaid. Jerome Singerman has been a wonderful editor, and Alison Anderson's patience and care with the manuscript have made my relationship with the press a very rewarding one. I would like to thank the editorial boards of *Criticism* and *Eighteenth Century: Theory and Interpretation* for permission to reprint some of the material from the first chapter, and the Indiana University Press for permission to reprint part of Chapter Three.

I have learned a great deal from others in the profession and am deeply grateful to them. Lenny Davis, Donna Landry, Gerald MacLean, Bob Markley, Joel Reed, Alan Richardson, Peter Stallybrass, James Thompson, and Sharon Willis have had profound influences on both the book and my work in general. I don't think I can ever fully express my gratitude to Pat Gill: her editorial genius and wit continue to leave me breathless with admiration. My greatest academic debt is to my most challenging critic, Tom DiPiero, whose intellectual virtuosity and grace have made my scholarly life a delight.

I thank Max for the past twenty years and my parents, to whom this book is dedicated, for the past forty-two. Above all, however, I thank Tom Pribyl for his ironic humor, his enormous talent, and his sustaining love. He thinks he has nothing to do with this book, but for me, his has been the most important presence.